SHANGHAI
key to modern China

Rhoads Murphey

SHANGHAI
key to modern China

Harvard University Press · Cambridge

1953

Distributed in Great Britain by
GEOFFREY CUMBERLEGE
OXFORD UNIVERSITY PRESS
LONDON

LIBRARY OF CONGRESS CATALOG CARD NUMBER 53–5073
PRINTED IN THE UNITED STATES OF AMERICA

TO MY MOTHER, EMILY SYDNEY MURPHEY

Author's Note

The great range of published materials bearing on the problems treated here has made for the usual difficulties which confront the student of China. In a narrower sense, neither scholars nor events have stood still since this book was first written. For example, S. F. Wright's *Hart and the Chinese Customs* might have been drawn on much more fully had it not come into my hands during that limbo between the supposed completion of a book and its actual publication. Recent works such as this are noted here wherever possible, but many of them could not be thoroughly used.

Having chosen a subject as dynamic as Shanghai, in a setting of violent and revolutionary change like modern China, I suppose that complaints about problems of obsolescence are clearly out of order. Realizing this in a more general way, I have tried to write about Shanghai and modern China in their geographic setting in a manner which will be meaningful and instructive regardless of changes which may occur, and are now occurring.

I am happy to record my indebtedness to the Social Science Research Council for a grant during 1948–50 which made it possible for me to do most of the research and the original writing of this book. My indebtedness to those at Harvard University and to others who have offered valuable criticism is so great, in kind and amount, that I can make only this gesture of thanks.

R. M.

Seattle, Washington
December 1952

Contents

MAPS

GRAPHS

1. Population of Shanghai, 1840–1936

There are no complete records of the population of Shanghai at any period. This graph has been compiled from a variety of estimates: Fortune (1846), Medhurst (1850 and 1864), Schmidt (1874), Mac-lellan (1889), Feetham (1931), *Shang-hai shih nien-chien* (1936), *et al*. The influx of Chinese refugees between 1852 and 1865 was an important matter for the foreigners, and most works covering the period give yearly estimates of the population of the foreign settlements. For the remainder of the period before 1928 the only consistently available estimates are decennial. Both sets of figures are approximations only, but those for the total urban area are especially imprecise.   22

2. Foreign Population of Shanghai, 1843–1936

Figures for the foreign population are reasonably accurate since each group of foreign nationals was the responsibility of a consul and since most of the foreigners lived within the settlements. Sources as for graph 1.   23

SHANGHAI
key to modern China

ONE

Introductory

This is the study of an anomaly. A city of four million people grew up in the short space of a hundred years out of the traditional agrarian economy of China, before the building of a modern railway network, before the development of a single national market, and before other Chinese commercial cities of metropolitan size had appeared. The city of Shanghai, born out of Western commercial enterprise and organized in its economic life largely along Western lines, was in effect superimposed on a peasant civilization. On this agrarian base, it erected first a trade which reached to all parts of the globe, and subsequently a manufacturing complex which put it among the leading urban industrial centers of the world.

In both respects, Shanghai has been the center of a vortex of economic change spreading from the city to engulf the rest of China, a process which is still in its early stages. Toward the close of the first century since its opening to foreign trade in 1843, Shanghai accounted for half of China's foreign trade and half of its mechanized factories. The city's four million people formed one of the first five or six metropolitan groupings in the world, and Shanghai was well over twice the size of each of its nearest urban rivals in China, Peking and Tientsin.

The rise of other great cities has in the main depended on either or both of two factors: the concentration of the administrative functions of a large empire or political unit in a single pre-eminent center (Rome, London, Peking); and the concentration of trade from and manufacturing for a highly integrated and commercialized economy in an outstanding urban location (New York, Rotterdam, Osaka), based on the existence of low-cost volume carriers. Shanghai has never performed any administrative functions beyond its own metropolitan limits, and the Chinese economy on which its trade is based remains far from integrated or commercialized, while railways are still perhaps China's most notable lack.

But Shanghai lies near the seaward face of the Yangtze delta, where the extensive water routes of a great river system are gathered into a knot, and where the coast of China extends farthest into the open sea. Goods which different local areas produced and for which foreign traders found overseas markets could thus move out for export through Shanghai, and foreign goods entering China in return could be distributed over a wide area from the city. Shanghai thereby became the commercial center for virtually all of the Yangtze basin, which includes the most populous and productive half of China. Not only did trade flow through the city, but Shanghai also became one of the world's leading financial centers. Its banks financed the Chinese government as well as the economic life of the city and of its commercial hinterland of half of China and all the Chinese ports. They controlled "at a very conservative estimate 90 per cent of the imports and exports between China and foreign countries." [1] As manufacturing developed in the city during the twentieth century, aided by the accumulation there of foreign and Chinese capital earned in trade, it was able to compete successfully with other manufacturing centers, despite the local absence of most industrial raw materials, because of the ease and cheapness of water transport for the materials of manufacturing brought from more distant places. Finally, Shanghai's four million people could be fed largely from rice produced in the fertile Yangtze delta.

Perhaps the most remarkable aspect of the city is simply its size. Dense populations have long been associated with deltas, and in southeast Asia nearly all of the notable population concentrations are on fertile deltaic soils where ample water is available for the irrigation of paddy rice. Each of the major deltas in southeast Asia also supports the largest or second largest city in its political unit (Hanoi, Saigon, Bankok, Rangoon, and Calcutta). But none of these cities approaches Shanghai in size; Calcutta, the largest, has a population of only about two and a half millions.

Two outstanding locational factors distinguish Shanghai from other delta cities in the lower and lower-middle latitudes: its central position on the coast of east Asia, and the great extent of its trade hinterland. With a similar delta agrarian setting for all of these cities, Shanghai is nearly twice as large as any of them because the trade of half, and that half the richer one, of the most populous political unit in the world is funneled through the city by the pattern of inland waterways and sea routes which focuses on it. In the pre-industrial economy of China, water transport is by far the most important volume carrier. While China remained agrarian, the stimulation of its external trade by foreign commercial enterprise produced an interregional flow of goods which moved largely through Shanghai. This situation continued to implement the physical advantages of the city's location to make it the major point of contact between China and the West.

Modern Chinese banking and finance, manufacturing, and commercial organization (and the new class of Chinese associated with them and divorced from traditional China) all got their start there, are still largely concentrated there, and for the last hundred years have spread out from there as from the center of a whirlpool. Of the whole process of Westernization in China, only railways came relatively late to Shanghai, a logical exception in view of the abundance of good water transport. Otherwise the city rapidly became, within the first decade of its opening to foreign trade, a physical and economic replica of the nineteenth-century Europe which had built it, and in time of the twentieth-century America which was also a prominent contributor.

Shanghai and the pattern of its development during the past century have been modern China in microcosm. In the city China for the first time learned and absorbed the lessons of extraterritoriality, gun-boat diplomacy, foreign "concessions," and the aggressive spirit of nineteenth century Europe. There more than anywhere else the two civilizations came together: the rational, legal-minded, scientific, industrialized, efficient, expansionist West, and traditional, intuitive, humanist, agrarian, inefficient, seclusionist China. The sequel, and China's response, began primarily at Shanghai, and there modern China was born.

China's economic revolution, as fully as Chinese nationalism, struck its first modern roots beside the Whangpoo, and these two have between them made the contemporary picture. Economically, the institutions, and still more the attitude and standard of values, which had grown up in the West with the end of the Middle Ages and reached a full flowering in the nineteenth century, were transplanted to Shanghai. As the city grew on this heady but nourishing diet, its growth set widening patterns of change in motion throughout the country. In the economic structure which developed at Shanghai, in the problems which economic development had to overcome, in the compromises and hybrid growths which arose, in the final maturing of a modern commercial, financial, and industrial metropolis, the city provides a key to what has since happened and is still to happen in China.

The events of the post-war years have thrown into relief the economic and political changes which have long been under way in China, but which have only recently made themselves violently apparent. Communism is merely the present vehicle, not the creator, of the revolution which has carried it to success. As a leading agent in modern China's revolution, Shanghai may claim a larger share than Moscow in the current product. War, civil war, and Communist victory have also ended the history of foreign Shanghai. The hundred years of its existence being ended, a larger perspective tends to emphasize the things about the city's development which seem most important in the light of what has followed. Hindsight would pick out evidences of Shanghai's role in stimulating Chinese nationalism and economic change, in teaching China the lessons of Western business, science, and industry, and in providing a sample of what these lessons might accomplish.

Nineteenth-century Europe was at its best in the pulpit or on the rostrum, especially when talking of its own accomplishments, and Shanghai belonged to it. A jubilee was held in the city on the fiftieth anniversary of the founding of the foreign settlements, in 1893, and the major address of the day was delivered in the park on the Bund by the Rev. Muirhead, a British missionary. His words are symptomatic of the West's attitude to the East and of Shanghai's characteristic part in it, and also perhaps enlightening toward an understanding of China's response.

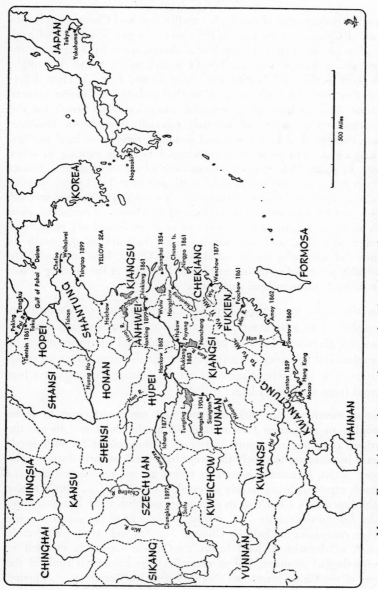

Map 1. East Asia, showing provinces and major cities and rivers of China. Dates refer to the opening to foreign trade as treaty ports of the cities so indicated.

Shanghai is the centre of our higher civilization and Christian influence for all of China. We are here in the midst of a people proud and prejudiced in favour of their ancient line of things, and what have we introduced amongst them, for their benefit as well as our own? We might well point to the English homes we have formed here. . . How different is this from what we know to be characteristic of Chinese homes? In front also we have these beautiful *hongs* (trading firms) for the transaction of business, and we may especially remark the Supreme Court, distinguished by the just and equitable conduct of legal matters, in striking contrast to what is represented to us as existing in other places. In short, look at the *tout ensemble* of the Settlement — houses and streets lit with gas and electricity, streams of pellucid water flowing in all directions, and sanitary arrangements according to the best medical advice. We have steamers, telegraphs, and telephones in communication with all the world; there are cotton and paper mills and silk filatures of Foreign invention, and last but not least, railways in the north as pioneers of what will yet be found all over China. Law and order are admirably preserved in the midst of 200,000 people at the instance of our own judicial and municipal authorities. . .[2]

In the same year, the (British) Commissioner of Customs at Shanghai wrote a trade report for a jubilee volume published by the *Shanghai Mercury* in which he also emphasized the prominence of Shanghai, but in which he expressed rather different views on other matters. The two sets of remarks are interesting to compare when viewed from sixty years later:

Chinese merchants are inclined more and more each year to make Shanghai an emporium for the trade of north China and to use the northern coast and river ports simply as landing places for such goods as may be necessary to supply the immediate needs of their districts. The largest native mercantile houses in China are all represented here. . . Chinese capital is being largely invested, not only in . . . purely native establishments . . . but also in companies established by foreigners and under foreign directorate . . . at least 40 per cent of the shares of some foreign companies are held by Chinese . . . (as well as) a considerable portion of deposits in local banks. . . Chinese capital is invested in foreign-flagged steamers, and of course a large amount is sunk in the shares of the China Merchants Steam Navigation Company. . . Having said so much, it should not surprise anyone if I express the opinion that probably in future Shanghai will furnish no such favourable opportunities for the investment of foreign capital as it has done in the past. . . To sum up, I think the future of Shanghai depends on China and the Chinese and their interests and that foreigners would be wise to run with them.[3]

The Commissioner and the missionary were in effect saying the same thing, although in different ways — that the most important thing about Shanghai was its relation to China; and that the city contained the seeds of great change for the entire country.

While it lasted, foreign Shanghai was an exciting and colorful place which travel folders could not exaggerate. It was for instance justly famous as one of the wickedest cities in the world, and we have the testimony of a duke for that as early as 1869. Following his visit to Shanghai, the Duke of Somerset referred to it in the House of Lords in that year as "a sink of iniquity."[4] His words pained especially the missionary residents of the city, and the Chamber of Commerce considered a formal reply through the foreign secretary, but matters never proceeded beyond the local press. The difficulty was that His Grace was right, and the city's own archives proved it. At the Landrenters' meeting in 1864, Sir Harry Parkes, then British consul at Shanghai, stated that of a total of 10,000 Chinese houses in the International and French Settlements, 668 were brothels, "while opium and gambling houses were beyond counting."[5] Seventy years later in 1934, a local Chinese newspaper estimated that Shanghai led the world's cities in prostitution as a specialty: in London, one person in 960 was a prostitute, in Berlin one in 580, in Paris one in 481, in Chicago one in 430, in Tokyo one in 250, and in Shanghai, one in 130.[6] It was indeed a major commercial enterprise in the city, and the fact that so many people earned their livings thereby stymied all attempts to eradicate or mitigate it. A special commission appointed in 1919 to investigate vice in the city recommended that all brothels be removed in five years, hoping that during that time other means of livelihood might be found. Licenses were issued in 1920 with the understanding that all licenses were to be withdrawn in 1925. But the plan was abandoned before the end of the five-year period as a complete failure. An earlier reform attempt also ended in failure when the first American judge of the United States Court for China arrived in

Shanghai in 1906 and began a crusade especially against American brothels. He became exceedingly unpopular in Shanghai, and finally felt obliged to sue the *Shanghai Gazette* for libel after he had abandoned both his crusade and his post and prepared to return to the United States.[7]

Opium dens in the two foreign settlements remained open long after those in the Chinese city had been officially (i.e., in many cases not actually) closed by imperial decree, and until at least 1935 these establishments flourished publicly. Subsequent regulations merely made them more circumspect. In the French Settlement opium vendors on the streets sold their wares in paper packets with labels giving their names, addresses, and telephone numbers. (Opium establishments were increasingly numerous and open in the Chinese city also after 1911, and into the 1940's). Kidnapping was another important enterprise, and a highly profitable one, since many wealthy Chinese moved into the foreign settlements where their property and persons were more secure but whence they or their children could be spirited over the short distance into Chinese territory and held for ransom. Organized commercial gambling was also a big business, and existed in Shanghai probably on a larger scale than in any other city in the world.[8]

Law enforcement was severely handicapped by the complex but ambiguous legal and administrative situation. Chinese police could not pursue suspects into the foreign settlements, and foreign police were similarly excluded from the Chinese areas. Foreigners in Shanghai lived under extraterritoriality, by which they were governed according to their respective national laws administered by their own consuls, but the law was seldom read to them with the same severity as it would have been at home. For one thing, the consul was often personally involved in business affairs in Shanghai, or was at least a personal friend of the defendant or plaintiff. Petty and grand swindles of all kinds tended to flourish under such conditions. It was easy enough for a foreigner to leave Shanghai if it became necessary, and he seldom had to face legal consequences at home. Chinese residents of the foreign settlements had unprecedented freedom of movement and activity. Foreign legal authority over them was tenuous, Chinese police could not operate in the Settlements, and extradition was possible only with the approval of the Shanghai Municipal Council (or the French Municipal Council for the French Settlement), which was not often granted. Police expenses accounted for 40 to 50 per cent of the annual budget of the Shanghai Municipal Council from 1855 to 1941, but even this remarkably heavy allotment did not achieve a rule of law and morality.

Shanghai was a place where two civilizations met and where neither prevailed. To the foreigners, it was out of bounds, beyond the knowledge or supervision of their own culture, where each man was a law unto himself, or where he easily adjusted to the prevailing *mores* with no qualms of conscience. Morality was irrelevant or meaningless in Shanghai, an atmosphere which was apparent to even the casual visitor. The fact that Shanghai was also a major port of call and naval station helped to prosper this attitude; sailors often formed a majority of the foreign population.* For the Chinese, Shanghai was equally off limits. Those who had chosen this new kind of life, like the merchants, were by that choice cut off from traditional China and from the sanctions which it imposed. Others who drifted to the city during famines or civil wars, or were kidnapped from the country as domestic servants, had by definition lost their family connections, which in traditional China was total physical and moral destitution. Small wonder that many of them turned to prostitution.

On top of this was the continually fluctuating population. Few people, Chinese or foreign, came to the city with the hope of remaining there long; most of them aimed to make a fortune in a few years and then to leave. Many of them did remain, but so did the frenzied atmosphere. The international, intercultural nature of the city added to its excitement. Foreign hotels found it necessary to advertise their ability to speak with patrons in English, French, German, and Russian as a minimum. Concerned missionaries and visiting judges contended with this tempting and stimulating situation in vain. It remained for the Communist administration of the city after 1949 to substitute their familiar order of austerity and

---

* The city gave its name to the practice of kidnapping men to work ships whose crews had found Shanghai's attractions too great. Both foreigners and Chinese were "Shanghaied" by roving gangs, often in search of coolie labor for East or West Indian plantations as well as of crews.

morality for the laxity and easy virtue which some Shanghai residents thought would prove a match even for the Peoples' Government.*

Another element which made life in Shanghai exciting, lawless, and profitable for the foreigners was the periodic flooding of the city by refugees from civil disorder in China. Shanghai was a tiny island of relative security at such times, where the presence of foreign consuls and troops and the quasi-independent status of the foreign settlements attracted large numbers of Chinese within its borders. The first great influx occurred at the time of the Taiping Rebellion (1850–1864), during which a local uprising of the Triad Society in 1853 and 1854 connected with the Rebellion virtually surrounded Shanghai, and even penetrated the Settlement until the troops were expelled by the foreigners. There were about 500 Chinese residents of the foreign settlements in 1852, 20,000 in 1854, and 500,000 in 1864.[9] Fortunes were made and lost in real estate and general speculation as the tide of refugees flowed and ebbed in response to the progress of hostilities in the Yangtze delta. Chinese capital from the hinterland also gravitated to the protection of the foreign settlements and added more fuel to the speculative blaze.

Legitimate (sic) business of all kinds received a great stimulus upon the expulsion of the Triads from the city, and a period of feverish and wellnigh fatal speculation set in. The price of land inside the Settlement and even without went up to an enormous pitch as thousands of wealthy Chinese from all sides flocked into the place for the security it offered. . . Great tracts of land were hastily built over with cheap shanties by the foreign speculators, who reaped a golden harvest. . .[10]

Land within the Settlements which sold for an average of £50 an acre in 1852 sold for an average of £10,000 in 1862. In 1862, for the first time since it had been built, the race course, pride of the Settlement, was idle. The foreigners were too busy to hold the races, and in the next year the race course was sold for tenement construction for twenty times its original price.† [11]

---

* The *China Monthly Review* records in its issue for January 1952 (p. 96) that at the time of the Communist take-over in May 1949 there were 800 brothels in Shanghai, which by November 1951 had been reduced to 71. In the latter month these were closed, and the 500 inmates sent to a special reorientation and training school, in accordance with the pattern established earlier in north China.

† Part of the proceeds was used to buy a new tract for a race course farther out

This pattern was repeated in most of its details whenever trouble threatened in China, as it did for example in 1884–85 (war between France and China), 1900 (the Boxer Uprising), 1911 (the republican revolution), 1915–18 (the first world war and Japanese intervention in Shantung), 1926–27 (the northern campaign of the Kuomintang), 1932 (Japanese attack on Shanghai), and most of the period of anti-Japanese and civil war from 1937 to 1949. It of course affected the economic life of the city in fundamental fashion, and understandably speculation flourished. It also meant that the foreigners lived in a state of some uncertainty and insecurity, since what brought the city prosperity could also destroy it. A foreign resident complained about this in a letter to the editor of the *North China Daily News* (published in Shanghai) which was printed the day before the Japanese attack on Shanghai in 1937, in a sense the last day of foreign Shanghai's existence:

Since I arrived in Shanghai some seventeen years ago I have been under arms as a member of the Volunteer Corps on a dozen different occasions in defense of the Settlement. Always these occasions have meant a cessation of business, a period of anxiety and possible danger, and no benefit to us as a community. 'Old stagers' of the mud-flat days will smile when one talks to them on the subject and say they have got used to the idea, but are we content to see this sort of thing continue indefinitely? We should organize ourselves as a community . . . that will enable us to have a more normal life. It is time the old idea that foreigners come to Shanghai for a few years and then go away with a fortune was abandoned. This is a place of permanent residence for most of us and we have a right to demand that same freedom and security which is the common possession of all civilized countries. . .[12]

The city's population, swollen periodically with refugees, was also an excellent source of cheap labor and an opportunity, or invitation, for labor abuses, especially after manufacturing became an important factor in the Shanghai economy during the twentieth century. The refugees had no bargaining power and lived in universal privation. Their presence in the labor force helped to account for the fact that factory conditions, wages and hours, and industrial

---

from the center of town. The present Communist administration has turned the race course, symbol of the foreign occupation, into its chief parade ground.

slums were as acutely bad in Shanghai as anywhere else in the world. Living standards among the Chinese were correspondingly low. A British visitor to Shanghai in 1843, one month after the founding of the foreign settlements, gave as his opinion in an account of the city that "in no other country in the world is there less real misery and want than in China." [13] This may be taken as a reflection of the state of Europe in 1843, and as a measure of what the second half of the nineteenth century, beginning with the Taiping Rebellion, did to China, but it also shows what happened in Shanghai (as it had happened in eighteenth-century England) when the industrial revolution came to a peasant society. Factory conditions and slum housing were bad, but scarcely worse than the condition of perpetual refugees who had neither factory nor slum to go to. In 1935, a comparatively peaceful year in China, the Shanghai Municipal Council collected 5,590 exposed corpses from the streets of the International Settlement alone. In 1937 the figure reached 20,746.[14]

An effective public health program under such conditions was impossible, and foreign residents lived in constant fear of epidemics. Cholera, smallpox, typhoid, dysentery and plague recurred periodically, and cases could not be restricted to the Chinese. The Council's attempts to improve the public health situation were also hampered by foreign and Chinese property owners. A code of public health laws was submitted to the Ratepayers' Association as early as 1903, but was voted down by "those with vested interests." [15] Later attempts met with similar obstruction, and nothing was ever done on the scale called for. Money dominated Shanghai, and everything gave place to it.

Even by 1941, however, it was still possible to walk from the center of the Bund to the unchanged agricultural countryside in three or four hours. It was less than ten miles, and the rice paddies and peasant villages could be seen clearly from any of the city's tall buildings. This was one of the sharpest and most dramatic boundaries in the world. Traditional China continued unbroken almost to the limits of the foreign settlements. It was hard to see there any sign of Shanghai's influence. The final proof of that influence came with the entry of the Communist armies into Shanghai in 1949.

PART ONE: The Setting

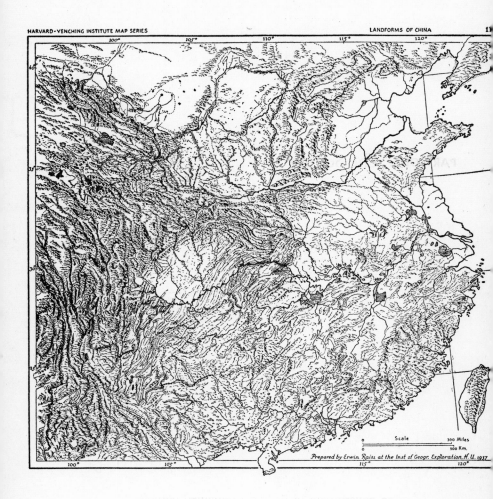

Map 2. Landforms of China (reproduced here by the courtesy of the Harvard-Yenching Institute).

TWO

Politics and Population

The Political Status of the City

In its physical aspect and in its economic organization, Shanghai was, and remains, largely Western. Foreigners governed most of the city. Yet the soil remained Chinese, and the legal or treaty powers of the foreigners were limited.[1]

The terms of the Treaty of Nanking in 1842 (between China and Great Britain at the close of the Anglo-Chinese war of 1840–1842*), which opened Shanghai, Ningpo, Foochow, Amoy and Canton to foreign trade, did not deal with the conditions of administration at the ports, and these were left to be negotiated separately. At Shanghai, negotiations in 1843 with the local Chinese officials established the right of foreigners to lease land within a small area set apart for the purpose outside the walls of the existing Chinese city. China remained sovereign at least in theory over the whole of Shanghai, and in effect delegated certain rights and powers to foreigners. The area of the foreign leaseholds was expanded by successive agreements with the local Chinese officials until it covered the greater part of the conurbation which developed at Shanghai, exclusive of the original walled city, but the administrative powers of the foreign government of this area remained tenuous.

The Shanghai Municipal Council, the chief organ of the foreign government at Shanghai, had the responsibility, granted by agreement with the Chinese officials, of maintaining order within the International Settlement, and this was taken to include policing and the maintenance of public works such as roads, drains, lighting, and later water, gas and electric services as these were developed. Powers of taxation, however, remained an unsolved issue until as late as

* Similar treaties were quickly negotiated by the other European powers and by the United States. See below, Chapter Five.

1899, when it was finally agreed (largely as a result of diplomatic pressure) that no Chinese taxes could be collected within the foreign settlements except maritime customs dues (administered by an organ of the Chinese Government staffed by foreigners and Chinese) and the land tax (since the land remained Chinese property), while the Shanghai Municipal Council was free to tax both foreign and Chinese residents of the Settlement.

Neither the Shanghai Municipal Council nor the foreign consuls at Shanghai were ever legally empowered to hinder the passage of Chinese troops through the foreign settlements, although Chinese troops were successfully excluded by *force majeure* and diplomatic bluff from the time of the first threat to the foreign settlements at the so-called Battle of Muddy Flat in 1853.* However, all of the Western powers having treaty relations with China claimed the right to land their own troops in the Settlements for the protection of the property and lives of their citizens. While this right was never formally enunciated in any treaty or agreement, it was practised on numerous occasions when troops landed from foreign warships in the harbor joined the Shanghai Volunteer Corps in defending the Settlement. The foreign settlements were never invaded by a hostile force (although bombs and shells landed there in 1932 and 1937), nor occupied by Chinese troops, from 1853, when the Volunteer Corps was formed, until Japan's assault on China engulfed all of the city after Pearl Harbor in 1941.

The most important right of the foreigners at Shanghai was extraterritoriality, which placed citizens of all powers having most-favoured-nation agreements with China under the jurisdiction of their own national laws wherever they went within China. This principle was first enunciated in the Treaty of Wang Hsia between China and the United States in 1843, and the law was in practice administered to foreigners by their own consular courts. Extraterritoriality gave the foreigners advantages in business and in security of person and property; at Shanghai it was the only solid legal basis

---

* An incident in the Taiping Rebellion (1850–1864), when Shanghai was for long periods surrounded by rebel or imperial forces. On this occasion, the foreign residents of the city, aided by crews from their ships in the harbor, cleared out a large encampment of imperial troops which had been established within the Settlement boundaries. See F. L. Pott, *A Short History of Shanghai* (1928).

of real significance for the existence of the city as a foreign enclave. (All special rights of foreigners in China, including extraterritoriality, were renounced by the treaty powers in 1944. Shanghai is now governed as a single unit by the Communist administration.)

The practice at many other treaty ports in China differed. At some, outright territorial concessions were made to each important foreign trading power; at others, the Chinese authorities established "international settlements" where foreigners might purchase land; at others, as at Shanghai, certain areas were reserved for foreign leasing (and later foreign purchase), with title deeds issued by the Chinese Government. Altogether, more than forty such treaty ports were established in China (some of them in fact inland centers far removed from navigable waterways), and administrative practice differed widely among them. The one common feature of all the treaty ports was that goods entering the "port" were exempted from all further taxation on their domestic movement by the payment of one inclusive tax. This provision was intended primarily to expedite the foreign trade of the treaty ports, but it also acted to encourage the movement of domestic trade through these cities with the streamlined tax system as compared with the multiplicity of local taxes which otherwise interrupted the movement of goods within China.

At Shanghai, there were three independent political units (map 3). First, the original Chinese city, to which were added, as the city grew after its opening to foreign trade, areas of predominantly Chinese occupancy outside the limits of the foreign settlements. This Chinese area was governed by the local Chinese county authorities until 1928, when the Nationalist Government established the Municipality of Greater Shanghai (map 5), a new administrative unit covering all of Shanghai outside the foreign settlements, responsible directly to Nanking and independent of local authorities. (It totalled 320 square miles, most of which remained open rural country outside the conurbation.) Second, the so-called International Settlement, which had originally been British and which was opened to all foreigners in 1854. This was the largest and most populous single political unit within the conurbation, and it included the city's commercial core, most of its manufacturing, and most of its shipping frontage. Third, the French Settlement, usually miscalled the "French

Concession," which was, like the originally British and later International Settlement, merely an area which by written agreement with the local Chinese authorities was set apart for the leasing and later for the purchase of land by French nationals. It was largely residential, and was governed by a Municipal Council in the same way and with the same powers as the International Settlement under the Shanghai Municipal Council. The population of both foreign settlements was overwhelmingly Chinese.*

One peripheral matter may be mentioned here in brief since it is a common difficulty in all great cities and since Shanghai's solution of it has been somewhat unusual. This is the problem of conveniently located space for suburban residential occupance. The development of large-scale manufacturing came relatively late in Shanghai, and was not a primary factor in the city's economy until about the first decade of the twentieth century. Most of the city's industrial area (map 3) has been occupied since that time, and while most of the Chinese industrial workers lived in the area of the factories (many of which were supplied with workers' dormitories on the premises), there was a growing need for conveniently located housing in residential suburbs for higher-income Chinese and foreigners engaged in the expanding economic activity of the city. A combination of circumstances had left such an area near to the city's commercial core only sparsely occupied until about the end of the first world war. This was the major part of the French Settlement, behind its narrow river frontage.

The last and largest addition to the French Settlement was made as late as 1914, and it covers substantially the area which had become residential by the 1920's. The French Settlement had not expanded earlier in this direction for a variety of reasons. In common with their practice in other colonial areas, the French had favored their own nationals in the granting and registering of title deeds to land in their Settlement. (Registry was managed through the French consul.) The choice sites went to French merchants, and most of the other foreigners took their business elsewhere, while the volume of French business alone was not sufficient to produce adequate grounds for territorial expansion. The French Settlement was further

---

* Wherever Shanghai is named here, it refers to the conurbation as a whole.

handicapped in its commercial and industrial growth by the very small extent of its frontage on the Whangpoo, on which most of the city's traffic moves, and French access to this waterfront was impeded by the interposition of the old Chinese city, which remained under Chinese control and through which no adequate roads were ever built. Just as important a handicap was the lack of navigable creeks running through the Settlement, since these have remained basic transport arteries in the modern economy of the city and have been important in locating many of its functions. Siccawei Creek (map 3) runs along part of the Settlement's southern border, but leaves it well before it enters the Whangpoo, and it has attracted industry along its southern bank rather than in the French Settlement. Finally, the French area is on the south side of the city, away from the Yangtze and the major industrial development reaching downriver toward Woosung, and upstream from the part of the harbor where ocean ships can dock.

Thus with the new addition in 1914, a relatively unoccupied area, free from industrial nuisances, but near to the center of the city and under the protection of foreign law and administration, was available for residential occupance at about the time when the suburban problem became acute. In addition to providing agreeable space for upper-income housing, it increasingly served as the entertainment center for the city and as a home for Chinese political figures in temporary retirement or for wealthy Chinese criminals who profited from the laxness of the French authorities and the ambiguous legal status of the Settlement. "Frenchtown," as the foreign residents of Shanghai called it, was famous before the war as the home of every variety of legal and illegal entertainment enterprise, as well as of most of the wealthy foreigners and Chinese in Shanghai.

Population Figures

Caution is the rule in the use of any statistics pertaining to China, and Shanghai, despite its measure of foreign control, is not an exception. The overwhelming majority of the city's population has always been Chinese (graphs 1 and 2), and census figures compiled by both the National Government and the Shanghai Municipal Council are admittedly estimates. In addition to the inaccuracy of totals at any one period, interpretation of the census figures must also consider the large-scale fluctuations in the city's population due to its role as a haven of security for Chinese (and, during the 1930's, foreign) refugees during periods of political unrest, and its subsequent loss of most of this floating population when order has been restored. The city has also contained at every period a large but unmeasured population of homeless Chinese and of Chinese families living in boats moored on the numerous creeks which dissect the city.

An accurate census of the foreign residents in the foreign settlements was not taken until 1870, when the Chinese population within and without the settlements was estimated in addition. This method of obtaining accurate figures for the foreigners and rough estimates for the Chinese continued until 1928, when the Shanghai Municipal Council began a yearly census for the entire city, using the machinery and figures of the Chinese government of the Municipality of Greater Shanghai for a count of the Chinese population outside the Settlements, with the understanding that these figures were only one step from rough estimates toward accurate counts. Since the foreign total for the whole city never exceeded 60,000, it is apparent that the grand totals for each period are guesswork.

One further factor has made population totals inaccurate: political limits of the foreign settlements have never coincided with conurbation limits. From 1870 to 1928, when the Municipality of Greater Shanghai was organized, Chinese residents of the conurbation outside the Settlements had constituted from one-half to two-thirds of the total population of the city, while after 1928 the new Municipality included much larger areas of farm land than of built-up area. Existing population figures for Shanghai, and the compilation made in graph 1 probably err on the conservative side.

Until 1895 Shanghai remained almost exclusively a trading city, with a consequent population which never exceeded half a million. The peak shown in graph 1 for the years 1860 to 1865 represents the influx of refugees from civil disorder attendant on the Taiping Rebellion. While the population doubled between 1843 and 1895 as a result of foreign-organized trade, this growth was slight compared with the increase which followed on the development of modern manufacturing in the city after 1895. The removal of overseas competition in the China and southeast Asia markets during the first world war gave this development a strong impetus and added to Shanghai's population some three millions to maintain the expanded economic activity in which mass Chinese labor was now the key. The prevalence of small-scale and under-capitalized industry in the city and the nature of industrial organization in China also meant that proportionately larger amounts of labor were necessary in Shanghai to maintain this industrial development than had been necessary to maintain the city's earlier and primarily trading activities.

Population figures after 1936 are increasingly inaccurate and are greatly affected by the alternate crowding and evacuating of the city by refugees from Japanese hostilities. It is probable that the total population rose to well over four million by 1941, and that it dropped to approximately the 1936 figure during the period of Japanese occupation after 1941. The influx of returning Chinese refugees beginning in 1945 probably boosted the population to its highest total in the city's history (variously estimated by the foreign press as between five and a half and six millions). Subsequent emigration from the unprecedently crowded city during 1946 and 1947 may have been nearly balanced by a new influx of refugees from threatened and actual Communist military operations in the hinterland during 1948 and 1949. The city's trade is still greatly reduced under Communist administration and under the Nationalist blockade and subsequent embargo by members of the United Nations. During 1949 Communist authorities offered free passage to their native towns in the hinterland to all refugees in Shanghai, and the offer was apparently accepted by about 400,000 of them.[2] It is likely that by the end of 1951 the city's population had dropped from the peak in 1946 to between four and a half and five millions.

The foreign population did not reach 1,000 until 1860, nearly twenty years after the city's opening to foreign trade in 1843, and until the end of the century its growth was slow (graph 2). Foreigners filled executive posts in the foreign-owned trading houses and provided specialized services such as medical care, legal and financial business, missionary work, and consular offices, but the great majority of services were performed by the Chinese, including the lower-ranking employees of the foreign trading firms. The development of manufacturing in Shanghai created a need for larger numbers of foreigners, to serve as technicians and administrators, and to operate the expanded banking and financial structure which industrial development required. And as trade increased with the growth of

POPULATION OF SHANGHAI, 1840-1936

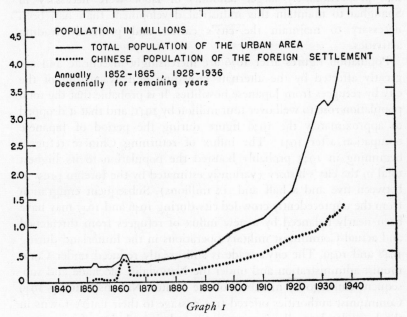

POPULATION IN MILLIONS

—— TOTAL POPULATION OF THE URBAN AREA

•••••••• CHINESE POPULATION OF THE FOREIGN SETTLEMENT

Annually 1852-1865 , 1928-1936
Decennially for remaining years

Graph 1

manufacturing and the widening of the China market for Western-type goods, a growing volume and variety of foreign imports were marketed in Shanghai and distributed from there throughout China by foreign firms.

In the period between the two world wars, Shanghai became a refuge haven for foreigners as well as for Chinese due to its ambiguous political status as an international oasis far removed in distance from political and racial problems in Europe. First to come there in large numbers were Russian refugees from the Bolshevik revolution, nearly a thousand annually from 1919 to 1930. After 1933, refugees from Nazi Germany found that Shanghai was the only world port which could be entered and resided in without a passport, and those who could afford the long trip formed a growing separate community in the city after 1934, many of them dependent on foreign charity.

FOREIGN POPULATION OF SHANGHAI, 1843-1936

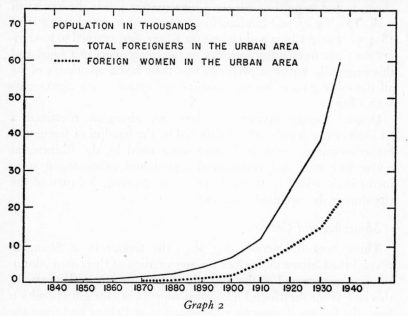

POPULATION IN THOUSANDS
——— TOTAL FOREIGNERS IN THE URBAN AREA
········ FOREIGN WOMEN IN THE URBAN AREA

Graph 2

In 1936 the approximate foreign total of 60,000 had as its most important constituents 20,000 Japanese, 15,000 Russians (predominantly White refugees), 9,000 British (who until about 1912, when they were surpassed by the Japanese, had always been the largest non-Chinese national group in Shanghai), 5,000 Germans and Austrians (most of them recent refugees), 4,000 Americans, and 2,500 French.[3] Foreign women were scarce before 1870 (graph 2) and never constituted much more than a third of the foreign total. Their presence did little to alter the prevailing adventurer's attitude of the

foreign community. It was only after 1900, when the Japanese became one of the leading groups in the foreign community, that the
proportion of foreign women reached even a third.

The Japanese are Shanghai's nearest foreign neighbors, and with
their industrial experience and their drive for economic expansion
overseas, they made Shanghai one of their most important industrial
centers, especially for the manufacture of cotton textiles, taking advantage of relatively cheap Chinese labor, locally grown cotton, and
cheap power to produce for the China market inside the low tariff
wall. The Treaty of Shiminoseki in 1895, which ended the war of
1894–5 between China and Japan over Korea, first granted to foreigners the right to establish factories in the treaty ports of China, and
this originally Japanese privilege was then taken advantage of by
all the other powers having most-favored-nation treaty agreements
with China.

Despite foreign investments, however, Shanghai remained a
Chinese city, still politically dominated by the handful of foreigners,
but economically more and more maintained by the Chinese, as
native industrial and commercial capital and management were
increasingly added to native labor in the growing industry of the
city during the twentieth century.*

Shanghai and China

Throughout the period 1843–1937, the foreigners at Shanghai
pressed the Chinese authorities for an extension of their own administrative powers and of the area of the two foreign settlements. In
this endeavour they found lukewarm support or outright opposition
from the foreign diplomatic representatives at Peking and from the
foreign offices in the home countries, who shied away from the
implications of full sovereignty over Chinese territory and who continually reminded the overzealous foreigners in Shanghai of their
precarious and equivocal legal position in asserting "rights" of taxation, defense, and administrative independence. The complex political and economic structure of modern Shanghai was erected primarily on the precedents resulting from bluff, maneuver, and *force
majeure* of the assertive foreign residents of the city.

* A majority of the city's industrial enterprises were Chinese-owned by at least 1920.

In this progress they were aided by the decline of the imperial government of China, the Ch'ing, or Manchu, dynasty. The military and economic impact of the West during the nineteenth century accelerated the decay of the Ch'ing, which had ruled China since 1644. The imperial government's attitude toward the foreigners at the time the first treaty ports were established was still, despite the Anglo-Chinese war of 1841–42 and its humiliating defeat for China, that these Western barbarians must be kept on the margins of the empire and that they must not be treated as equals by receiving them at Peking. Negotiations at each treaty port for the establishment of foreign settlements or concessions were accordingly left in the hands of local officials, but by the time it became apparent that the foreigners could not be contained by such methods, the Ch'ing government was too weak to prevent their further encroachment. It was the hesitancy of the foreign offices at home rather than the lack of opportunity in China which stopped the process short of colonialism.[4]

With the downfall of the imperial system and the rise of republican China under the leadership of the Nationalist party, Chinese nationalism became increasingly jealous of Shanghai as a foreign creation which was an excrescence on the Chinese body politic. While the Chinese were wrong in assuming that twentieth-century Shanghai was primarily a foreign creation, they were right in fixing on the city as the outstanding symbol of the economic exploitation of China by Western commercialism, and as the principal reminder of China's unequal-treaty status with the Western powers. This reaction against Shanghai and against what it stood for was one of the few points on which Nationalists and Communists have consistently agreed. Despite the fact that he and prominent members of his party earned considerable wealth out of the Shanghai economy, and despite the profitable existence in Shanghai of a major segment of China's manufacturing and trading firms as well as its leading banks, Generalissimo Chiang Kai-shek (Chairman of the Nationalist party) had this to say about the treaty-ports in 1943:

year after year our country's life was increasingly concentrated in these areas. . . Within the concessions the only ones that prospered were the compradores (Chinese agents for foreign firms) . . . and no productive enterprises developed in these ports because they could not absorb people

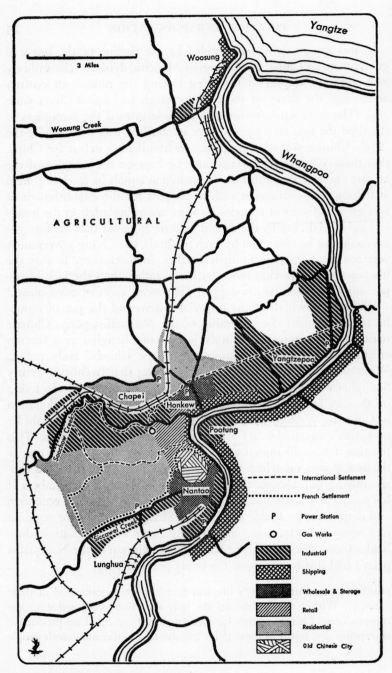

Map 3. Land Use at Shanghai, 1936

from the agricultural villages . . . Economic reconstruction must have its foundation in the national economy. . . This abnormal development of the national economy could not be adapted to the defense needs of the state. . . The main communication routes were based on these easily blockaded cities . . . the imperialists could have strangled the country's economic life. . . The state could not protect itself and the people could barely exist. . .[5]

The Communist condemnation is even more specific:

Shanghai must break off its dependence on the imperialist economy and must be changed from a city where imperialism, compradores, and bureaucrats oppress and exploit the people to one which produces for the domestic market and serves the people. . . Shanghai is the concentrated, typical expression of the colonial or semi-colonial nature of old China's economy. Its so-called prosperity in the past was not founded on an independent, sound economic basis, but on bureaucratic capitalism and on imperialism and its compradores. Shanghai's production was mainly for the selfish interests of a handful of foreign exploiters and domestic compradores and bureaucrats. Most of Shanghai's key enterprises were in the hands of foreigners or Chinese bureaucratic capitalists. The raw materials and power of many industries had to depend on foreign supplies. Such colonial or semi-colonial economic status must be discarded before Shanghai can become a truly prosperous new peoples' city. . .[6]

The Communist armies took Shanghai on May 27, 1949, and in the following months plans were discussed for the relocation of some of Shanghai's manufacturing and population to inland centers where they would be less exposed to outside attack and where their economic activity would redound more generally to the welfare of the country as a whole. These plans were given additional impetus by the Nationalist blockade of the coast and by the United Nations embargo which has followed it, which at present writing appear to have curtailed industrial production in the city to a considerable extent. Writing in late August of 1949, the then mayor of Shanghai, General Chen Yi, stated that the official Communist program for Shanghai was to "change (its) industrial policy from that of dependence on imperialism to that of serving the Chinese people." In order to accomplish this end, and to minimize the effects of the blockade, "we must evacuate the population of the city systematically and transfer factories to the interior wherever possible." [7] While no details have been published on Communist plans for the relocation of Shanghai factories, this has been a recurrent theme in general policy statements. How much will be done about it remains to be seen, and may depend in large measure on how long the current trade restrictions remain effective. While such relocation might be dictated by non-economic considerations, it is the writer's opinion that it would economically be unwise, at least at the present stage of the Chinese economy as a whole.

But the foreign Shanghai which Nationalists and Communists alike have castigated is now a thing of the past. As much a Chinese as a foreign creation by at least the time of the first world war, the city has now become politically and economically an integral part of China. The course of Chinese nationalism and of the Westernization of the Chinese economy, both developments begun in and stimulated by the growth of Shanghai, have reclaimed the city.

THREE

Site

The Delta

In common with most delta ports, Shanghai has achieved its prominence in spite of the disadvantages of its site. Some indication of this may be found in the title of the first governing body set up in the city by its foreign residents in 1845: "The Committee of Roads and Jetties." The Yangtze delta, which in the vicinity of Shanghai extends westward to a low range of hills along the western shore of Tai Lake, is in process of rapid growth.

The delta as a whole comprises the level lowlands east of Tai Lake and of Chinkiang, and north of Hangchow; north of the Yangtze, the river's delta merges with that laid down by the Huai, and by the Huang in its several courses at different periods south of the Shantung peninsula. The delta is truncated on its seaward front, like other deltas formed on the coasts of open oceans, by coastal and tidal currents. The usual delta characteristics are present, in particular the long, relatively straight stretches of natural levee along the lower course of the river (although these are rather low and may periodically have been removed by the local farmers for grading and soil renewal), and the gradual foundering of the lower-lying areas behind the levees, in which lakes have formed.

It can be empirically assumed that the Yangtze is more silt-laden and is extending its delta faster during the last 2,000 years since the beginning of intensive farming and accompanying denudation of slopes in the river's watershed then before agricultural occupance. At Shanghai, unconsolidated alluvium covers the site to a depth averaging about 1000 feet, and the level of the almost flat plain as far west as Tai Lake is less than one foot above spring high tide in the Yangtze estuary. Calculations based on the average silt content of the Yangtze at its mouth, the velocity of the river, and the slope of the river bed indicate an average of about one foot added overall to the elevation of the bed at the river's mouth in each twenty-year period, or about one mile added to the coastline in each sixty-year period.[1]

On this basis, the site of Shanghai would have been on the seacoast about 500 B.C., an empirical estimate which agrees with the record of Chinese history. All cities in the delta area east of the line of Sungchiang (map 5) for which there are adeqaute records were founded after the third century A.D.[2] Records of the Eastern Han dynasty (25 A.D. to 220 A.D.) speak of Kunshan, now 80 miles from the sea, as the seaport of Soochow in the second century A.D., but Shanghai has served as Soochow's port since about the fifth century A.D. Tsungming Island in the Yangtze estuary, according to the official gazetteer of the island, first emerged as a habitable sand spit in the tenth century A.D. By the thirteenth century it was sufficiently densely populated to be made a separate *hsien* (county), and at present measures approximately 43 by 8 miles.[3]

Building and Drainage

The material on which Shanghai rests is thus totally unconsolidated and presents serious problems for building. An average vertical section shows silt from the surface to about 20 feet, sand to 300 feet, and gravel mixed with sand and silt to about 1000 feet, where some consolidated conglomerate is reached. The water table lies between five and eight feet below the surface of the ground.[4] It may be assumed that before the draining and filling done by the foreigners since 1843, the water table was considerably higher, and that even before 1843 the canals dug by the Chinese provided enough drainage to keep the water table lower than it would otherwise have been considering the soil and elevation of the site.

Foreigners were discouraged to find in 1875 when a bridge was built across the mouth of Soochow Creek * that one blow from the small pile driver employed buried the pilings out of sight in the

---

* "Soochow Creek" is the name given by foreign residents to the Woosung Chiang, originally a much larger stream, which drains into the Whangpoo at Shanghai and connects the city with Soochow, some sixty miles inland. In the interests of clarity and consistency it will hereinafter be referred to as Soochow Creek, the name by which it has most generally been known in Shanghai itself.

silt.[5] A foreign resident writing in 1915 took a gloomy view of the city's future because he considered that six storeys was the maximum possible for buildings on this site.[6] These problems have been overcome, at considerable expense, by floating the taller buildings on concrete rafts in order to provide a stable foundation adequate to support structures which would otherwise sink into the alluvium. Until the first experiment with this method in the building of the new Shanghai Club in 1910, large buildings had been set on wooden pilings driven into the silt, and great care was necessary to prevent unequal settling. Shanghai's twenty-storey hotels and public buildings, erected during the 1920's and 1930's, float on their concrete rafts in this jelly-like subsoil, a scant 800 miles from the major earthquake belt running through the Japanese islands, but fortunately in the hundred-year history of the foreign settlements, no serious shocks have occurred.

Surface drainage has also been a constant problem in the development of modern Shanghai. The original site [7] (adjoining the walled Chinese city — map 6) as the British found it in 1842 was a typical agricultural landscape of the Yangtze delta: wet rice paddies and dry cotton fields, crisscrossed by creeks and canals, and with occasional clusters of family villages. This land was subject to frequent floods at high tides by the tidal inflow of water from the Yangtze and the resultant backing up of fresh-water outlets (primarily Soochow Creek and the Whangpoo), and until recently it was still flooded nearly every year in late summer by typhoon winds from the east and accompanying heavy rains. The land within the metropolitan area was gradually raised by filling to permit the building of roads and houses. Filling was easier and cheaper than artificial drainage for all but the swampiest areas and proved adequate for the growth of the city, but it was accomplished only at a considerable expense of money and energy.

The commercial core of the city, concentrated along the Whangpoo frontage, remained regularly subject to flooding. One of the first public works projects to be carried out under the Communist administration (which has attempted to make Shanghai a showplace of efficiency as an advertisement of the virtues of the new regime) was the filling of the lowest places in this downtown area, particularly its major commercial artery, Nanking Road, which follows fairly closely the course of a small creek culverted early in the period of foreign occupance (map 6). It was thus one of the most frequently flooded areas in the city. Paving along this heavily traveled street through the heart of the hotel and retail district was removed for nearly a mile back from the river, and replaced after the ground level had been raised sufficiently to protect it from all but the worst floods.

The numerous tidal creeks (map 6), characteristic of the lower delta, were useful in the early days of the Settlements as master drains and for demarcating legally and defending militarily Settlement boundaries. They were also used for carrying off sewage, where their tidal ebb was an advantage, and for movement of goods within the city and to and from the hinterland. The so-called Defense Creek at the western limit of the British Settlement of 1848 (map 6) was culverted and covered with a roadway in 1906, a few years after the Settlement had reached its greatest areal extent in 1899, but the Yang Ching Pang, which formed the boundary between the French and International Settlements on the south, remained an open sewer and transport artery until 1915, when as an enclosed culvert it was covered over with a broad boulevard named Avenue Edward VII as a gesture of ideological if not political unity between France and Great Britain. The remaining uncovered creeks are still important transport arteries, and as such key factors in the economic life of the city. While Shanghai has at least to this extent turned its delta site to advantage (and in a largely unique way as we shall see below), the problems which the delta has presented far outweigh its benefits.

The City

The site of the original British Settlement, on the left bank of the Whangpoo at its confluence with Soochow Creek, was determined by the existing walled Chinese city just upstream, whose trade had attracted British interest in a concession there (map 6). Soochow Creek, the original natural and later canalized waterway to the leading delta city of Soochow for which Shanghai served as the port, was the primary factor fixing the Chinese city, and it was naturally built on the outside of the bend in the Whangpoo, where tidal scour cut a channel and where it could tap a larger hinterland than on the inside of the bend. It may be assumed that the Chinese city was originally at the junction of Soochow Creek and the Whangpoo, and that since its founding in approximately the fourth century A.D., deposition and alterations in the character of both Creek and River (see the next section of this chapter) have left the city on the Whangpoo about 5000 feet upstream from the Creek's mouth. A considerable area was thus left between the city walls and the mouth of Soochow Creek, and here the British Settlement was established.

Sir Henry Pottinger, head of the British delegation at the Treaty of Nanking, selected the site for the British Settlement at Shanghai on his way back from signing the Treaty, his choice being influenced by strategic considerations.[8] The area he fixed on was the little square bounded on three sides by defensible waterways and on the fourth by the navigable Whangpoo (map 6). The main suburbs of the Chinese city lay between its wall and the Yang Ching Pang, while north of this creek the land-use was agricultural.

The boundaries of the original British leasehold of 1843 and later additions, and of the original French leasehold of 1849, made close use of existing waterways. These were useful not only for demarcation and defense, but also for sewage disposal, drainage, and transport, although not for drinking since they were both brackish and polluted. Roads (including Nanking Road) were built over many of these streams, but they continued to act as sewers. The course of Defense Creek and its junctions suggest that it was canalized for at least part of its length and diverted to supply the moat of the Chinese city, supplementing the water also received from the three other creeks emptying into the moat.

There are no contemporary accounts of natural levees anywhere on this site in 1843, and the possibility of their existence is lessened by the contemporary pattern of streams and canals as it can be reconstructed from period maps and records. Possibly the material which must have been deposited by Soochow Creek and Whangpoo flood waters along their respective banks was continually removed by local farmers in order to spread the alluvium over their fields (a common practice in the delta), or to maintain proper ground levels for the flooding of rice paddies. It is therefore unlikely that foreign settlement was fixed in any respect by the protection or by the higher and drier ground which natural levees would have afforded.

A frontage on the navigable Whangpoo, completing the water defenses around the British Settlement, was an additional source of security for the foreigners, since it permitted British naval vessels to command the entire site with their guns. George Balfour, the first British consul at Shanghai, in expressing his approval of Pottinger's choice of a site, stressed the importance of the Whangpoo on this point: "By our ships our power can be seen, and if necessary, felt." [9] This consideration may have been a factor in the decision to retain the prohibition against building on the river side of the Bund, a problem which is discussed in more detail below. Certainly foreign naval vessels have been prominently anchored off the Bund at every period of Shanghai's history from 1843 until the Communist takeover in 1949.

Along the Whangpoo and Soochow Creek, the muddy tidal foreshore was not usable for buildings or wharves until embankments had been constructed. This process, known in all the China treaty ports by the Anglo-Indian term "bunding," was a continuing job requiring large sums of money. In the case of the famous Bund along the Whangpoo frontage of the International Settlement from Soochow Creek to the Yang Ching Pang, the terms of the original grant of lease rights by the Chinese government to British subjects prohibited building within thirty feet of the high-water mark, which space was to be reserved as a tow path for the use of Chinese trackers pulling boats upstream.

When the rights of the Chinese trackers lapsed by the mid-1850's in the face of the growing foreign stake in Shanghai and the demands of steam navigation, the Shanghai Municipal Council inherited this waterfront strip by default and successfully defended it against the designs of foreign traders who wished to make commercial use of the area for warehouses and offices which would be convenient to the river.[10] The Council undertook the bunding of this strip in 1862, and in the process extended it beyond the high-water mark to make an overall width more than double the original thirty feet. At the northern end of this embankment, at the mouth of Soochow Creek, the Council made use of some gratuitous real estate, deposited by the Creek around the hulk of a sailing ship wrecked there in 1851, and soon made part of the mainland by continued deposition, for the establishment of a park on the river side of the Bund. A broad boulevard was built from Soochow Creek to the Yang Ching Pang along the new embankment (later extended by the French into their Settlement), and this artificially preserved freeway has been maintained by the modern city as its chief showplace and promenade ground, lined to landward by hotels, banks, trading houses, and public buildings, but on the river side by unsightly floating wharves (necessitated by the annual tidal range of 13.6 feet) and mud flats exposed at low tide.

On this problem also the Communist administration of the city have expressed themselves in another project to dress up China's modern front door to the West. The current project for the Bund (now largely completed) calls for the removal of the railway and street car lines which have run down the middle of the broad embankment, with attendant rickshaw stands and cargo stations, and their replacement by an island to be planted with grass and trees, in a reversion to the original late nineteenth century pattern. Planting is also to be added on the river side of the Bund, to provide some screen in front of the harbor functions which are too important to move, however unsightly.

Water Supply

Water for drinking and for the manifold needs of a large city has been a perennial difficulty, since the brackish Whangpoo is high in carbonates and indifferently potable, while most local wells yield an even less desirable and more limited supply. Only the relatively modest demands of most of the Chinese population and the absence of any large pure-water consuming industries make the water supply adequate for such a large city on this site.

Until 1883 all water used by the foreigners for drinking (aside from that drawn from the few local wells) was dipped from the Whangpoo or Soochow Creek (and by the Chinese from the other creeks and canals as well) and settled in earthen jars with the help of alum to precipitate the mud. The water was then boiled and cooled, but this beverage was not held in much favor by the foreign community, and beer, wine and spirits imported from abroad filled most of the needs of at least the male foreign residents, aside from the missionaries. In 1883 a foreign-owned and directed water company under contract to the Shanghai Municipal Council began to supply water to the foreign community in pipes, and this service was gradually extended to Chinese residents of the Settlement after 1884, primarily to help prevent disease, which could so easily spread. This water, pumped from the Whangpoo, was purified by slow sand filters, alum, and chlorine, but it remained unpalatable and was distributed to less than 10,000 users in all until the turn of the century. The intake for this plant has remained on the Whangpoo below the city in south Yangtzepoo.[11]

Location downstream from the city enables the plant to draw on the tidal inflow from the Yangtze, which is less contaminated, fresher, and less muddy near the surface than what the Whangpoo brings down. The widespread use of city refuse of all kinds for fertilizing fields and for filling low-lying land makes a downstream location so near the city less of a danger than it would be in most Western cities. The Whangpoo may originally have been a tidal salt water creek which later benefitted from stream piracy in making connections with a fresh-water stream or streams farther inland as its own headwaters. Such a possibility is suggested by the Whangpoo's short total course compared with the volume of water it carries, by the sharp right-angle bend it makes in flat alluvial country about ten miles above Shanghai (map 5), and by what is known of the hydrographic history of this area, which is discussed in greater detail below.

This private British-owned company, the Shanghai Waterworks Ltd., continued to provide about half of the piped water supply of the entire city until 1936, by which time it distributed a daily average of about 54 million gallons. It was supplemented in 1903 by a company owned by the government of the French Settlement with an intake above the city on the Whangpoo, and also using sand filters, alum, and chlorine to supply a daily average of about 32 million

gallons by 1936. Two Chinese-owned waterworks were also in operation, one in Chapei (part of the Chinese municipality — map 3)
established in 1921 and drawing water from an intake on the
Whangpoo just above Woosung. This was the largest Chinese-
owned waterworks in China, and supplied an average of about ten
million gallons daily. The other Chinese waterworks was built in
1906 in Nantao, with an intake just upstream from that of the
French company, but it operated intermittently until 1930, and by
1936 supplied only about three million gallons daily. These two
Chinese waterworks served a tiny fraction of the Chinese population
outside the foreign settlements, primarily in the areas immediately
adjoining the Settlements on the northwest and south. Both plants
used sand filters and chlorine to purify their water, but in 1926 the
supply of the Chapei company was found to be grossly polluted and
probably responsible for a cholera epidemic in that year in which several foreign as well as several hundred Chinese cases were reported.[12]

Aquiferous sand strata with water pockets of some size underlie
parts of the city's site at depths of 100 feet or more, and most of the
textile and paper factories have tapped this relatively pure and soft
water by wells deeper than those dug during the early days of the
Settlement. Drilling in the alluvium is cheap, but while water thus
obtained appears to be satisfactory for soft-water using industries,
it is questionable whether it is renewable and will not soon be ex-
hausted, and certainly whether it is adequate to supply even a small
part of the city's needs.

Despite the chemical purity of the water supplied by at least the
two foreign companies, most foreign residents continued into the
1930's to boil and filter it before using it for drinking, an old habit
which died hard and which was doubtless prolonged by the unpleasant taste of the heavily treated water. The total piped and
treated water consumption of the entire city in 1936, approximately
100 million gallons a day exclusive of private wells, would not have
supplied New York in the same year (with a population a little less
than twice that of Shanghai) for more than two and a half hours.*

---

* New York used approximately one billion gallons a day in 1936, according to the
1936 edition of the New York *World Almanac*.

The Harbor

This is a delta city, and its consequent site problems are nowhere more apparent or more serious than in the matter of its harbor. The tidal inflow from the Yangtze which brings in relatively fresher water also brings in and deposits large amounts of silt. Shanghai maintains its position as a port fourteen miles from the Yangtze estuary only by constant dredging. Until approximately the eighth century A.D. Soochow Creek was the major stream at Shanghai and much larger than the Whangpoo, which up to that time remained about the same size as the present Soochow Creek.[13] However, mud brought in by the Yangtze and brought down by Soochow Creek from its upper course increasingly silted up the latter's lower reaches, and in 446 A.D. a canal was dug along its lower course in order to maintain the water link with Soochow, then the leading city of this part of the delta and at the time dependent on Shanghai as its port. Flood gates were also erected in Soochow Creek against the inflow of Yangtze mud. These are first mentioned in the thirteenth century, and were apparently replaced about 1735 by stone gates a quarter of a mile upstream from the Creek's mouth.[14] The gates had disappeared by the time the British arrived in 1842, but the Creek has remained navigable as far as Soochow for boats up to 80 tons cargo capacity.

As Soochow Creek lost its primacy, the Whangpoo became the master stream, possibly aided by capture of fresh headwaters, and with the additional help of tidal scour, cut a deep channel to the Yangtze. On the outside of the sharp bend in the Whangpoo at the mouth of Soochow Creek the currents maintained a depth adequate for sailing ships of the nineteenth century, and in 1842 there was a channel in the Whangpoo between Shanghai and the Yangtze estuary with a minimum navigable depth of about fifteen feet. By 1905 silting had reduced this to ten feet, and in that year dredging work was begun by the Whangpoo Conservancy Board, an organ of the Chinese Government staffed by foreigners and Chinese and administered by the Commissioner of Customs at Shanghai, also a foreign employee of the Chinese Government.

Three main bars had by this time formed: Woosung Outer Bar at the point where the Whangpoo empties into the Yangtze,

Woosung Inner Bar about half way between the mouth of the Whangpoo and Soochow Creek, and Wayside Bar, opposite the mouth of Soochow Creek. A Dutch hydraulic engineer worked as technical chief of the Board from 1905 to 1911, by which time a minimum navigable depth of 19 feet had been obtained between Woosung and Shanghai. Training walls were built at the mouth of the Whangpoo to concentrate the current and scour a channel. The old ship channel at Woosung Inner Bar (where a large island divided the river) was dammed and the river straightened at that point to permit maximum effective scour in the new channel. At Wayside Bar continuous dredging was instigated. This program, and the widening of the channel between Shanghai and Woosung to a least width of 900 feet was continued after 1911 under a Swedish engineer, Heidenstam, who published several short scientific papers based on his work with the river. By 1928 a controlling depth of 26 feet at neap low tide within the 900-foot channel had been obtained, but the daily tidal range of six feet made a 32-foot depth available for a few hours every day in the year.[15]

33,700,000 cubic yards of mud were removed by dredging between 1905 and 1930. About a third of this was used to fill in the old ship channel at Woosung Inner Bar. About half was dumped at sea, and the remainder was used for filling low-lying land adjacent to the river between Yangtzepoo and Woosung.[16] However the greatest obstacle to shipping using the port has been the Fairy Flats, a very large bar area at the entrance to the Yangtze estuary, where the silt deposition of the river is particularly concentrated as the delta grows seaward (map 5). Prior to 1932, when dredging work was begun there, ships drawing more than 26 feet were obliged to wait for high tide on every day of the year, those drawing 30 feet could arrive in Shanghai only at the time of spring tides, and those drawing 32 feet or more could not enter the harbor at all. While the deepest-draft ships regularly in the Pacific trade were the "Empress" boats of the Canadian Pacific Steamship Line drawing 31½ feet, the majority of trans-Pacific shipping entering the harbor drew between 26 and 30 feet and were thus frequently delayed by as much as a day at the Fairy Flats. This condition also caused considerable congestion in the harbor. Turn-arounds were slowed and money was lost.[17]

Work was begun in 1932 by the Board on cutting a channel of 33 feet at mean high tide through the Fairy Flats, which required the removal of nine feet of silt from the bar as it then existed, including an allowance of three feet for clearance in heavy seas and one foot for fall of the tide during the passage of the ship. By 1936 about three of the nine feet had been removed for half of the distance of the channel. Dredging was suspended during the Japanese occupation and has not yet been resumed during the blockade conditions of the post-war period. Much of the earlier work has thus been lost.

Ebb and flow currents at Shanghai average about three knots for a total of eight hours during each 24-hour period. Six major bends in the Whangpoo (the one at the mouth of Soochow Creek being almost a hairpin turn) and the narrowness of the channel make these tidal currents a problem for ocean-going ships, both in docking and in maneuvering for anchorage. None of the ocean vessels (except for foreign warships, which usually anchored off the Bund) dock above Soochow Creek, and most of them find it easier to unload cargo onto lighters in midstream, taking on cargo at wharves farther down the river in Yangtzepoo.* The wharves along the Bund are used for lighters and for river shipping. Roadsteads within the harbor are severely limited, and collisions and congestion are common.

There have been periodic suggestions that the main harbor be moved to Woosung, but even here conditions are far from ideal. There is a large anchorage in the open roads of the Yangtze with a minimum depth of 30 feet at mean low tide, measuring two miles by six miles, but tidal currents average about a knot stronger than at Shanghai, and these together with the winds across the open sweep of water prevent loading or unloading by lighter about 30 per cent of the time. Existing wharves at Woosung can accommodate only vessels drawing less than 18 feet. Cargo unloaded at Woosung by lighter or at the wharves is mainly carried to Shanghai directly by lighter on the Whangpoo, but there is also some shipment by rail. The expense and inconvenience of transshipment would probably

---

* Because of the angle and direction of the tidal currents and the set of the channel, loaded ships can be maneuvered out of the wharves and down the Whangpoo more easily than up the river and into the wharves.

not be overbalanced by the questionable virtues of Woosung as a harbor, although as trade volume grows port development at Woosung may help to relieve congestion. Up-river ports are always inconvenient, but only when a clearly preferable alternative is available, as for example at Bremerhaven, or the much earlier ascendancy of Shanghai over Soochow, is the original port city likely to be eclipsed in its maritime functions. In 1937 the Chinese Municipality completed preliminary work on a new wharf on the left bank of the Whangpoo just below Yangtzepoo. The river is slightly wider there and the problem of Wayside Bar is avoided. The ship channel was adequate at that point in 1937 to allow the largest Pacific ships to dock parallel to the shore, and the new wharf was designed especially for passenger traffic. By surfaced roads then under construction, Shanghai center could be reached by car in about thirty minutes. Under the Japanese occupation, work on this new wharf was continued, and post-war Chinese plans for the Greater Shanghai of the Future (i.e., the plans of the Nationalist Government) called for the transfer of all the passenger and most of the freight traffic from Honkew and Yangtzepoo to this new area, where facilities were to be greatly expanded.[18] If the city continues to grow in the direction of Woosung, this would be a logical change and would make it possible to handle a greater volume of deep-draft shipping with less delay and without sacrificing unduly the convenience of central location. Under the Communist administration, no more work has been done on this project, in the virtual absence of ocean shipping.

The inconveniences of congestion are marked at Shanghai, which in the 1930's had riverside shipping frontages (wharves with a minimum depth of 12 feet and more) totalling only nine and a half miles. Hamburg, in the same period, with approximately the same annual volume of shipping entered and cleared, had nearly forty miles of similar shipping frontages, and New York, with less than twice Shanghai's annual volume of shipping during this period had 260 miles of similar shipping frontages.[19] Shanghai in 1936 (the last year of regular dredging operations), with a permanent through ship channel of 26 feet at mean low water, was by far the shallowest as well as the most confined and awkward harbour among leading Far Eastern ports.[20] The fact that from 1920 to 1936 it remained sixth or seventh in rank among world ports, in terms of annual net registered tonnage entered and cleared, points to its characteristic role as a delta port. The trade of the Yangtze basin requires a major outlet to the sea, and Shanghai, despite its poor site, offers the only practicable deep-water harbor near the mouth of China's greatest trade highway, the Yangtze River.

The harbor has a few advantages. At latitude 31° 10′ and where it is also influenced to some extent by the warm Kuroshio, or Japan Current, Shanghai is the northernmost port on the China coast to be free from ice at all seasons in most years. This gives it an advantage over the two leading ports of north China, Tsingtao and Tientsin, where floating ice is usual for parts of January and February. Location fourteen miles up the Whangpoo gives the harbor protection from typhoons, which are a significant menace to shipping in all south China ports during late summer. Shanghai averages about one typhoon annually, but with the adequate warning provided and the degree of protection afforded by its up-river location, damage to shipping is never more than negligible. In the period before the growth of the foreign city, this inland location was also important as a measure of protection against frequent coastal raids by Japanese and Formosan pirates. Finally, fog adequate to delay shipping in the harbor or in the approaches in the Yangtze estuary is quite infrequent.

Prophecies of Shanghai's isolation from maritime shipping by the seaward growth of the delta have not been lacking at any period in the history of the modern city. As each new difficulty arose however, means were found to overcome it, for the advantages of the city's location have greatly outweighed the disadvantages of its site and have made extensive dredging worthwhile. There is no reason to believe that the undoubted accumulation of silt, especially on the Fairy Flats, during the war and post-war years will present an insuperable problem once dredging is resumed. The great volume of water discharged by the Yangtze into the sea and the scouring action of tidal currents will assure some kind of channel in the estuary on which dredging can concentrate. The neglect of dredging over such a long period may make it necessary to relocate the main ship channel, but what dredging has accomplished before it can accomplish again. As long as water transport retains its basic place in the Chinese economy, a harbor for ocean ships will be maintained at Shanghai as the commercial center of the Yangtze basin.

Relief and Climate

The site has only two advantages of importance: it is almost completely flat, and it has a more favorable climate than rival south China ports. Ample level ground was useful during the purely commercial phase of the city's development in allowing adequate space for storage of goods, for half of China's foreign trade passed through Shanghai from 1865 on, but it was more important in allowing the development of manufacturing after 1895. The commercial center which began in an area of 43 acres along the Whangpoo in 1843, demarcated and defended by creeks, was able to grow outward toward the west, south, and north as both political and economic conditions provided the impetus for metropolitan industrial development. Level ground continues unbroken within a twenty-mile radius of the city. While the site's liability to floods is a notable disadvantage, level ground must in general be counted an asset, especially as against the lack of it in Hong Kong, Foochow, Amoy, and other south China ports.

Shanghai's climate is influenced alternately by cold dry air from inner Asia and Siberia, and by warm moist Pacific air; it is tropical for one third of the year and temperate for two thirds. Rainfall averages 45 inches annually, 14 inches of which falls in June and July, but with no very marked seasonal concentration. July and August are uncomfortably tropical, and while rains keep the temperature below 90° for at least a quarter of these two months, the relative humidity throughout this period averages 84 per cent. Temperatures rarely exceed 98°. Vital statistics for foreign residents of the China treaty ports included in the yearly medical reports published since 1870 by the Maritime Customs give Shanghai, with a death rate averaging 16 per thousand annually for the period 1870–1930, a relatively good record. Most of the foreign residents considered it among the healthier treaty ports despite its uncomfortable summer, during which as many of them as were able left the city for the central mountain belt or the Shantung beaches. The accompanying table com-

pares temperatures and relative humidity at Shanghai with selected
cities in different climatic regions.

	Mean Annual Temperature	Mean Annual Rel. Humidity	Dec.-Jan.-Feb.		June-July-August	
			Temp.	R.H.	Temp.	R.H.
New York	54	60	30	61	79	62
London	49	79	39	82	61	76
Canton	64	82	48	56	83	89
Shanghai	59	78	39	36	78	85

Shanghai's is a moderate climate compared with south China,
especially in respect of the greater effect in winter of the Siberian
high, and with daily and seasonal changes in which Chinese and
foreigners can work under reasonably favorable and familiar conditions.

In sum however, the growth of Shanghai must be regarded as an
illustration of the extent to which the advantages of an exceptionally
favorable location can overcome the disadvantages of an exceptionally unfavorable site. While most of the city's site problems are
common to many delta ports, its locational advantages are unique.
These will now be examined in the following chapter.

FOUR

Location

■

Shanghai's Hinterland

"The first and most natural root of a great city is the labour and populousness of the adjacent country, which supplies the materials of subsistence, of manufactures, and of foreign trade." [1] Shanghai is a great city primarily because it stands at the apex of the most fertile and populous area of comparable size anywhere in the world, the lower Yangtze basin.

The Yangtze watershed totals 750,000,000 square miles, or half of China proper, and has a population of approximately 200,000,000. The section of the river's basin which we may call the fertile triangle, bounded by Chinkiang, Hangchow, and Shanghai, an area of about 20,000,000 square miles, has an estimated population of 40,000,000, or an overall average of about 2,000 inhabitants per square mile. Nearly 80 per cent of the total land area is cultivated (map 10), and this region stands out as one of the three most widely cultivated in China (the Red Basin of Szechuan and the north China plain being the other two). Nodes of commerce are thickly scattered over the fertile triangle, which contains three cities of over half a million population (Hangchow, Soochow, and Shanghai — map 5). The Yangtze delta supports by far the densest single concentration of population in China for an area of similar size (map 7). The river's course is marked by successive clusters of settlement, terminating westward in the densely peopled Red Basin of Szechuan.

Of the other major cities of the lower Yangtze basin, Hangchow, Soochow, and Nanking were all at one time imperial capitals, and all have remained important commercial and industrial centers. Hangchow and Soochow are still among the three or four leading cities in China in silk reeling and weaving, and both act as central places for the surrounding rice and silk areas of the delta. Nanking

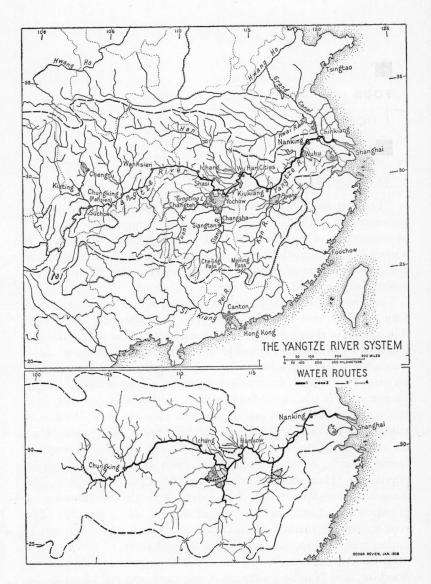

Map 4. The Yangtze River System (reproduced here by the courtesy of *The Geographical Review*). Numbers refer to: 1, regularly scheduled, all-year steamship runs; 2, waters open to all-year service by steam launches and tugs with barges; 3, waters navigable all year by large native boats; 4, waters navigable all year by small boats.

is above the delta proper, and its water connections are limited compared with those of its delta rivals. It has profited primarily from its location at a break in transport routes (including China's major north-south railway, which breaks at the Yangtze — map 8), and from its periodic function as a political capital.

All three cities have been hampered in their modern development by the lack of harbors adequate for ocean ships. At Hangchow an impressive tidal bore and many shoals in Hangchow Bay preclude use of the Chientang estuary by ocean shipping, and the river itself is navigable only for small boats. Soochow, once a maritime trading center, is now effectively land-locked, and was in any case superseded as a port city by Shanghai by at least the eighteenth century A.D. Nanking, 210 miles from the sea, must contend with silting, river currents, and an exposed anchorage. Both Nanking and Hangchow are handicapped as commercial centers, especially in a region where most goods move by water, by the rugged country around them (map 5), which contrasts with the extensive lowland focused on Shanghai. While all three of these cities were larger than Shanghai before the opening of China to foreign trade and to Western commercial exploitation, they were quickly outstripped by Shanghai under the new economic conditions, where access by water to the entire Yangtze basin and to the major ocean lanes of world commerce gave it a decisive advantage.

The city lies topographically at the focus of the east China lowland, converging on it from both the west and the north, and of the Yangtze basin as a whole (map 2). The river and its tributaries, draining the productive heart of China, all feed ultimately to the mouth of the Whangpoo. In the mainly pre-industrial economy of China, the great majority of goods moving beyond purely local markets do so by water. No other location can marshall a fraction of the advantages of Shanghai on this crucial point.

Of China's two other major river systems, the Huang (Yellow) in the north is navigable for steam launches for 25 miles above its mouth and for a small part of its course through Honan, but it is otherwise useless for navigation except in short stretches by small boats. The Hsi (West) River in the south is navigable for some 230 miles in the high-water season (spring and summer) for vessels drawing fifteen feet and for the same distance at low water for vessels drawing six feet. Smaller steam launches use the river for about 700 miles at all seasons. The Hsi system, however, drains only about 210,000 square miles, and contains no such extensive lowland as the Yangtze basin (map 2).

On the Yangtze there is an all-year ship channel for 5,000-ton ships as far as Hankow, 600 miles from the river's mouth, and a summer (high-water period) channel to Hankow for 10,000-ton ships. Above Hankow, permanent steamship service is maintained as far as Chungking, 1400 miles from the sea, by vessels up to 2,000-tons, and river steamers also operate to Suifu (Ipin, Süchow), 150 miles farther upstream where the Yangtze leaves the mountain mass of central Asia and is joined by its navigable tributary, the Min, from the western part of the Red Basin of Szechuan. Map 4 shows the extent to which the river's tributaries are navigable by different sized ships (Suifu on this map is referred to as Süchow). The total of inland waterways navigable from Shanghai by junks at all seasons (excluding the canals of the delta) is nearly 30,000 miles, reaching approximately 200,000,000 people. This transport network is reflected in the fact that Shanghai between 1865 and 1936 handled between 45 and 65 per cent of the total foreign trade of China by value.

The Yangtze system feeding Shanghai is reproduced in miniature within the delta itself (map 5). A maze of canals dissects the fertile triangle, connecting with natural waterways to form through water links between every village and town in this area and from all of them to Shanghai. The canals are used primarily for transport, but they also serve as sources of irrigation water for wet paddies and as community water supplies, in addition to providing drainage, which may have been their original purpose.[2] The alteration of the natural environment which the canals represent has been in progress for at least the last 2,000 years, and now constitutes probably the largest concentration of artificial waterways anywhere in the world.

When the canals are added to Tai Lake and the chain of smaller lakes to its east, the Yangtze, the Whangpoo, Soochow Creek, and many smaller rivers in this area, the landscape becomes an enormously magnified Venice. Within a radius of at least 100 miles from Shanghai it is possible to go from any village or town to any other village or town entirely by water, and in most cases in no other way. According to existing estimates,[3] and on the basis of the incomplete cartographic data, the delta area must contain at least half a million miles of canalized or artificial waterways. The railway between Shanghai and Nanking includes in its 193 miles 164 bridges over navigable rivers or canals.

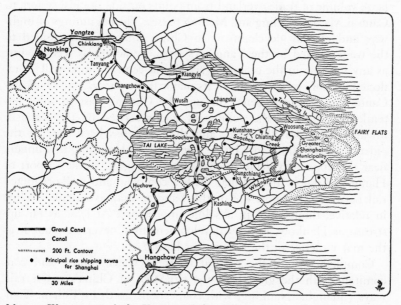

Map 5. Waterways of the Yangtze Delta. All waterways shown are navigable. Provincial boundaries are indicated by a dotted line.

The use of water routes is reflected in the sparseness of roads compared with other level areas of China and in the fact that such roads as exist run in most cases at right angles to major waterways. In addition, carts and barrows are scarce in the Yangtze delta, in marked contrast with other areas of China, or with most pre-industrial regions. Traditional Chinese bridges in the delta area are nearly all of the single span hump-backed type, reflecting the virtual absence of wheeled traffic as well as the need to provide adequate clearance over waterways for the passage of masted vessels.

The opening of the Yangtze to steam navigation by about 1862 following the Treaty of Tientsin (in 1858 between China and Great Britain; the commercial section of the treaty was not completed until 1860) ensured the ascendancy of Shanghai over rival southern ports by allowing the trade of central China to drain by its natural route, and within a very few years reduced to a trickle the formerly large volume of trade overland from points outside the Hsi system to Canton, via the Cheling and Meiling passes. The beginnings of highway and railway development in China (map 8) have added to the trade carried by the Yangtze system, by acting as feeders, just as any increase in the economic activity of central China will be reflected in more intensive use of its major trade artery. The Hankow-Canton railway, completed through the Cheling pass in 1936, has tended to augment the volume of goods carried by the Yangtze toward and from Shanghai, and the same has been true of the older railway built in 1910 by the French from Kunming in Yünnan, near the upper navigable reaches of the Yangtze, to the seaport of Hanoi in French Indo-China. With a complete and well-organized rail network, transport use of the Yangtze may eventually decline in relative, though not in absolute importance. At least as far upstream as Hankow, railway development may never supplant it as the major carrier in the lower river basin.*

Complemetary to the natural focus of water routes, and concomitant with the growth of the city, two of China's major railways (Shanghai-Nanking, with connections north to Tsinan, Tientsin, and Peking, and west to Chenghsien and Sian; and Shanghai-Hangchow-Ningpo, with connections west to Nanchang and Hankow and south to Canton) terminate at Shanghai (map 8), and a small network of motor roads links the city with most of the other centers of the lower Yangtze basin. The gathering of rail and highway routes at Shanghai is however a reflection of rather than a

---

* The importance of the Yangtze as a carrier in future competition with well developed railways may perhaps be compared with the current importance of the lower Rhine, below Mannheim. Although it runs through the heart of a major industrial region with one of the densest and most heavily traveled rail nets in the world (including lines along both banks of the river), the Rhine and its tributaries consistently carry a larger volume of goods than the combined railway lines through its basin.

factor in the pre-eminent location of the city. Peking, Tientsin, and Chenghsien are all more important rail centers than Shanghai.

Sea Routes

Shanghai's orientation to the sea is almost equally favorable. It lies less than a hundred miles east of the great circle route followed by shipping between west coast North America, and Japan, China and southeast Asia. All of the major commerce lanes of the western Pacific meet there. Midway on the China coast between north and south, Shanghai has the further double advantage of accessibility from the Chinese hinterland and nearness to Japan and the trans-Pacific trade. The China coast at the Yangtze delta extends farther eastward into the open sea than at any other point. The Yangtze keeps Shanghai in close relation to the hinterland despite its sea-ward extension, which in turn gives it an advantage over ports south of the coastal bulge, or north China ports on the enclosed Gulf of Pohai.

For the coasting trade it is a natural terminus. A foreign observer noted in 1843[4] that it was the division point between the carrying trade of junks from northern and southern ports, and that it acted as the leading entrepot on the China coast for the concentration and exchange of goods from the two major regions of China. This function Shanghai has retained to the present at least for the coasting trade carried in native junks, which is considerable though largely unmeasured. All direct coastal routes between northern and southern ports must touch the Yangtze estuary.

Shanghai is approximately equidistant in shipping time and distance from western European and eastern United States ports. Shippers must compete there on equal terms, and goods arriving via Suez or Panama can be laid down at competitive prices. Shanghai is not the terminus of either route (Singapore serving this function for west-bound traffic and Nagasaki for east-bound), although it is a major port of call for both. But most important is its focal position for Far Eastern shipping, and its median location between Atlantic Europe and America.

Rival Ports

The maritime trade of south China is divided among several ports, each serving a small and well-defined hinterland outlined by mountains as separate river basins, of which the basin of the Hsi is by far the largest. The Ta Yü and Wu Yi ranges extend almost to the coast from Hong Kong north to Ningpo. Their ridges form a barrier over which very little trade passes, and the rivers which flow from their crests to the sea have cut neither easy passes across them nor extensive flood plains. The relatively short Han, Min, Wu, and Chientang Rivers, interrupted by falls and rapids over most of their courses, are navigable only for small boats, and none of them makes easy connections with other river systems. The high relief extending down to the coast, except for the few small river flood plains, makes food production as well as transport difficult. The area as a whole (southeast coastal China) must import rice, but its important exports are limited to tea and timber. The configuration of east Asia and the submerged character of the south China coastline, bring these southern ports much closer to the continental mountain mass and leave them a hinterland which is hilly, thinly populated, and unproductive compared with the Yangtze basin.

The submerged coastline of the south includes a number of good harbors, notably Foochow (the estuary of the Min River), Amoy, and Swatow, but they are too small for any volume of modern ocean shipping, and their topographically limited hinterlands do not make harbor extensions worthwhile. Railways have not yet penetrated this area, aside from the single line from Hankow to Canton, with a spur to Kowloon (the mainland adjunct to the Crown Colony of Hong Kong), a reflection of its commercial unproductiveness more than of the engineering problems which it presents.

The outstanding exception among south China ports is Hong Kong, possessed of the finest harbor in the Far East, a deep and well-protected roadstead between Hong Kong island and the mainland, flanked on all sides by shielding islands. Location just off the mouth of the Hsi, whose basin is the most extensive and productive lowland in south China and contains its only major transport artery, is a further advantage. The port of Hong Kong however owes its ascendancy as much to its political status as to its physical advantages. Acquired by the Treaty of Nanking in 1842 at the close of the first Anglo-Chinese war as a British rival to the Chinese-controlled trade at Canton, it has since its founding served as an entrepôt for the entire China coast. Since at least 1865 it has transshipped annually between 20 and 25 per cent of China's total foreign trade by value, aided by its treaty status as a free port.* Hong Kong has nevertheless yielded first place as a port to the greatly inferior harbor of Shanghai, located on the mainland and more closely oriented to China's productive areas and transport routes.

The coastline becomes emergent at about the mouth of the Chientang River in Hangchow Bay. There is only one natural harbor on the coast north of Hangchow used regularly by a large volume of ocean shipping: Tsingtao, on the rocky promontory of Shantung. Chefoo, also on this promontory, has a good, though somewhat shallow, natural harbor, but it has been relatively little used or improved. Weihaiwei, near the tip of Shantung and thus one of the most seaward ports in China, is a largely artificial harbor constructed by the British at the turn of the century for their naval vessels (following a decade of "concessions" by the crumbling Ch'ing government to the European powers), but its large protected roadstead has attracted little commercial shipping.

It is an unfortunate circumstance that these few adequate harbors are in effect isolated from the body of north China by the crystalline mountains of Shantung and by their out-of-the-way location. This situation is responsible for the small importance of Chefoo and Weihaiwei as ports, as well as for the fact that they still have no railway connections. Shantung, originally an island in the Yellow Sea, has been land-linked by silt deposition from the Huang, yet its harbors are economically cut off from the mainland. In a more highly industrialized economy, these harbors would probably be more important, but the almost complete lack of water transport links between them and the north China hinterland decrees for them under present conditions a relatively minor role.

Tientsin, the leading port of north China, forty miles from the sea on the Pei River, fight a losing battle against silt. Two rivers flow-

* Hong Kong is not included in the customs figures for China.

ing from the semi-arid plain of north China, navigable for small boats only with difficulty during the summer and autumn, and subject to severe spring floods, feed into the Pei just above Tientsin. The combined deposition of all three has forced the removal of the port from Tientsin itself to Taku, at the mouth of the Pei, where an offshore bar is forming with a minimum navigable depth at mean low tide in 1936 of fifteen feet. Dredging there is barely able to keep pace with deposition, and the open roadstead at Taku affords inadequate protection to shipping. Ships drawing over fifteen feet discharge cargo onto lighters six miles out at sea.

During their occupation of north China, the Japanese began work on a new artificial harbor just south of Tangku (map 1) on an ambitious plan which remained largely unfinished with the end of the war in 1945. This work has now been resumed by the Communist Government of China, which aims to complete the project in 1953. The harbor, to be known as Hsinkang ("new port"), is planned to receive vessels up to 10,000 tons, which will be able to discharge their cargoes onto wharf-side railway lines. The total protected roadstead will be about ten square miles, but its projected depth would still exclude the largest trans-Pacific carriers.[5]

Haichow, in northern Kiangsu, terminus of the east-west Lunghai railway, is an artificial harbor nine miles from the sea. Work was begun on dredging the small river which connects it with the sea, and on the building of wharves, in 1933, and by 1936 the port could handle ships drawing up to fourteen feet. It thus remained largely limited to the coasting trade. Coaling facilities are available on the coast just south of the river's mouth where a group of islands provides some shelter, but again controlling depths exclude most large trans-ocean shipping. Peking, without access to navigable waterways (aside from the Grand Canal, which contains several unnavigable stretches in Shantung and southern Hopeh) has relied on Tientsin (Taku) as its port. Primarily an administrative center and rail junction, Peking's population had not reached a million and a half by 1936.

The configuration and relief of north China make it difficult for any one deep-water port to serve it all. As it is, while Tientsin (Taku) acts as the port for most of north China, a considerable proportion of the trade especially of the northwest (Kansu and Shensi) and the north China plain south of the Huang moves through Shanghai.

Along the Yangtze itself, potential ports for ocean shipping must contend not only with the Fairy Flats in the Yangtze estuary, as does Shanghai, but with silting problems and river currents farther upstream. Chinkiang, at the head of the delta, has been crippled as an ocean port by silting. Nanking, where silting is an equally great problem, has relatively few water connections with its hinterland. Hankow and Kiukiang-Hukow profit from their location where major tributaries join the master stream, but their harbors are relatively small and shallow. Hankow, despite its location and the all-year channel for 5,000-ton ships from the sea, has never been an important rival of Shanghai in either foreign or domestic trade. The other Yangtze ports do not stand at notable route foci, and their harbours are equally handicapped for space and depth. Navigation on the river and within its unsheltered harbors must cope with a summer current averaging nearly five knots at Hankow and nearly four at Nanking. These confined waters are difficult and costly for deep-draft ocean shipping, especially in terms of insurance rates.

Shanghai's trade hinterland is the largest in the world. Nowhere else does a population or area of this size depend for its commercial intercourse on one master river system and one primate city. The accompanying table compares the estimated populations of China's major cities and ports in 1930.[6]

Shanghai	3,300,000	Nanchang	500,000
Peking	1,400,000	Wenchow	450,000
Tientsin	1,300,000	Tsingtao	350,000
Hankow	1,200,000	Tsinan	300,000
Canton	950,000	Amoy	250,000
Hong Kong	800,000	Ningpo	250,000
Nanking	650,000	Chinkiang	200,000
Changsha	600,000	Swatow	200,000
Chungking	600,000	Weihaiwei	200,000
Foochow	500,000	Chefoo	100,000
Soochow	500,000	Haichow	20,000
Hangchow	500,000		

Raw Materials

The basic industrial raw materials lacking in its immediate hinterland are Shanghai's major problem after the disadvantages of its site. Coal must come from north China, Japan, or Indo-China. Finished steel is largely imported (from Japan and the United States), as are petroleum products, sulfur, rubber, copper, and all other non-ferrous metals except antimony and tungsten, which are supplied from the metaliferous belt running through Honan, Kweichow, and Yünnan. Shanghai is industrially out of gear with the rest of China, and in the absence of an exploitable local resource supply maintains its industrial position on imports from kindred economies overseas. China supplies the market, and the labor, for Shanghai's industrial production, both factors of considerably more locational importance for manufacturing in general than raw materials alone. Closely oriented to major ocean routes, Shanghai can economically produce goods whose raw materials must be assembled from great distances, since the cost of sea transport, especially for these bulk commodities, is a relatively minor item in total costs of production. From the Chinese hinterland, the Yangtze also transports to the city at low cost industrial raw materials produced by agriculture within the river basin: cotton, silk, vegetable oils and tallow, hides and skins, hemp, tea, bristles, wheat, tobacco, and eggs.

Aside from steel (which until recently had not been economically produced from ore anywhere in China proper), industrial machinery, and petroleum products, admittedly large cost-items in its production, Shanghai has not suffered industrially to any great extent from the local absence of resources. The city's transport connections as outlined in this chapter have been largely responsible for this, and have made possible an industrial and commercial metropolis in an agricultural economy poor in resources and in land transport.

FIVE

The Opening of the City to Foreign Trade and its Early Development

Canton and the Treaty Ports

The treaty ports * were an answer to the expansionist foreign pressure for trade with seclusionist China. The Ch'ing government (1644–1911) hoped that by granting trade privileges only in these cities it could confine the scope of the Westerners and protect the body of China from their disturbing activities. But when the Canton system was broken by the Anglo-Chinese war of 1841–42, the foreigners envisaged a continually expanding trade with the potentially immense China market. Sir Henry Pottinger, chief of the British delegation at the Treaty of Nanking, stated that the treaty had opened to trade "a market so vast that all the mills of Lancashire could not make stocking stuff enough for one of China's provinces." [1] Western economic enterprise, once given a foothold and an opportunity under its own laws to buy and sell with the Chinese, was a dynamic growth which could not be checked by treaty provisions.

The Canton system of the eighteenth century, under which the British East India Company and later private American firms were permitted to establish trading factories in a limited area of the city set aside for them, was an increasing annoyance to foreign merchants. Several diplomatic missions to Peking, including that of Viscount Macartney in 1793 and of Lord Amherst (who was not even received by the court) in 1816, all failed to obtain a relaxation of

* Canton, Amoy, Foochow, Ningpo, and Shanghai were opened to foreign trade by the Treaty of Nanking in 1842, and eleven further ports, including Hankow, Kiukiang, Chinkiang, Nanking, and Tientsin were added by the Treaty of Tientsin in 1858, although the actual opening of Nanking was deferred until 1899, a reflection of its poor location compared with Shanghai (see map 1).

restrictions on the trade at Canton or the opening of further ports
to foreign trade. These changes finally came about only as a result of
the Anglo-Chinese war of 1841–42. Under the old system at Canton,
foreign traders were virtually confined to their trading factories,
were forbidden to bring in women or arms, and were allowed in
Canton at all only during the trading season, which largely as a
result of monsoon winds essential to overseas trade movements by
sailing vessels, and particularly favorable to shipping in and out of
Canton, lasted from September to April. However, the foreigners
thus avoided the uncomfortably tropical summer in Canton. They
spent the hot months for the most part in Macao, a remnant of the
once extensive Portuguese empire in the East, at a distance of
some 75 miles southeast of Canton and on the tip of a hilly and
narrow peninsula jutting into the sea, where the breeze seldom
failed.

Most cramping of the restrictions was that requiring all foreigners
to trade only through the Canton merchants' guild, or Cohong, established with official support in 1720 as the principal instrument for
controlling the foreigners, armed with full governmental powers of
enforcement of the factory regulations, as well as the monopoly of
trade with the foreigners under conditions which yielded them enormous profits. Disputes between Chinese and foreigners arising out
of the trade were settled by the Cohong, and protests against abuses
could be made by foreigners to the Chinese government only through
the Cohong.[2]

One of several attempts to break out from this system independently of the Government at Peking was made in 1832, when
the British East India Company (shortly before its monopoly of the
British trade with China was removed by Parliament in 1834) sent
the ship Lord Amherst with a commercial mission under Hugh
Lindsay (with the Rev. Karl Gutzlaff as interpreter) to request
trade privileges from the local officials at other ports on the China
coast. Lindsay was refused entry at Amoy, Foochow, and Ningpo,
but he obtained an interview with the taotai (Intendant of Circuit,
or chief local official) at Shanghai. The taotai informed Lindsay
that Canton would remain the only port where foreigners could
trade, but Lindsay was enthusiastic about the possibilities of Shang-

hai and his report indicates that its location had already made it a large trading city.[3]

He counted 400 junks, averaging between 100 and 400 tons, entering the port of Shanghai weekly during July. If this count was representative of the whole year, it makes Shanghai at that time one of the leading ports of the world.[4] Lindsay stated that the native trade of Shanghai was greater than the total trade of Canton, and described the large wharves and warehouses, and the remarkable accessibility of the port to the hinterland. While the trade was primarily domestic, it included large numbers of junks from as far as Manchuria and Kwangtung, and relatively smaller numbers from Java, Indo-China, and Siam. "The advantages which foreigners would derive from the liberty of trade with this place are incalculable . . . It is the seaport of the Yangtze River and the principal emporium of eastern Asia." [5]

Lindsay noted that British textiles brought in via Canton were on sale in Shanghai shops, and he saw a market for British woolens in this colder climate, a market for which the British had long been hoping since they had been able to exchange only Indian opium in any appreciable volume for their purchases of tea and silk.* Multiplying the estimated population of the Yangtze basin and north China by the expected consumption of woolens, Lindsay voiced one of the earliest expressions of recurrent trade dreams about the China market, none of which have yet materialized on the scale hoped for. He also commented on the extensive crops of cotton within sight of the city, the carding, spinning, and weaving of cotton cloth in every home, and the superior quality of the nankeen cloth made at Shanghai and exported from the city. While this did not appear to discourage him about the prospects for imports of British textiles (which until about 1840 remained inferior in quality and dearer in price than Chinese nankeens),[6] he counted it another advantage in trade with the city.† Lindsay concluded that "considering the extraor-

---

* For a recent study of the familiar problems of the China trade before 1842 and its balance of commodities and payments, see Michael Greenberg, *British Trade and The Opening of China 1800–42* (1951).

† An 1850 account says that Shanghai's production of cotton cloth supplied "several of the neighbouring provinces." W. H. Medhurst, *A General Description of Shanghai* (1850), p. 15.

dinary advantages which this place possesses for foreign trade it is wonderful that it has not attracted more observation." [7]

The lack of attention to Shanghai of which Lindsay complained had been beyond the powers of the foreigners to remedy, as Lindsay discovered for himself when his request for trade privileges there was refused. The tension at Canton finally resulted in open hostilities nine years later. Early in the course of the war of 1841–42 the British occupied the Chusan Islands at the mouth of Hangchow Bay, and interest was revived in making that well-protected site the principal base for British trade, as earlier surveyors, including Lindsay, had suggested.* However the further progress of the war required British occupation of the mainland ports, and a fleet under Sir William Parker, after taking Amoy, Foochow, and Ningpo, arrived off Woosung June 13, 1842, and captured the forts commanding the mouth of the Whangpoo. The British planned to invade the Yangtze valley and by appearing in force on the river and capturing Chinkiang block the movement of rice via the Grand Canal to Peking.

Shanghai was taken, and then evacuated by the troops on June 23, in order to concentrate on the advance to Chinkiang and Nanking. The treaty, signed at Nanking on August 29, created the treaty ports already named, where British merchants and their wives could reside permanently, with their own consuls, and importing goods into China under a fixed and nominal tariff (it averaged about 5 per cent *ad valorem*) without any requirement to trade through a Cohong or under official supervision. Article II of the treaty contained the provision that "British subjects shall be allowed to reside, for the purposes of carrying on their mercantile pursuits, without molestation or restraint, in the cities of Canton, Amoy, Foochow, Ningpo, and Shanghai . . . Her Majesty, the Queen of Great Britain (etc.) will appoint superintendents or consular officers to reside at each of the above mentioned cities to be the medium of communication between the Chinese authorities and the said merchants . . ." [8]

No other mention was made in the treaty about foreign rights of

---

* This plan was not abandoned in favor of Hong Kong until the very end of the war.

settlement or holding property, and certainly areal concessions were not in the mind of either of the parties. The right to lease land was left to be negotiated in each case through the local officials at the treaty ports, a reflection of Peking's lack of interest in relations with the foreigners. Article XI of the Treaty of Tientsin in 1858 legalized this practice, already developed in the treaty-ports "including the right of residence, of buying or renting houses, of leasing land, and of building churches and cemeteries." [9] On this flimsy legal basis, the political and economic structure of foreign Shanghai was erected.

Trade had escaped from its traditional Chinese cage at Canton, and was able at Shanghai to develop on a Western pattern by Western rules instead of being regulated at every point by semi-official Chinese merchants. The Treaty of Nanking between China and Great Britain was followed in 1843 by the Treaty of Wang Hsia between China and the United States, which extended trade and residence rights in the treaty ports to United States citizens and which also stated explicitly for the first time the condition of extraterritoriality. Similar treaties were negotiated by France and Russia in 1844 and 1858 respectively.

The Settlements at Shanghai

George Balfour, the first British consul at Shanghai, arrived November 8, 1843, and declared the port open to foreign trade on November 14. His primary job was arranging for the leasing of land to foreign traders. His original agreement with the taotai in 1843 provided for an area of about 43 acres within the site selected by Pottinger where foreigners might lease land in perpetuity, since the Chinese at that time refused to sell. The western boundary of this area was extended by similar agreement in 1845 to include a total of about 180 acres, and in 1849 the boundary was moved farther west to Defense Creek, bringing the area of the British Settlement to 470 acres (map 6). The maps attached to each of these agreements were lost when the Chinese city was taken by rebel forces in 1853 and when the British Consulate burned in 1870, and the boundaries of the Settlement were not demarcated at all until 1889.

Foreign merchants who leased land within this Settlement had to agree by contract to allow the former Chinese owners to visit their

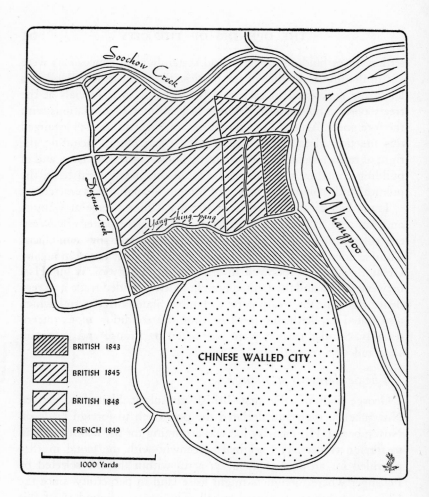

Soochow Creek

Defense Creek

Yang-ching-pang

Whangpoo

BRITISH 1843

BRITISH 1845

BRITISH 1848

FRENCH 1849

CHINESE WALLED CITY

1000 Yards

Map 6. Early foreign settlements at Shanghai

ancestral graves at will. During the first months after November 1843, many of the Chinese owners refused to vacate houses and land already leased to foreigners and had to be paid a fee or were forcibly ejected. The numerous disputes over the property rights of foreigners resulted in the Land Regulations of 1845 negotiated between Balfour and the taotai which, *inter alia*, forbade Chinese residence within the Settlement and made foreigners responsible for its upkeep and policing from their own funds. These were raised by a committee of foreign merchants, appointed by the British consul, which assessed each foreign landrenter and controlled community expenditures.

An American Settlement in Honkew, never defined or legally established, amalgamated with the International Settlement in 1863. The French merchants, however, proceeded independently and negotiated with the taotai their own set of Land Regulations, issued in 1849, for an area set apart for French leasing immediately south of the International Settlement, between the Yang Ching Pang and the city wall. This Settlement, and its later extension, inaccurately titled the French "Concession," remained under separate French administration until the rendition of all foreign rights.[10]

While the position of the foreigners at Shanghai fell far short of actual sovereignty, it was a long step from their confined position at Canton. Travel into the surrounding country was permitted on condition that the travelers return to Shanghai the same day, and there was no requirement for the foreigners to leave at the end of the trading season as formerly at Canton. Most important, however, was the escape from the Canton Cohong. Foreign traders were now free to deal with any Chinese merchant they wished, and could employ their own Chinese agents for buying and selling in the hinterland, a significant advantage which the foreign firms soon put to use. Business could be conducted without the semi-official supervision of the Cohong and its function as the watchful eye of Peking in all dealings with the foreigners.

This monopoly, so useful both economically and diplomatically, died hard. In Canton, the Cohong continued in effect in disguised form by the simple device of preventing the appearance of other Chinese firms in the market. All trading with the hinterland was managed through the Cohong firms as before, and foreigners could not employ their own agents.[11] At Shanghai, Consul Balfour found himself unwittingly involved in an attempt to create a local Cohong when after some difficulty in finding a house available for leasing as the consular residence on the day after his arrival in November 1843, he accepted the offer of a prosperous Chinese gentleman. His landlord leased him a large house in the Chinese city, and then established himself in the gate house where he carefully observed the comings and goings of his tenants. When Balfour was approached by his host on trade matters, it was revealed that the gentleman was a prominent Shanghai merchant and that by agreement with the taotai he had planned to acquire a monopoly of trade with the foreigners and to keep them conveniently under supervision in polite house arrest. Balfour quickly made other housing arrangements, and in 1846 moved the consulate to quarters rented outside the city in the foreign leasehold.[12]

By the end of 1843, eleven foreign trading firms were in business at Shanghai, most of them branches of British and American firms originally established at Canton. The new conditions under which they now operated were unique in the history of the China trade. Escape from the Cohong meant moreover a large saving in customs duties. Average total duties per ship exacted at Canton between 1800 and 1840 were estimated by the foreign merchants at 240,000 taels, of which 200,000 taels represented officially connived-in "squeeze." (The tael was a unit weight of pure silver which remained fairly constant from 1800 to 1860 at the equivalent of seven shillings.) At Shanghai the merchants estimated in February 1844 that since the port had been opened average total duties per ship had been 50,000 taels, of which only about 15,000 represented "squeeze."[13] During 1844 a total of 44 foreign ships entered and cleared the port, and by 1855 the figure had risen to 437.[14]

The three great trade commodities of this period were tea, silk, and opium (tables I and II), and for all of them Shanghai was advantageously located. The major silk-producing regions of China lie in the lower Yangtze basin. Tea for export was grown primarily in the belt of hills which forms the Yangtze divide on the south, and waterways connected the northern slopes of this region (where the best teas were grown) with Shanghai more easily and directly than with any other ocean port. Opium could be distributed domestically to greater advantage from Shanghai, via the Yangtze, than from any other coastal port. In 1846, within three years of its opening, 16 per cent of China's export trade passed through the city, and by 1861 its share was 50 per cent.[15]

With its natural advantages, and doubtless helped as well by the veiled continuance of the Cohong system at Canton into the 1850's, Shanghai overtook its nearest rival in total value of foreign trade in 1864, two years after the effective opening of the Yangtze to steam navigation. By 1870, Shanghai was responsible for 63 per cent of the total external trade of China by value, as against 13 per cent for Canton, still its closest competitor. The opening of Japan to foreign trade in 1859 brought into play the locational advantages of Shanghai for this new and rapidly expanding market, and was credited by Shanghai merchants with an important part in the quick rise of the city's commerce.[16]

As imports became more diversified with the relative decline of opium, they were more easily shipped to and distributed from Shanghai as the primate commercial center, but exports, which became diversified more slowly, could in many cases move out as cheaply from other ports which might in particular cases be better oriented to production areas. This situation was of course the usual one for the movement of commodities into and out of any trade area. The accompanying table shows Shanghai's place in China's foreign trade from 1870 to 1930, by value percentages of China's total external trade in each category passing through the city.[17]

	Imports	Exports	Total Foreign Trade
1870–1880	65%	59%	62%
1880–1890	58%	48%	53%
1890–1900	56%	52%	54%
1900–1910	54%	48%	51%
1910–1920	51%	45%	48%
1920–1930	50%	40%	45%

Robert Fortune, an English botanist sent to China by the Royal Horticultural Society to collect plants and seeds of ornamentals not found in England, spent most of November and December of 1843 in Shanghai, and visited it again late in 1848, this time under commission from the British East India Company to introduce the tea shrub into India. (He also made two later trips to the Yangtze basin, in 1853–1856 and 1861–62.) He was as much taken with the natural advantages of the place as Lindsay had been, and provided a neat and prophetic summary of the factors which have been responsible for Shanghai's growth:

No other town with which I am acquainted possesses such advantages. It is the great gate to the Chinese empire and a place of vast native trade . . . The convenience of inland transit is unrivalled in any part of the world. The country is one vast plain intersected by many rivers, and these again joined and crisscrossed by canals, many of them nearly natural and others stupendous works of art. The port of Shanghai swarms with boats of all sizes employed in the inland traffic. Since the port has been opened these boats bring down large quantities of tea and silk and return loaded with the manufactures of Europe and America which they have taken in exchange. From what we know of the geographic nature of the country there can be no doubt that all the green teas and most of the black can be brought to Shanghai at less expense than they can be taken to Canton or any of the southern towns. The large silk districts of central China are also close at hand. The proximity of Shanghai to the large towns of Hangchow, Soochow, and Nanking forms a further advantage. Lastly, viewing this place as an immense mart for our cotton manufactures, which we already know it to be, there can be no doubt that in a few years it will not only rival Canton but become a place of far greater importance.[18]

Fortune however estimated the population of Shanghai in 1843 as only 270,000, while he gave figures of one million for Hangchow and about 500,000 for Soochow, Nanking, and Ningpo. He credited six other delta cities with populations equal to Shanghai's (Sungchiang, Chiating, Changshu, Kashing, Huchow, and Wusih — map 5).

Chinese Shanghai had risen as the port of Soochow, from a small fishing village at the junction of Soochow Creek and the Whangpoo. When silting, and presumably advance of the coastline, made maritime access to Soochow impossible by the eleventh century A.D. despite the canalizing of the Creek's lower course in

A.D. 446, ships began to dock at Shanghai, or Hu Tu as it was then called and in 1075 an official was stationed there to administer the customs. In 1279 the town, now called Shanghai (which may be translated as meaning "up from the sea") declared itself independent of Soochow and sent its taxes direct to Peking. It was however still too small in the thirteenth century to be mentioned by Marco Polo, who gave a detailed account of all cities of importance in south coastal China. The city walls were built in 1544 following the sacking and burning of the city in the preceding year by Japanese pirates.[19]

By the beginning of the nineteenth century, Shanghai was the principal port of the Yangtze basin, and was also the center of the coastal trade between north and south China. Southern junks were not permitted to trade north of Shanghai, and vice versa. (This official regulation may have been influenced by the difference in the nature of the coast north and south of the city.) In 1812 the official gazetteer of Shanghai estimated the population of the *hsien* (county), which included an area of about 400 square miles, at 528,000.* Despite its commercial prominence, it did not seriously rival the older delta cities in size because they were in varying degrees administrative centers, a function which Shanghai has always lacked beyond its own metropolitan limits. They were as well or better situated for domestic or regional trade, but administration more than commerce was the consistent basis of urban existence and growth in the bureaucratic framework of traditional China.

Shanghai before 1843 had grown primarily on the trade of its immediate delta hinterland: tea, silk, cotton, and rice, and on its key position in the coasting trade which enabled it to act as an entrepôt and to distribute goods received by sea within the densely populated delta. But the wider water network, both sea and river, of which it stands at the focus was not fully exploited. It remained for foreign traders and foreign economic organization, implemented by the steamship, to realize the geographic potential of Shanghai's location.

---

* Ch'ing dynasty population figures of this period are, however, suspect, partly because of the practice of padding the census in order to impress the emperor with the prosperity resulting from his reign.

Settlement and Trade

The foreign population of the city, swollen to 100 in 1843 by the presence of British troops, fell to 50 in 1844, but by 1849 had risen to 175 traders, missionaries, and consular staff, who built the first Settlement roads, following the small winding creeks. The first foreign buildings were mainly godowns (warehouses) and residences combined in one large establishment within two-or-three-acre compounds along the landward side of the Whangpoo Bund. No foreign architects were available, and the plans were drawn by the merchants and modified by Chinese builders to fit local materials and Chinese techniques, so that the resulting structures were of the simplest design.

On the river side of these compounds was a perfectly square bungalow-type building which contained bedrooms, mess hall, and offices. In order to shut out the summer sun and keep the inside as cool as possible, the stamped earth or native sun-dried brick walls were at least three feet thick and plastered or stuccoed in white on the outside, while an open verandah with wide arches ran around the outside of the first two stories. Overhanging roofs shielded the two or three upper stories. In the rear of the compound were usually four or five godowns (for the different trade goods), dwellings for the Chinese assistants, the residence and office of the compradore * (the chief Chinese assistant or agent), and the

* The compradore was a treaty port institution which epitomized the hybrid economy and business order produced where China and the West met. It originated with the Portuguese in the East Indies in the sixteenth century, who supplied the term. In the China treaty ports, the compradore was usually a banker or merchant who was acquainted not only with the China market and with indigenous business methods and conditions, but had also learned enough from and about the foreigners to be an invaluable aid. He usually had his own Chinese staff, and guaranteed their honesty by his personal and verbal bond, in the Chinese tradition, but in keeping with Western usage also deposited a cash security with his employing firm. He was paid a fixed salary, plus a commission, and was seldom in want of funds. More than once a foreign firm was saved from bankruptcy by the generosity of its compradore. Such men were highly respected by the foreign community as shrewd and scrupulously honest business men, and as friends. Their standing in the Chinese community depended on the prevailing attitude toward the foreigners (see pp. 25-7 above). As a group they were quick and apt students of Western civilization in all of its practical aspects, and from their number was recruited a majority of modern China's political and economic leaders (among them, T. V. Soong and H. H. K'ung) until the final success of the Communist revolution. By about 1930 most

stables.[20] Within a few years bricks began to arrive in ballast from England, and the brick work prominently displayed in verandah arches facing the Bund provided an indication of the search for Chinese markets for foreign goods in return for China's wealth of tea and silk. This architectural style, common to all the nineteenth-century treaty ports in central and south China, was wittily and fittingly christened the "Compradoric," for it was a necessary blend of Chinese with foreign methods.

The larger foreign firms had two or three partners and eight or ten foreign clerks, plus fifty or sixty Chinese staff (with families), all living in the compound. Among the foreigners there was a notable preponderance of Scots, including the partners of Jardine, Matheson, Ltd., the largest trading firm in Shanghai and known universally as "the muckle house." Apparently the enterprise of these perennial pioneers had conquered Shanghai as it had conquered London. William Jardine, the firm's founder, had been a surgeon on one of the East India Company's ships trading to Canton. He found trading more profitable than healing, and in 1828 persuaded his compatriot James Matheson to join him in his new company at Canton. A Jardine ship carried the first cargo of "free" tea from Canton after the old Company's monopoly was removed by Act of Parliament in 1834. William Jardine was said to keep only one chair (his own) in his office, to encourage his clients to state their business and leave.*

All the large foreign trading firms were divided into six departments: 1. tea; 2. silk; 3. "Manchester goods" (predominantly cotton piece goods); 4. shipping and insurance (understandably a profitable enterprise); 5. land and house agency; 6. "muck and truck" (all the other trade goods, which seldom amounted together to more than 5 per cent of any firm's total goods transactions).† Each

---

foreign firms in Shanghai found compradores no longer necessary as employed agents. By that time the compradores had taught them almost as much as they had unwittingly taught the compradores.

* See Greenberg, British Trade, for a detailed account of the history and operations of this and other private firms in the Canton trade, based on contemporary letters and business records.

† Until 1890, overseas exports in this category were primarily hides, leather, bristles, horsehair, China grass, and art objects; imports, aside from opium and textiles, were largely limited to hardware, cotton yarn (for Chinese household and small-scale industry), and machinery.

foreign firm employed a tea expert, usually a foreigner, who went every year in the tea season of late April and early May to the local collecting centers in the hinterland at Kiukiang, Hukow, Hankow, Siangtan, and Hangchow (map 9), where he made his own selection and bought according to the anticipated state of the London market. By the time of the Treaty of Tientsin in 1858, the original provision that foreigners must not be away from the treaty ports for more than one day had yielded to foreign assertiveness and the demands of trade. Under the new treaty, foreigners were permitted free movement to all parts of the empire, and required a passport only beyond 100 *li* (approximately 33 miles) from the treaty ports.

For the silk trade at Shanghai, there was also an expert attached to each foreign trading firm, again usually a foreigner, but since the main silk-producing areas were in the delta it was not necessary for him to travel so extensively, and he did most of his appraising and buying of silk in Shanghai. Kiangsu and Chekiang silk was considered by these men to be the finest in the world, a quality which they ascribed to the favorable effects of the climate and soil on the growth of the silk worm and on the excellence of its diet of mulberry leaves. The silk was brought to Shanghai by Chinese silk merchants in the city, who bought it at hinterland collection centers, notably Soochow, Wusih, Huchow, and Hangchow.

Much depended on the accuracy of predictions about the London market. In the early days of the Settlement, letters from London arrived via Bombay or Calcutta by the opium clippers, forerunners of the tea clippers, which carried a cargo of such high unit-value that they could sacrifice size and weight to speed. By 1840 they had supplanted the slow-moving and cumbersome East Indiamen of the old Company, and at Woosung they discharged their cargo into hulks anchored in the Yangtze, since the importation of opium had been made illegal for American, French, and Russian nationals by their treaties with China after 1842, and declared illegal for British subjects by Sir Henry Pottinger in 1843. The opium was illegally distributed from Shanghai by the Chinese dealers to whom it was sold there. Mail was at the same time dropped off at Woosung, and rushed to Shanghai by pony express, whose riders galloped up the

Bund and slung off at each firm's compound the mail bags addressed to it. After 1860 when a British mail service was begun by steamship to Singapore and Hong Kong, Jardine's managed to get its mail two days before its competitors by arranging for its own line of faster ships to take its own mail from the mail boat at Hong Kong or Singapore while the mail boat was coaling and bring it at full speed to Shanghai, where it was put ashore farther up the Yangtze above Woosung and brought secretly to the firm's offices, thus giving them a valuable jump on buying and price transactions.

This advantage was, however, shortlived, since a telegraph line was completed into Siberia by 1871, and messages could be sent from London to Kiachta on the Mongolian frontier of Siberia, relayed from there by courier to Tientsin, and thence by coastal steamship to Shanghai in three weeks total, while the regular sea mail from London, even with Jardine's short cut, took seven weeks. In at least one case these dramatic but often uncertain improvements in communication proved disastrous. Early in 1876, a telegraph and marine cable line was completed to Shanghai via Singapore and Hong Kong, and in June came the news that half of the French and Italian silk-worm crop had been destroyed by violent thunderstorms. This stimulated frenzied buying of silk by the foreign firms, but the cable broke early in July a few days before the London market (which supplied the continent with Chinese silk) collapsed, and two foreign firms at Shanghai were ruined by their continuance of buying in the expectation that the cable would soon bring more good news.[21]

It was an alternately lazy and frenzied life for the foreign merchants during the days when tea, silk, and opium were the only important trade goods and before the advent of cables and steamships. During the "season" of about two and a half months (the silk-buying season lasted from mid-May to late June), foreign merchants worked twelve or fifteen hours a day seven days a week arranging for the buying, transport, packing, and shipping of tea and silk. For the rest of the year they kept leisurely hours, seldom opening their offices before ten or closing them after four, and taking two hours or more for a heavy lunch in the mess. They placed great emphasis on violent exercise as the only way for a Westerner to keep healthy in China, and nearly every foreigner in Shanghai rode, hiked, or took part in team sports.

The Chinese were amazed at this waste of calories. " 'Belong foreign man custom' they would say as they turned to their diet of rice and cabbages," according to the memoirs of an early foreign resident.[22] Certainly the foreigners ate well, but while they brought spirits and special foods from home at great expense, the bulk of their food came from the delta area, according to the records of the same early resident, who was for a time during the 1870's in charge of the mess at one of the foreign firms and lists the sources and prices of the most important items which supplied it.[23] Foreign merchants and assistants would often be gone for weeks at a time on shooting excursions in the hinterland. Wherever they wanted to go in the delta area they found they could travel by houseboat, to the smallest village or the most remote bird-feeding grounds. And wherever they went they found these waterways clogged with Chinese craft carrying both domestic and foreign goods to and from Shanghai.[24]

W. H. Medhurst, an early British missionary (and later consul) at Shanghai, took a trip into the tea and silk districts of Kiangsu, Chekiang, Anhwei, and Kiangsi in 1845, disguised as a Chinese. His account of the trip laid emphasis on the waterways of this region, and since his journey never took him far from the waterways of the delta or of the Yangtze system, he attributed what he saw over this large area to the whole of China:

Canals have been dug in all directions, and spread like veins and arteries to almost every part of the empire. As far as the experience of this writer goes, the Chinese have no walled cities or large towns except in places which are accessible by water.[25]

He noted that the major canals, used by grain junks, averaged about 40 feet wide and 6 to 8 feet deep, and that bridges over them were at least 20 feet above the surface of the water at the center of the arch so that the grain junks could pass under them with their masts lowered.

By 1863, the original foreign leasehold at Shanghai of 43 acres had been expanded through agreements with the taotai to a total of

2094 acres (including the French Settlement), and Shanghai was indisputably the leading port and commercial city of China.

Struggles with the Harbor

The problem of an adequate harbor, however, was a matter of increasing concern to the foreign community through the latter half of the nineteenth century, if not to the Chinese authorities. It was openly stated by the ranking Chinese government official at Shanghai in 1874 that Woosung Outer Bar was in fact a "heaven-sent barrier intended to prevent war vessels of heavy draught . . . from entering the harbour." [26] But foreign residents realized with alarm that the city could not hope to remain an ocean port if the silting process were allowed to continue, and they had yearly evidence of the speed with which the Yangtze was extending its delta. Blonde Shoal, near the mouth of the Whangpoo, was covered with ten feet of water at low tide in 1850, and by 1890 rose three feet above mean low water. The history of Tsungming Island, already referred to above, was well known, as well as the fact that the site of Shanghai had originally been on the seacoast and that it was rapidly being cut off from access to the sea.

A local resident writing in 1894 estimated that silt deposition in the Yangtze estuary would lessen the depth of the water about one foot in every eight years if spread evenly, and that while tides and currents provided some scour in certain channels, these too were filling up, although at a slower rate. The same writer, however, pointed a lesson later acted on by the Whangpoo Conservancy Board after 1905 by calling attention to the fact that when a small coasting vessel had been rammed and sunk in mid-stream just above Woosung Outer Bar in 1892, the Whangpoo current had apparently been diverted and concentrated sufficiently to scour a new and deeper channel through the bar.[27]

Shanghai's environmental dilemma was intensified by the progress of steam navigation in the latter half of the nineteenth century. The most economical ocean carriers were increasingly those of larger draught, and by 1885 or 1890, most of these new steam freighters could reach Shanghai only with difficulty or not at all. Shipping lists published in the *North China Herald* at Shanghai

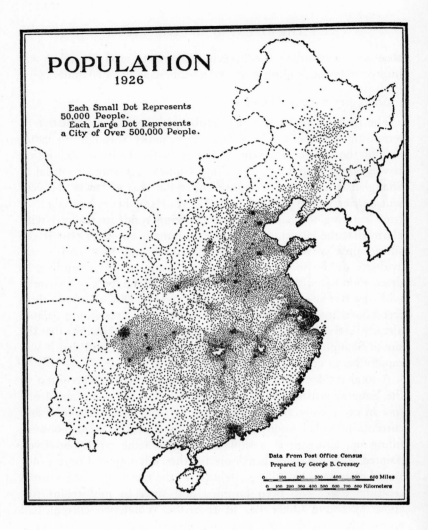

Map 7. Distribution of Population in China (reproduced here by the courtesy of the McGraw-Hill Book Company, Inc., from G. B. Cressey, *China's Geographic Foundations* [1934]).

show an average size of ocean-going ships entering Shanghai harbor between 1850 and 1860 of about 1,000 gross tons. In the decade of the 1860's, this figure reached 2,300, and by 1880 had exceeded 4,000. The original harbor regulations, published by the *North China Herald* in 1852, limited the overall length of ships to 165 feet if they wanted to come as far as Soochow Creek, in view of the narrow channel and confined anchorage. However, between 1850 and 1930 the width of the river at Shanghai decreased from about 2300 feet to 1450 feet, and while dredging had widened somewhat the original channel and anchorage by 1930, the harbor was little more commodious than it had been in 1850.[28] The advent of steam did however make the harbor's overall size and the narrowness of the channel less of a disadvantage than it had been for sailing ships, and it further removed the special advantage of Canton accruing from the monsoon winds.

As early as 1873, representatives of the major foreign shipping firms in Shanghai pointed out to Robert Hart, Inspector General of Customs, the need for dredging the Inner and Outer Woosung bars. Hart approached the Chinese authorities, but could not persuade them to take any action. In the following year, the British chairman of the Shanghai General Chamber of Commerce, in a letter to the British Minister to China, T. F. Wade, asked whether permission might not be obtained for the foreign ratepayers of Shanghai to tax native and foreign shipping in order to dredge the harbor if the Chinese government refused to do anything about it, but Wade also had no success through Peking channels.[29]

As a result of this controversy, Hart in 1875 published his opinion on the problems raised by the vanishing ship-channel, which read in part as follows:

The trade consequent on opening the Yangtze basin has so far been diverted into a false channel by the vested rights or money spent in Shanghai. The agency is in turn counteracted by the opening of the Suez Canal, through which steamers have begun to pass, making London and Hankow their termini . . . Teas will be shipped at Hankow and Kiukiang, and Shanghai silks and Ningpo teas at Chinkiang. They will be the return cargoes of the steamers which carry what China will continue to demand from Europe. In twenty years' time Chinkiang will have taken the place of Shanghai as a semiterminus and transshipment port . . . Thus looked at, as it affects and is affected by natural and artificial agencies now at work at the mouth of the Yangtze, the question of the Woosung Bars is seen to mean that dredging may possibly be nothing more than a means of making the last days of Shanghai a little more comfortable than they would otherwise be; it will not prolong or avert the commercial death of the place, but it will make a show of vitality during its declining years more possible . . . Given the natural and commercial agencies at work, it may be taken for granted that, certainly for ten, or perhaps twenty or thirty years to come, the commercial status and foreign community of Shanghai will be such as to make it worthwhile to prevent the river from being blocked up at any one point, for instance by the Woosung Bars. Dredging can do this, and then only for a time. It cannot secure for Shanghai either a navigable channel or a continuance of commercial prosperity . . . The circumstances of Shanghai, its present position as a commercial centre, the interests of the community and the revenue it yields China, are in themselves sufficient reasons why the demand for dredging ought to be assented to, but it must be borne in mind that no one can say how soon commerce may cease to ask for access to Shanghai, or natural forces acting elsewhere make dredging operations at Woosung useless.[30]

Hart could not of course foresee the degree of improvement in dredging methods and machinery which have kept Shanghai, as well as many other world ports, open to ocean commerce where natural processes would long ago have cut them off or where the dredging equipment of 1875 would have been unequal to the task. He also failed to appreciate that the locational advantages of Shanghai were sufficiently great in relation to other possible centers in the Yangtze basin to make large-scale efforts to combat the disadvantages of its site worthwhile, or to permit its continuance as a major port despite its poor harbor. He may have been influenced in his judgment by the fact that in 1875 the only three trade commodities of importance were opium, tea, and silk. These high unit-value goods were relatively less dependent than bulk or low unit-value goods on precise locational advantages in their transport. As they lost their dominant position in the foreign trade of China, the more diversified and relatively lower unit-value agricultural exports and the equally diversified and low unit-value imports created a much greater need for an ocean port with the best possible location. Shanghai's water route connections through the Yangtze system made it the obvious choice.

Hart also did not consider the fact that while the progressive rise in average tonnage of ships in the Pacific trade increasingly emphasized the limitations of Shanghai, it even more pointedly revealed the barriers to navigation on the Yangtze above Shanghai. Chinkiang, Hart's choice as the port most likely to become the major Yangtze basin entrepôt, declined to insignificance in ocean shipping handled by the turn of the century. On the other hand, within twenty years of Hart's prophecy, and while he was still Inspector General of Customs, the gross value of the trade of Shanghai doubled.

As the foreigners continued to see new mud banks rise out of the Yangtze and the Whangpoo, dry out, and be settled and farmed, other gloomy predictions were added to Hart's.[31] Partly as a result of indirect foreign pressure, the Chinese Government purchased a German dredge and began work on the Woosung Outer Bar in 1881, but little was accomplished and work was stopped in 1889. By 1893, the situation led the foreign Commissioner of Customs at Shanghai to remark:

The Woosung Bar dredging has I think convinced most people that the bar there must always be with us and that business must adapt itself to things as they are . . . The largest vessels which come to port never come any nearer than Woosung. I expect to see development of business there, but the available anchorage is not too capacious, and the distance from go-down is a considerable source of expense.[32]

In addition to the factors mentioned here by the Commissioner, the presence of the Fairy Flats in the Yangtze estuary is probably as much responsible as the progress of dredging in the Whangpoo for the fact that Woosung has never become Shanghai's port in any significant respect.

With the beginning of permanent dredging operations on a large scale by the Whangpoo Conservancy Board in 1905 (see above, Chapter Three), the locational virtues of Shanghai in effect dictated an ultimately successful attack on the city's major site problem.

Once Western economic enterprise had established itself at this strategic center of modern China's key economic area, neither treaties nor Chinese officials, neither isolation nor mud, could prevent Shanghai from realizing its wider geographic advantages.

SIX

The Political Factor

The opening to foreign trade of ports in China outside Canton required for the first time purely commercial cities of metropolitan size. Within the treaty ports, a blend of Western and Chinese business methods developed under the dominance of foreign commerce and the protection of foreign order which provided entrepreneurs with security of investments and freedom from bureaucratic control for the first time in the history of China. This new economic activity was largely created out of the traditional economy of China, still pre-industrial but highly developed, and it was natural that in each treaty port the presence of foreign traders and their capital attracted Chinese middlemen and merchants to the foreign settlements, where commerce under Western rules and legal protection was more profitable than under traditional conditions elsewhere.

Provided with a merchandizing outlet, the trade of the Yangtze basin flowed in increasing volume through Shanghai and created there a rising structure of Western-style commerce. Risk capital for commercial investment, earned both in the new market of Shanghai and in traditional enterprises in the hinterland, notably in land, became concentrated in the city, where opportunity and security were uniquely combined. For the first time, safe and productive investments were available to capital which under the traditional system was almost exclusively, and unproductively, invested in land. Capital and trade were mutual catalysts in this situation, and when foreign capital was permitted to invest in industry in the treaty ports after 1895, Chinese capital was soon attracted to this further profitable outlet. The marked concentration of China's trade through Shanghai after 1860 had also tended to foster the accumulation of both Chinese and foreign capital in the city, which after 1895 was available for investment in industry. The political independence of the foreign settlements was a key factor in all of this, as well as in the development in the city of banking, exchange, and an international money market, all profiting from financial enterprises by no means limited to the city's trade and industry but conducted under the advantages of foreign law and of free circulation of foreign and Chinese currencies.

Trade, industry, and finance thus were given an original impetus and were helped to maintain their mutual and cumulative effect of attraction by Shanghai's political status. Location has, however, been the predominant factor in the growth of the city at every period, and distinguished Shanghai from other treaty ports which, with the same economic opportunity derived from their political status, were rapidly outdistanced by Shanghai. Hong Kong's location was equally favorable at the start (before north China and the Yangtze valley were opened to foreign trade) and the city had the further early advantage of insularity, where full British sovereignty gave to trade the security an entrepôt requires. If political status were the primary factor, Hong Kong would have displaced all its rivals. Hong Kong's trade is still second only to Shanghai's, but following the usual pattern, as commercial development proceeded in the wake of treaties opening new ports and granting new rights to foreigners, a mainland site became increasingly advantageous. At the same time, the center of trade shifted inevitably to its natural focus in the Yangtze basin after the collapse of the artificial Canton system.

A vigorous controversy among foreign and Chinese businessmen in Shanghai over the economic importance of the city's political status was touched off in 1931. The Shanghai Municipal Council (at that time composed of five British, two American, two Japanese, and five Chinese members), had for a decade received increasingly explicit requests from the Shanghai Chinese and from the national government to consider means of returning to China full sovereign rights over the entire city, including the abandonment of extraterritoriality. In 1930 the Council invited the Hon. Mr. Richard Feetham, a judge of the supreme court of the Union of South Africa, to appraise the situation as an impartial investigator and to make detailed recommendations "with a view to assisting them in formulating some constructive plan for the future of the Foreign Settlement which, while giving full consideration to the aspirations of the Chinese people will at the same time afford reasonably adequate protection to the great commercial and business interests which have been developed in Shanghai." [1]

In the course of his investigations, Justice Feetham consulted virtually every prominent foreign businessman and business organization, including those which had been demanding the rendition of foreigners' special rights, legal and territorial. Justice Feetham asked these individuals and organizations to give their several opinions on "the nature and extent of the business interests concentrated in Shanghai, particularly in the foreign Settlement, and the main causes which have led to such concentration." [2] Whether or not Feetham intended this as a leading question, the replies from foreigners were almost unanimous in stressing that the political status of the foreign settlements had been the only factor of importance in the growth of the city.

Their argument, as far as it went, was convincing. They pointed out that trade and investment could prosper only under orderly conditions, and that the security offered to business by the foreign settlements was not only physical but legal, embodied in courts of law free from political interference and upholding the sacredness of contract. They neglected to point out that the law, originally administered to each national group by its own consular officials who were often themselves members of the business community as well, and later for the larger national groups by specially appointed judges from the home country, was frequently read to the particular advantage of each national group, at the expense of other foreigners and of their Chinese competitors or customers. There was nevertheless protection, by the due process which obtained, against seizure of property, extortion, excessive taxation, illegal practices, and other phenomena common in contemporary China, where military requisitions, arbitrary government regulations, dues and fines, official and unofficial "squeeze," and wholesale expropriation were the daily risks of the businessman.

Even the Chinese enterprises outside the settlements profited from the special rights of foreigners by sharing the protection of foreign ships and troops against threatened occupation of these areas by Chinese forces in times of civil disorder or rebellion. Under Chinese control, the foreigners argued, public utilities would quickly deteriorate, and illegal and disastrous business operations would disrupt commerce and industry. The enormous investment in land within the settlements, legally protected by deeds and free from expropriation, was a prominent source of new capital for investment in the city's expanding economy. Title deeds to real estate in the settlements, registered with the foreign consuls, were important as security for loans to both foreign and Chinese entrepreneurs. Foreigners cited the gradual drop in interest rates in the Settlements since 1843, a healthy condition for business, and attributed it to the security attendant on foreign political control, comparing it with interest rates elsewhere in China often exceeding 50 per cent per annum. Some of the statements from foreigners cited "the superior geographic location of Nanking" (an assertion which they did not substantiate and which hardly can be upheld), arguing that it was nevertheless "backward" solely because it lacked the advantages of security on which Shanghai had grown.

There were two dissenting voices among the foreigners. Germany had lost her special rights in China, including extraterritoriality, in 1915, and the statement of the German Chamber of Commerce [3] gave first importance to geographic location in the rise of Shanghai, taking the view that its political status had been a minor factor. "In our opinion, the geographical situation is the vital point . . . The position of Shanghai as a commercial centre greatly depends on the situation in the interior." Most of the city's imports are transshipped to the interior, and most of its exports originate there. This trade is "not protected by Shanghai's special administration, still there is an ever-increasing total of trade figures, a phenomenon which evidently is not entirely due to the status of Shanghai." [4] It was natural that the German businessmen should prefer to see the special treaty advantages of the other foreign merchants removed, but the recovery of German trade at Shanghai after 1919, despite the handicap of dealing on equal terms with the Chinese, was quick, and by 1930 it amounted to a larger percentage of the business of Western nationals than it had in 1913.[5]

Professor C. F. Remer, a noted student of Chinese economic problems then on the faculty of St. John's University in Shanghai, contributed the only impartial and certainly the best informed opinion on the questions raised by Justice Feetham.[6] He allowed the early importance of political (and thus economic) security in favouring the concentration of capital and commerce in Shanghai, "but it does not follow that the abolition of extraterritoriality would destroy Shanghai as a financial center. China's trade would still be financed. The degree of difficulty would depend on the Chinese government regime, and here the Chinese bankers, merchants, and industrialists would exert great influence." Emphasizing that China appreciated the geographic advantages and importance of Shanghai and would not let them lapse, he pointed out that "what would go primarily would be the present free opportunities for foreign investment and foreign financial operations, and possibly the concentration of silver and specie in the Settlement, which would limit speculation and general financial operations, but not necessarily seriously. Financial dislocation could easily be avoided by intelligent Sino-Foreign cooperation, and China's financial center would remain at Shanghai."

Statements from Chinese civic and business organizations ranged from polite Chinese phrases claiming that "the problem is too intricate for an immediate or complete answer" to outright demands for the immediate rendition by the foreigners of all special rights. Most of them played down the importance of political and economic security in the growth of the city, or maintained that it could adequately be provided under full Chinese sovereignty, and all of them stressed the natural advantages of Shanghai as the key factor. Justice Feetham's final recommendations were that immediate rendition would be fatal to the economic life of the city, and that although it must come eventually in order to satisfy Chinese national aspirations, it should be delayed until the rule of law and constitutional government was accepted in China.[7] This was of course a conveniently ambiguous phrase, and no provisions were made for determining when the conditions had been met. It remains to be seen how the surrender of special privileges in China by all of the nations having treaty relations with China (completed by 1944), and the full sovereignty of the national government of China over the whole of Shanghai will affect the economic development of the city.

Jealous of their threatened treaty rights, which undoubtedly gave them as foreigners an advantage in business and investments over the Chinese, the foreign business community of Shanghai overstated the importance of the political factor in the rise of the city, especially by implying that the special status of the Settlements and their foreign residents worked equally to the interests of Chinese and foreigners. Primarily, they failed to evaluate correctly the locational factors which, once the Yangtze basin was opened to foreign trade by treaty agreements, played the predominant role in the growth of modern Shanghai. A city of this order of magnitude and volume of trade could not have and did not develop anywhere else in China, and this condition was in large part responsible for the mushroom growth of Shanghai as the one dominant commercial center for most of the country.

The security provided by foreign control was an important stimulus to economic development at a critical time, during the early years of the foreign settlements when capital began to concentrate there. In this respect it had the effect of a protective tariff for the infant Western-type economy born into a strange land. Once this economy had matured and acquired its own momentum (based increasingly on Chinese participation according to Western economic methods), the tariff was characteristically retained although it was no longer necessary to the healthy functioning of the economy and now operated merely to protect special sectors (in this case the foreign businessmen), which could continue to operate on a non-competitive basis. It is not necessary to deny that removal of the tariff would cripple "special interests" to maintain that the net effect of removal on the overall functioning and prosperity of the economy would be slight.

A new group of Chinese businessmen had learned Western commercial methods from their intercourse with foreigners in the treaty ports. Shanghai was the leading school, and by the turn of the century, foreigners in business there were in general limited to the heads of firms and their executive assistants. Chinese were responsible in the foreign firms for the bulk of buying and selling and for the essential groundwork of financing in addition to maintaining their own trading firms. Private Chinese entrepreneurs took a prominent part in the growth of industry in the city after 1895, and modern Chinese banks modeled on Western methods rivaled the foreign banks after 1920 as the leading Shanghai financial institutions. Strong foreign, especially Japanese, competition, profiting from treaty advantages, was more responsible than Chinese lack of experience or ability for the fact that the Chinese did not dominate the originally foreign economic life of the city more completely than they did. Chinese capital for investment was a problem, but it was increasingly being produced by Shanghai's own economy, and capital could be borrowed abroad without requiring foreign control over its investment.

It could be argued that while Chinese methods in business and industry were in many cases different from those of the West, they were better adjusted to the particular conditions of the Chinese economy and society and if given free competitive opportunity would be at least equally successful.* In any case, it could not be assumed that if left in sole control of the complex economy of Shanghai which they had helped to build, the Chinese would allow it to run down to any significant extent. Conscious planning to relocate industry is another matter.

The prolonged controversy leading up to Justice Feetham's investigations included a special number of the *China Weekly Review* in 1926 devoted to "Greater Shanghai" in which the following argument for rendition appeared: "Shanghai would have been a great city had there never been a foreigner in the place. It would continue to be a great city even if the foreigners should vacate their modern buildings and go home." [8] While the first sentence is an overstatement of the case, the second sentence is undoubtedly accurate.

* Carl Crow, *Four Hundred Million Customers* (1937), and *Foreign Devils in the Flowery Kingdom* (1940), an American businessman of nearly thirty years' experience in Shanghai, tends to take this view.

PART TWO: Key Functions

SEVEN

Transport Routes and Trade in
the Hinterland

The commercial ascendancy of Shanghai was due in large measure to its favorable orientation to the major sources of China's leading trade goods. This specific locational advantage will now be examined in a more detailed analysis of the production and transport of the staple articles of trade. In the interests of clarity, the main transport routes leading to the city will be treated first so that the discussion of production and movement of goods which follows it may be read in the light of the environmental conditions which directed their flow.

Transport Routes

The first railway connection with Shanghai was the Nanking line (193 miles or 308 kilometers), which was opened to traffic in 1908. It was followed in 1909 by the line to Hangchow (118 miles or 188 kilometers), and these two have remained the only rail connections aside from the spur to Woosung. By 1936, the total length of railways tributary to Shanghai was about 600 miles, as against 1900 for Peking and 1300 for Tientsin (map 8). From 1930 to 1936, the Hangchow and Nanking lines each carried annually about one million tons per mile of line, or about the average for a moderately important branch line in the United States. The same figure for the main line of the Pennsylvania Railroad during this period was about 38 million tons.[1]

Despite the fact that Shanghai is by far the largest and most completely industrialized city in China, the total haulage of the two railway lines connected with it averaged between 1930 and 1936 only 7 per cent of the total kilometer/tons hauled by Chinese railways (exclusive of Manchuria).* The role of railways in the growth of Shanghai has clearly been minor, and they have never become large volume carriers on a Western scale, despite their connections with most of the several large cities in the delta, and despite the relatively great agricultural and industrial productivity of the lower Yangtze basin.

The highway pattern is also relatively little developed. Two roads run south from Shanghai to Hangchow (both opened to traffic in 1932), and one runs north to Nanking. A large proportion of the highway mileage runs beside the railway lines, which makes the highways less useful than if they ran independently of or as feeders for the railways. The northern and southern highway routes are joined by a road from Kashing to Soochow, but the few remaining roads are either short-distance feeders or dead ends. There is no direct road connection between the major cities of Soochow and Wusih or Nanking. With minor exceptions in the vicinity of Shanghai, none of these surfaces were paved, and nearly all of the mileage is two-lane only.

The paucity of roads is presumably not due either to construction difficulties or to lack of general trade volume, although level ground in this area is usually accompanied by a dense network of natural and artificial waterways over which bridges must be built. The roads were constructed primarily for tourists and for general automobile travel rather than for commercial haulage. At least two of the major links (the shore road from Hangchow to Shanghai and the northern road from Shanghai to Soochow) were legally closed to vehicles over three tons gross weight from the time of their construction.[3] Due partly to the high cost of fuel, trucks, and parts, and partly to the generally pre-industrial nature of the economy, the volume of truck haulage on all of these roads has remained slight.[4]

Within the delta, however, and within most of the Yangtze basin, goods can move so easily and cheaply by water that there is little

---

* The total length of railways in China proper in 1936 was 9,712 kilometers, of which the two lines discussed above accounted for 753 kilometers (including sidings, loops, branches, and 112 kilometers of second track in and on the outskirts of Shanghai, Nanking, and Hangchow), or 8.3 per cent.[2]

need for mechanized carriers even to supply a city the size of Shanghai. The Shanghai Municipal Council made a traffic count in 1919 on Soochow Creek near its mouth and found a 24-hour average of 1858 cargo boats between 10 and 90 tons cargo capacity

Map 8. *Railways of China, as of 1936* (reproduced here by the courtesy of *The Geographical Review*).

and 807 freight sampans passing the point of count.[5] Assuming that half of these boats were empty and half were loaded to capacity, and assuming arbitrarily that the sampans had half of the average cargo capacity of the cargo boats, these figures show a volume of haulage on this one creek (the main water connection with the delta hinterland, although there are several others as well) between five and ten times greater than on either of the two railway lines.

In addition to the Yangtze and the Whangpoo, three major water routes connect Shanghai with the delta: Siccawei, Soochow, and Woosung Creeks (maps 3 and 5). The lower reaches of Soochow and Siccawei Creeks were periodically dredged by the Whangpoo Conservancy Board until 1936, and on the former a minimum depth of five feet at low water within a 100-foot channel was maintained as far as Soochow, where the Creek terminates. This enabled boats up to 80 tons cargo capacity to reach Soochow, and to move from there into the wider water network of the delta. Siccawei Creek provides a through route for boats up to 40 tons cargo capacity as far as Tsingpu and from there to Tai Lake. Woosung Creek makes similar connections as far as Kunshan, where it joins several other navigable waterways. Five daily "boat trains" (barges towed by a steam launch) left Shanghai for Soochow during the 1920's and 1930's, a journey of ten to twelve hours. The "trains" carried freight as well as passengers, but more deck-passenger space was available west-bound, presumably because outward-bound Shanghai manufactured goods took less space than inward-bound rice, silk, cotton, or other agricultural raw materials.

There were no railway wharves inside the harbor limits. Those at Woosung and Lunghua (both outside harbor limits) were relatively little used, and the Woosung railway wharves handled almost entirely inbound ocean and river cargo destined for Shanghai rather than for other cities. On the right bank of the Whangpoo there was not a single motor road before 1936.* Three large creeks, however, connected the river's right bank with the sea and with the district southeast of Shanghai. The barrier represented by the Whangpoo, and the relatively small and unproductive countryside east of the river were largely responsible for the smallness of commercial and manufacturing development in Pootung. The shipbuilding, wharves, and manufacturing located there were maintained entirely by water transport.

---

* In 1936 a short road was built in Pootung, extended to 37 kilometers in 1948, paralleling the river behind the wharves.

The Yangtze system, of which the delta's waterways are a part, has been outlined above in chapter four. With its channel for ocean-going ships as far as Hankow, for river steamers to Suifu, and for smaller craft still farther, in addition to navigation on its tributaries, the Yangtze is in turn tributary to Shanghai. The hills and mountains which define its watershed are in most cases barriers sufficient to prevent volume movements of goods by land across the divides. The Cheling and Meiling passes (map 4) connecting Canton and the Hsi basin with central China, are the only two exceptions of importance, aside from the open coastal lowlands. By 1890 steamships had become more important carriers than native junks on the Yangtze and the lower reaches of its major tributaries for all but local hauls, but junks have continued to operate over the entire navigable length of the river and are of course particularly important in its upper reaches and along the tributaries.

Junks of the type in use on the lower Yangtze average about 100 tons cargo capacity, and draw between six and eight feet of water, so that they can also use the major delta waterways and most of the Yangtze tributaries. Large rafts are also used on the Yangtze for transporting general goods as well as the timber of which they are made, the rafts being broken up and the timber sold at the end of the downstream trip, as on the Mississippi during the eighteenth and nineteenth centuries. Such rafts were until recently often so big that not only families but entire villages, including barbers, tinsmiths, and restaurateurs lived on them during the downstream trip to Shanghai, which was slowed by the size of the rafts.

While the winter low-water period limits the range of steamships, it tends to make junk navigation easier because of quieter waters and because the easiest towpaths are then exposed along the river bank. Steamships using the river above Ichang in winter frequently tie up for the night, but along many stretches, especially in the gorges immediately above Ichang, junks cannot move with safety during the summer because of the current and because the flood waters covering the winter towpaths are confined between nearly sheer rock walls. On the lakes within the Yangtze basin, notably Tung Ting and Poyang Lakes, strings of barges towed by steamships are the major carriers.

The usefulness of the Yangtze system for the transport of goods is due in large measure to the number of navigable tributaries feeding the master stream, each draining its own highly productive area (maps 1 and 4). Of the major tributaries, the Kan, entering the Yangtze at Kiukiang, is navigable for steamships for 100 miles from its mouth at all seasons, and for 300 miles in summer. Both figures are exclusive of the navigation on Poyang Lake. Steam navigation on the Han from Hankow is possible for 150 miles in winter and for about 375 in summer. Junks and sampans make connections via the Han with southern Shensi. Steamships operate on the Hsiang (Siang) from its mouth in Tung Ting Lake, Hunan, for 150 miles in winter and for 250 miles in summer. On the Chialing, there is steam navigation for about 100 miles from Chungking in winter, and for 280 miles in summer. The Chialing also provides a navigable connection for sampans with southern Shensi and southeastern Kansu. On the Min, regular year-round steamship service is maintained for 80 miles from Suifu. The steamships operating on the Yangtze and its tributaries are predominantly registered in Shanghai, an indication of the extent to which the trade of the river's basin drains to the city.

These waterways of the Yangtze system were collectively the backbone of China's transport facilities in the nineteenth century, and they have remained so. Their limitations are in general those of unreliability. Stream regimens fluctuate widely through the year in all mid-latitude continental climates. In the moderately monsoonal climate of western and central China, the denuded watersheds of the Yangtze and its tributaries, where intensive agriculture has centuries ago removed most of the original forest cover, make for further seasonal extremes in stream levels. Snow melt-water from the northern and northwestern parts of the Yangtze watershed, and the rains of late spring and summer, drain rapidly into stream channels, and produce a yearly range of 90 feet in the level of the Yangtze at Ichang, and 60 feet at Hankow.

In addition, the Yangtze cuts across the major north-south mountain range of central China in its progress from the Szechuan basin to the east China lowland. Between Chungking and Ichang (the gorges of the Yangtze where it has cut through the mountains are between Wanhsien and Ichang), a distance of about 400 miles, there is an average drop in elevation of 14 inches per mile and a total of 15 major rapids. These gorges and rapids are responsible for the break from orthodox ocean and river steamships to special shallow-draft and high-powered steamships at Hankow, which because of its location at the mouth of the Han is a more convenient shipping and commercial center as well as a breaking-point in transport than Ichang, whose hinterland is relatively unproductive and poor in waterways. On all of the Yangtze tributaries beyond the reaches navigable by steamships, navigation by native boats is increasingly seasonal toward the headwaters, and as we have seen above, steam navigation is considerably restricted during the winter low-water period.

The Chinese of the Yangtze basin have learned to make maximum use of existing waterways, with the technical means available to them, and are accustomed to floating rafts and even specially designed junks on one or two feet of water.* Such rafts can carry up to 20 tons of goods and remain waterborne in one foot of water. Spring and summer floods present more of a danger for them than does the winter low-water period. In southwestern Shensi and southeastern Kansu, a region which produces wool, cotton, and hides for export, these products are sent to market during the time of the spring floods by making them up into bundles around which the hides are sewn in a waterproof covering. The bundles are then put into the headwaters of streams leading eventually into the Chialing or Han Rivers, down which they float to collecting centers near the head of junk navigation.

Despite such ingenious adjustments to an environment poor in easy overland routes and rich in waterways, movement of goods along many reaches of the Yangtze system virtually stops during the lowest low-water and highest flood periods, and is seriously hampered even on the master stream by currents, gorges, and rocks. Merchants of Ichang, just downstream from the main gorges of the Yangtze, estimate that about 20 per cent of east-bound boats and

* See Baron von Richtofen, *Letters to the Committee of the Shanghai Chamber of Commerce* (1871), p. 7. He describes navigation in the upper waters of Yangtze tributaries in the central mountain belt on two inches of water.

cargoes between Wanhsien and Ichang are damaged in transit, and about 10 per cent of west-bound boats.[6] Rates of course vary according to the season and to whether the cargo is to be moved up or downstream.

More than a few villages along the Yangtze between Ichang and Chungking depended for their livelihood largely on salvage from boats wrecked on the rocks or in the rapids. Many of these villages were engaged in neither agriculture nor fishing. Hsin Tan (the characters mean "new rapids"), some eighty miles upstream from Ichang, was described by the delegates of the Shanghai Chamber of Commerce in 1869 as a large and prosperous town whose wealth derived mainly from its location at one of the most dangerous rapids along the upper Yangtze. The original channel there was blocked by a landslide in the fourth century B.C., and shortly thereafter Hsin Tan was founded a few hundred yards from the new channel, which contained a series of rapids. The new town presumably acted as a lay-over point for boat trackers, but the rapids also yielded another form of income. Navigation on this stretch was originally forbidden by the provincial authorities between November and April, but the inhabitants of Hsin Tan cleared a channel adequate for the passage of boats during the low-water period but not adequate enough to prevent frequent wrecks, from which they realized most of their livelihood.[7]

Trade within the Yangtze basin has to adjust itself to the seasonal limitations on navigation. Merchants in each trading place, including Shanghai, are obliged to keep large reserves of goods on hand to tide over the periods of flood and low water, and to be ready to ship in large quantities when navigation is possible. Water transport is also liable to interruption by civil disorder (peasant risings, troop movements, bandits), since boatmen fear expropriation of their craft and cargoes at such times. Foreign traders in Shanghai found that most of the Chinese dealers in the hinterland had insufficient capital to buy goods adequate to ensure a uniform supply, and that it was therefore necessary for local branches of the Shanghai firms in inland trade centers such as Hankow or Kiukiang to keep on hand at all times a minimum of 18 months' supply of goods. Under such conditions, only the largest foreign firms could afford to operate, since only they could make such large investments, and could spread the risk of loss over many distribution centers in the interior. Only the largest firms could also keep prices reasonably uniform throughout the year by balancing seasonal and regional losses against seasonal and regional gains.

These operations could not be conducted by foreign firms from a non-Chinese port (such as Hong Kong, or such as was at one time envisaged on Chusan Island), where customs dues and handling charges would be added costs, and because much of the Yangtze trade can best be conducted by junks which are usable over most of the basin's waterways but are not suitable for coastal navigation. Junks drawing between five and eight feet can navigate both the upper and lower Yangtze (i.e., above and below Hankow) as well as most of the major tributaries and the larger waterways of the delta. Their shallow draft and unseaworthiness eliminate them from coastal navigation; a dual-purpose junk would be an overly expensive carrier. Cargo packed at the Shanghai headquarters of foreign firms for shipment to inland centers can be packaged more cheaply for river transport than would be possible for non-Chinese entrepôts dependent on coastal shipping for their connection with the transport routes of the mainland.*

All of these factors, in particular the advantages accruing to the largest firms from the seasonal variations in water transport facilities, redounded to the benefit of Shanghai, since the great majority of the largest foreign and Chinese firms engaged in the import and export trade had their headquarters there. Hankow was handicapped in its direct foreign trade by the low-water period of winter, during which most ocean ships could not reach the city. Shippers preferred to operate out of Shanghai as the only year-round ocean port for the Yangtze basin.

The advantages of unfettered access to this trade artery were apparent to the early foreign traders at Shanghai before the Yangtze was opened to foreign steam navigation by the commercial section

---

* A statement from a "businessman of wide experience in China," cited in R. C. Feetham, *Report to the Shanghai Municipal Council* (1931), I, 289–90, makes many of these points. What is discussed here is of course the "break-in-bulk" theory. The statement goes on to say that "fully 80 per cent of cargo delivered to ultimate consumers in China moves via waterways."

of the Treaty of Tientsin in 1860. (Large-scale foreign trading on the river was in effect delayed until after 1862 by Chinese recalcitrance resulting in a second British campaign in 1860, this time to Peking itself, and by the progress of the Taiping Rebellion in the Yangtze basin.) Rutherford Alcock, British consul at Shanghai in the early 1850's, was of the opinion that "it is vain to look for improvement in British imports while these great trunk lines of inland commerce [i.e., the Yangtze system] are closed to the transit of our goods." [8] The British campaign of 1858 against the Ch'ing Government, and its sequel in 1860, had as one of its chief objectives the opening of the Yangtze to British trade and the addition of Chinkiang, Kiukiang, and Hankow to the list of treaty ports. All three were opened by 1861, and with free navigation on the Yangtze, Shanghai was at last able to implement its location to the full.

Graph 3 suggests the effect of these changes on the foreign and domestic trade of Shanghai. Both total trade and re-exports of foreign goods increased only slightly between 1859 and 1862 owing to the problems referred to in the preceding paragraph, but by 1865 there was a ten-fold increase over the figure for 1859 in the value of foreign goods re-exported to Chinese centers. The total value of trade rose in the same period by nearly 34 per cent. The trade report of the British consul at Shanghai for 1864, commenting on this growth, attributed it entirely to "the large and increasing trade from ports opened on the Yangtze." [9]

The same report pointed out that from a total of 34 million Hai-kuan taels' worth of foreign imports to Shanghai in 1864, 26 million was re-exported to Chinese centers, by virtue of the city's newly-opened water connections with the interior. Consular trade reports in the early and middle 1860's from the newly-opened treaty ports on the Yangtze indicate that these ports shipped the bulk of their exports to Shanghai for re-export, and received from Shanghai the bulk of their imports of foreign goods, principally opium.[10] Hankow, the largest trade center among the Yangtze treaty ports after Shanghai, despite its channel to the sea for ocean-going ships, carried on its exchange transactions with Shanghai rather than with London, and all of the foreign and most of the

Chinese commercial houses in Hankow were branches of Shanghai houses.*

The foreign merchants at Shanghai, aware that their trade was increasingly based on the commercial exploitation of the entire Yangtze basin now made possible by the new treaty, combined in 1868 to finance an expedition under the leadership of Alexander Michie and Robert Francis to explore the trade of the upper Yangtze. The leading American firm in Shanghai, Russell and Company, paid the travel expenses of the expedition by steamship as far as Hankow, and the remainder of the expenses were met by the Shanghai Chamber of Commerce, from which body the members of the expedition had been selected.

The report of these delegates, published in 1869, stressed the importance of water transport in the trade of major commercial centers along the Yangtze, and in the overall movement of domestic trade to and from Shanghai. They noted the extensive tea shipments moving via the Kan River and its tributaries and Poyang Lake to Kiukiang and Hukow and thence via the Yangtze to Shanghai. They commented on the widespread water connections of Hankow, via the Han River system, which brought tea, hides, hemp, timber, and vegetable oils for transshipment to Shanghai, and via the Hsiang River system, which brought mainly tea and cotton. Szechuan sent hemp, hides, bristles, tea, vegetable oils, and opium via the Yangtze to be transshipped at Hankow for Shanghai, these goods having originally been assembled at Chungking via the Chialing, Yangtze, and Min Rivers.[11]

British dominance of the trade of the newly-established treaty ports was secure, but the organic connection between the growth of their primary stronghold at Shanghai and a similar dominance of the Yangtze hinterland which fed it was perhaps the most compelling reason for the early development of Britain's traditional sphere of influence in central China and throughout the Yangtze basin. In north China they could better afford to give ground later in the nineteenth century to Russia and Germany, and in the south to

---

* The British consul at Hankow notes this pattern in his trade report for 1865, which further emphasizes the conditions of Yangtze trade favoring a monopoly by the large Shanghai firms.

share hegemony to a degree with France, but along the Yangtze British preponderance was the logical accompaniment of Britain's trade investment in Shanghai. Without the Yangtze, Shanghai was merely an indifferent harbor.

Two major changes in trade movements resulted from the opening of the river and its tributaries to foreign navigation, aside from the overall increase in foreign trade moving to and from Shanghai. First, the diversion of the export trade of central China (including the Yangtze basin) from Canton to Shanghai, as indicated above in Chapter Four. Under the artificial Canton system, goods for export from central China were obliged to move across the grain of the country in order to reach the only port where foreigners were permitted to trade. The opening of the Yangtze allowed this trade to drain by its natural channels. Two major routes had led from central China to Canton: one from Hankow to the headwaters of the Hsiang River and over the 1400-foot Cheling Pass with a land portage of 26 miles into the headwaters of the Pei River, and one from the lower Yangtze basin via the Kan River to its headwaters near the Meiling Pass at 1000 feet, with a land portage of 24 miles to the headwaters of a tributary of the Pei (map 4). Canton had drawn its trade goods of silk and tea from central China for export via these two routes, but the opening of the Yangtze short-circuited the bulk of this trade to the much closer port of Shanghai.

Goods from central China began in fact, after the effective opening of the Yangtze in 1862, to move to Canton via Shanghai by coastal shipping instead of by the former overland routes. Chungking in Szechuan, which before 1862 had drawn all of its foreign textiles via Canton, was by 1869 entirely dependent on Shanghai for this supply. The delegates of the Shanghai Chamber of Commerce were sufficiently impressed by this indication of the greatly expanded markets which the opening of the Yangtze created for Shanghai that they succumbed to the old dream of British traders of finding buyers for British woolens. Szechuan, they reasoned, had a climate colder than any of the areas where British trade had theretofore reached, and a boom in the woolens trade there could consequently be expected. Like the earlier grandiose expectations of the East India Company days, it never materialized.*

Second, the opening of the Yangtze was a leading factor in permitting the increasing native opium production, notably in Szechuan, to acquire the major share of the China market by the 1870's, at the expense of opium imported from India. Opium was not introduced into China by the Europeans. It had been consumed domestically, from both domestic and foreign sources, since at least the early eighteenth century, and the first Imperial Edict against the import and smoking of opium was issued in 1729. Small amounts of the Szechuan production had continued to find their way as far as Canton by overland routes well into the nineteenth century, despite new Imperial Edicts of 1821 and later making opium smoking and trading in opium capital offenses. But by 1868, with free navigation on the Yangtze, Szechuan opium undersold Indian opium in Shanghai by about 40 per cent, although its quality was inferior, and it was already beginning to rival the sales of the imported drug.[12] This was true despite the fact that consular records show Shanghai in 1864 accounting for 72 per cent of China's total imports of opium, by virtue of its access to the central China market.[13] By 1882, the Maritime Customs estimated that opium production in China amounted to 224,000 piculs (one picul equals 133 pounds) (of which Szechuan accounted for 177,000 piculs), as against foreign opium imports of only 67,000 piculs.[14]

Though opium was no innovation of the Europeans, it is true that it was they who first organized its import on a large scale. That the trade was avidly taken up by the Chinese is indicated by the rise of Szechuan opium, as well as by the well-known history and complements of the Canton trade.† Foreigners and Chinese alike were eager

* The woolens consumed in north China have continued to come from local industry, both household and factory, which can produce goods of a quality and price better suited to the China market.

† For a discussion of the role of opium in the China trade before 1842, see Greenberg, *British Trade*, especially chapter 5. He includes an analysis of the conditions within and without China which stimulated it, and of the close relationship between the trade in tea and in opium. The revenues of Great Britain and of India, the profits of the British East India Company and of the private trading firms at Canton, and the viability of the tea and silk trade are discussed as they depended in varying, but significant or decisive degree, on the import of opium from India to

for the large profits always associated with an illicit traffic. Chinese edicts against it were matched by foreign pronouncements in the wake of the "Opium War" of 1840–1842 (see above, p. 70) to make the trade doubly lucrative. The Chinese drug dealers profited both from its distribution from coastal ports of entry, notably Shanghai (an undertaking from which foreigners were explicitly barred by their own governments), and also from the growing domestic production and its distribution. (Opium came domestically not only from Szechuan but also from the northwest [Kansu and Shensi] and Yünnan, areas of limited arable land remote from the market where high unit-value production was essential and where local taxes and requisitions added to the incentive to grow opium.) Using both sources Chinese drug merchants built up a system of distribution and marketing which was later to implement the penetration of the China market as a whole by the variety of goods which increasingly entered domestic and foreign trade channels after the opening of the Yangtze.

Shanghai's key role in this process is evident from its command of the Yangtze trade artery, and it was the principal market for the distribution of both imported and domestic opium. The drug trade was profitable, and it was conducted on a very large scale. Concentration at Shanghai played an important part in the process of capital accumulation in the city, which was in turn a significant advantage in its continuing acquisition of commercial (and later industrial) dominance. These aspects of the opium trade have been little studied or described, for obvious reasons. Opium remained a live issue in which important sectors of the economy and important bureaux and personalities have been involved until very recently. One cannot consider the issue closed for China until Communist control had been thoroughly established. But it seems likely that opium played as great if not a greater part in Shanghai's rise than did tea or silk (see table II), and that it continued to stimulate the growth and concentration of capital and commercial activity in the

China. This trade, with its consequences for commercial development, was largely inherited by Shanghai after the breakdown of the Canton system. For an earlier standard work on opium, see David Owen, *British Opium Policy in China and India* (New Haven, 1934).

city long after tea and silk had lost their commanding positions. The import of opium into China was legally abolished in 1917 by the terms of an international convention (see below, Chapter Eight), and it disappeared from customs figures at that time. But it was clearly still a powerful generator of capital and trade in the Shanghai of the 1930's. Opium also became a highly profitable export from Shanghai once its import had been officially banned, though as a then wholly illegal trade its volume and mechanics can only be guessed at.*

It also appears likely that the activities of Chinese opium merchants and distributors during the period from about 1800 to about 1870 helped to pioneer the commercialization and integration of the China market for sales of foreign goods, and that the later rapid spread of merchandizing, especially from Shanghai, was in some measure due to this earlier development of the techniques of commercial exploitation. Concurrently, opium continued to flow into Shanghai for domestic marketing and even for export, a trade which under the circumstances was increasingly profitable.

Tea and Silk

However, it was the trade in tea and silk, the two dominant staples of China's export trade until the close of the nineteenth century (table I), whose contribution to the commercial growth of Shanghai is clearest. The city's original near-monopoly as a result of the concentration of tea and silk production in or near the delta was further implemented by the opening of the Yangtze and its ports by the Treaty of Tientsin.

Transport costs for tea and silk by overland routes were high, averaging during the 1860's and 1870's 13 taels per bale of silk (approximately six bales to the ton), and 12 taels per hundred chests of tea (approximately 100 chests to the ton), for 200 miles. Taking the tael at this period as equivalent to about 6s 2d, these rates work out at about £24 per ton of silk (US$.56 per ton/mile), and £21 per ton of tea (US$.50 per ton/mile), as compared with

* See R. d'Auxion de Ruffe, *La Farce de l'Opium* (Paris, 1939), for a somewhat bitter *ad hominem* account of opium smoking and the opium trade in Shanghai, against the background of local and international measures designed to suppress it.

average per-ton costs over similar distances in the same areas for ordinary goods of about £12 (US$.30 per ton/mile).[15] Tea and silk required special handling, and neither was supposed to get wet or to touch the ground during its transport.* These rates compare with an average of about £14 per ton for tea and silk over similar distances by water transport.[16] Shanghai's water connections were thus a vital advantage in securing for it the lion's share of foreign trade in these two leading commodities. Robert Fortune estimated in 1848 that transport costs for tea from the hinterland to Shanghai averaged about 50 per cent of total costs to that point, while he estimated the figure for Canton at 70 per cent.[17]

A desire on the part of the Ch'ing Government to continue the diplomatic and economic advantages resulting from the monopoly system of the Canton Cohong was apparently combined with a desire for increased revenue from the newly expanded trade with the foreigners in a movement to tax tea and silk exported via Shanghai at the same rate as would have been applied if these had moved out via the much longer route to Canton. The resulting Imperial Edict of 1845 ordering the imposition of extra transit dues on this basis had, however, only a nominal effect, since the locational advantages of Shanghai meant that the saving in transport costs and interest charges on tea and silk shipments more than made up for the additional dues.[18]

Map 9 shows the major tea-producing areas of China in the nineteenth century. The Yangtze itself runs through the northern part of the area producing the best quality teas, and its tributaries and the Chientang River (with its mouth at Hangchow, from which multiple waterways lead to Shanghai) drain most of the remainder. In spite of its river connections into this area, Wenchow was not a major tea exporter. This was certainly due in part to its relatively late opening to foreign trade, but that fact is in itself related to the high relief in Wenchow's hinterland, through which interrupted navigation provides the only adequate means of trans-

---

* For overland transport, they were carried in special frames mounted on porters' backs, with a supporting stick attached so that the load could be rested without being set down on the ground. For water transport, special care was taken to see that tea and silk were kept in clean dry holds or securely under cover. See Robert Fortune, *A Journey to the Tea Countries* (1852); Richtofen, *Letters to the Committee.*

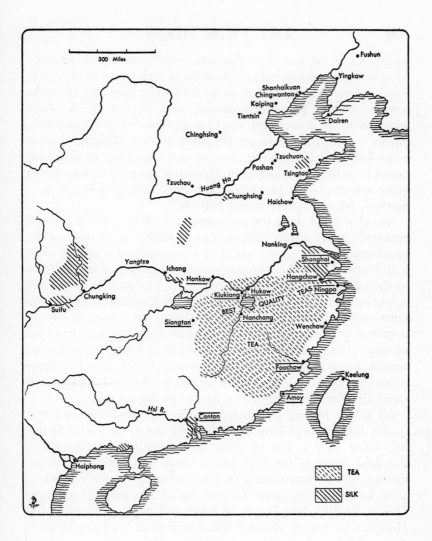

Map 9. *Tea and Silk Areas of China in the Nineteenth Century, and Coal Mines Mentioned in the Text.* Major collecting centers for tea underlined. Major ports for overseas exports of tea underlined and overlined. Data from China: Maritime Customs, *Silk* (1881); *ibid.*, *Decennial Reports*; Robert Fortune, *A Journey to the Tea Countries* (1852); Richtofen, *Letters* (1871); *et al.*

port. Most of the teas from this area could move out more easily by water to Ningpo, or to Hangchow for transshipment to Shanghai. Foochow and Amoy drew their tea for export primarily from the southern part of the chief producing area, by way of the rivers which terminate at each port, and Canton depended for its tea supply mainly on the route through the Meiling Pass. Ningpo, situated on an indifferently navigable river, in fact drew some of its tea for export from the Chientang basin, via a canal from the Chientang ten miles upstream from Hangchow, but even so three portages were necessary between the river and Ningpo.[19]

Shanghai could draw tea from almost all of the chief producing area with much greater facility. Tea in China, as in most of the important tea areas of the world, is a mountain or a hillside crop. It is displaced from the lowlands by grain crops, and it is considered by the Chinese that a more fragrant leaf is produced on slopes and at higher altitudes, where drainage is good, nights are cool, and mists are frequent.[20] In the chief producing area, most of the tea is grown at elevations between 1000 and 2500 feet, and was thus necessarily transported by portage to the local curing and collecting centers. From these local centers, however, the tea moved to larger collection places and to ports of export predominantly by water, especially after the Yangtze was opened to foreign trade.

All of the leading tea districts of the area producing the best quality teas (map 9) have through water connections with Shanghai, while only a few of them have similar connections with Foochow, Ningpo, or Wenchow. Amoy and Canton have no through water connections with this area except by sea.[21] Hankow acted as a collecting center for the teas of Szechuan, Hupeh, and Hunan, brought there largely by water and largely transshipped to Shanghai for export, although direct exports of tea from Hankow during the late nineteenth and early twentieth centuries amounted to about one quarter of the amount transshipped to Shanghai for export.[22]

The tea of central China is grown in the northern and southern highlands of the hill and mountain ranges south of the Yangtze (called by Cressey the "South Yangtze Hills"), with the better quality teas coming from the northern highlands. The tea leaves are picked as a rule three times a year: in April, May, and September, so that the bulk of export shipments comes during the summer high-water period, but occasional picking and regular shipments from the collecting centers continue through most of the winter. The stream pattern is better developed in the northern highlands than in the southern, and it focuses ultimately on Shanghai, either directly via the Yangtze, or via Hangchow. The less well developed stream pattern of the southern highlands drains to at least five separate ports, each in its own isolated river basin.

Along these streams, as along all of the rivers in China, successive trading centers developed at each break in navigation necessitated by rapids or by a change in the depth of the water where junks gave way to sampans or sampans to bamboo rafts. More of these trading centers which acted as collection places for tea are located north of the divide than south of it, and they naturally tended to ship their teas to northern ports for export, although the normal routes were occasionally abandoned in favor of roundabout routes in order to avoid excessive local transit taxes or arbitrary dues, as for example the shipment of tea from the upper Chientang basin overland to Ningpo and thence by sea to Shanghai.[23]

The cargo capacity of the boats, and hence the freight rate from these local centers to larger regional collecting centers, varied sharply with seasonal changes in the water level. In a tea area approximately 150 miles up the Chientang River from Hangchow in 1870, rates for transporting 100 chests of tea to Hangchow varied during the year from Mex$20 in summer to Mex$50 in winter.* During the summer the average time for tea in transit to Hangchow was five days, as against ten days in winter, while goods moving from Hangchow to the area in question took about twenty days at all seasons.[24] The use of water transport in this case is clear from the fact that these rates and transit times follow so closely the conditions of stream navigation, and are the only ones quoted for the tea trade in this area.

W. H. Medhurst in the account referred to above in Chapter Five commented on the fact that tea, at that time marketed entirely by Chinese merchants at the treaty ports, moved to Shanghai from the

* Mex$1 at this period equaled about US$.80

producing areas by water, but that many of the routes to Canton began on land and were interspersed with portages. Medhurst also noted that tea was being shipped in large quantities from the northern highlands of the divide to Shanghai, via the smaller tributaries of the Yangtze in Kiangsi and Anhwei.[25] Robert Fortune (see above, Chapter Five) visited the same areas a few years later, also in disguise as a Chinese. His account corroborates in more detail the general impression of Medhurst that tea from nearly all of the collecting centers in the area producing the best quality teas moved to Shanghai by through water routes, while some part of all of the routes to Canton lay on land.* [26]

By 1867, the British consul at Shanghai, in commenting in his trade report for that year on the greatly increased trade of the port resulting from the opening of the Yangtze, gave his opinion that the greater ease, cheapness, and speed of transport for tea to Shanghai had resulted in a decline in the quality of the tea. He considered that less care was taken with grading and packing the tea for the short haul to Shanghai (where its cost price was of course considerably lower than it had formerly been at Canton), and that it therefore often arrived stale and poorly sorted. This may illustrate in reverse the common association of high unit-value and high-quality goods with high transport costs. He added that before the opening of Shanghai, tea from the northern slopes of the divide frequently spent six months in transit to Canton, but that the average transit from this region to Shanghai after the opening of the Yangtze was approximately six weeks.[27]

However, it was as much the great increase in the volume of the tea trade through Shanghai, in which many more producers were able to enter the export market with the drop in transport costs, which accounted for the decline in quality of the tea. This was no longer a small-scale, specialized, luxury business, but a large commercial enterprise, made possible by uninterrupted water connections. It was clearly these transport advantages of Shanghai as much as its relative nearness to the tea-producing districts which were

* Tea grown along the Hsi-Yangtze divide (the area known as the "Bohea Hills") was necessarily moved to collecting places north or south of the divide by porter.

responsible for the city's commanding position in the tea trade. Its tea exports rose from one million pounds in 1844 (the year after it was opened to foreign trade) to 80 million pounds in 1855. Smaller amounts continued to be exported direct via Hankow, Kiukiang, Ningpo, Foochow, and Canton, but by 1855 Shanghai accounted for 58 per cent of the total, and in 1864 (two years after the effective opening of the Yangtze) for 64 per cent.[28]

For the silk trade, Shanghai was even more favorably located. From the opening of the treaty ports through the 1930's, there were four principal silk-producing areas in China (map 9): the Canton region, producing so-called "soft" silk; central Szechuan, producing "yellow" silk; northeastern Shantung, producing "tussah" silk; and southern Kiangsu-northern Chekiang.* This last was by far the largest producer, and its silk (known generically to the foreign merchants as "China" silk) was considered by both Chinese and foreign traders to be the finest in the world.† Kiangsu and Chekiang together accounted for about half of the total production of raw silk in China through the nineteenth century and into the 1930's, while the Canton region accounted for about 20 per cent, Szechuan for 15 per cent, Shantung for 5 per cent, and Hunan and Hupeh together for 5 per cent.[29]

The area around Tai Lake was the major center within the Kiangsu-Chekiang silk region. In certain districts there, notably around Wusih, Soochow, and Huchow, mulberry displaced rice as the first crop, and nearly all of the farmers were engaged in silk culture during the six-week worm-rearing season in April and early May. Hangchow was also a leading silk center, and was especially important in silk reeling and weaving. The cocoons were reeled and the silk spun into yarn either in these cities (and lesser centers), or in Shanghai, but nearly all of the silk produced in this

---

* Silk for export also came in smaller quantities from Honan and Anhwei (notably Wuhu). Hopeh and Liaotung (southern Manchuria) were important "tussah" producers in addition to Shantung.

† The study of the silk industry and trade published in 1881 by the Maritime Customs (Special Series #13) includes an account by the Rev. Mr. Milne, a British missionary who traveled around the delta and a little beyond in the mid-1840's, disguised as a Chinese. He details the nature of silk worms and describes their care and the production of silk according to the traditional Chinese ideas and practices, expressed in picturesque language in the spirit of the Chinese texts.

"China" silk area for foreign trade was marketed in Shanghai, through both Chinese and foreign trading firms, who sold it for export. Steam filatures for the reeling and spinning of silk had largely replaced domestic reeling and spinning by 1920, but this did not affect the concentration of silk marketing in Shanghai, since the reeling centers remained tributary to Shanghai and since the silk-reeling industry was also concentrated, in differing degrees at different periods, in the city.

After the introduction of cotton from India in the Yüan dynasty (1260–1368) and the manufacture of cotton cloth in China on a large scale by the end of the Yüan, this much cheaper fabric largely displaced silk, which previously had been produced in almost every region of China and was universally worn. The quality of the silk also declined. By the end of the eighteenth century only the four major areas listed above were important silk producers, but the great increase in China's foreign trade, especially in tea and silk, which followed the opening of the treaty ports stimulated both the quantity and quality of silk production in these areas, most of all in the chief silk region of the Yangtze delta, where foreign traders were closest on the scene.

The leading silk areas within the delta coincide closely with the areas where navigable waterways are most numerous. The upland districts south of Nanking and west of Tai Lake, where waterways are relatively sparse, are largely avoided by silk culture. This is mainly due to the fact that silk culture is a painstaking and time-consuming process which requires prodigious amounts of hand labor. It is therefore heaviest in lowland areas with a dense population, as is the case with nearly all of the silk producing regions of China, but such a location facilitates a virtually exclusive dependence on water transport for marketing the silk. This in turn tends to make Shanghai, as the primate commercial center of the delta, the dominant market for silk exports, since it can draw silk from the producing areas by water transport nearly as easily and cheaply as can inland centers.

Every important cocoon and filature center in the delta has multiple water connections and depends on them for the collection of cocoons and for the marketing of silk. Liu Ta-chün in his study of the silk industry makes this clear, and uses the case of Huchow as an example. No less than sixteen navigable waterways connect Huchow with the local silk culture districts, and with Shanghai, where the bulk of its cocoons and spun silk was marketed.[30]

Shanghai was also the primary market for the silk exports of Szechuan, Shantung, and Hupeh-Hunan. Before 1843, and to a lesser extent until 1862, the silk exports of these areas went to Canton via the Cheling and Meiling passes, or from Shantung by coastal junk, but after the opening of the treaty ports, and particularly after the opening of the Yangtze, these exports moved out via the much nearer port of Shanghai. The silk areas of the upper Yangtze basin, notably in Szechuan, are closely related to the Han and Chialing Rivers, or to the Yangtze itself. With free navigation throughout the river system, it was natural that this silk should be marketed through Shanghai.

Before the abolition in 1834 of the East India Company's monopoly of the British trade with China, yearly exports of silk from China averaged under 6,000 bales. By 1840 the figure had risen to 16,000 bales, largely as a result of the new volume of trade by private firms out of Canton.[31] However in 1844 Shanghai, one year after its opening to foreign trade, exported alone 6,433 bales, and by 1855 the figure for Shanghai had risen to 92,000 bales, or over 60 per cent of the total exports of silk from China.[32] By 1864, after the opening of the Yangtze, Shanghai accounted for approximately 64 per cent of China's silk exports, and in 1930 for 62 per cent, as against 29 per cent in 1930 for Canton.[33] Canton was left with only the local silk areas in Kwangtung to draw on, while Shanghai in 1925 drew 30 per cent of its spun silk exports from filatures in the city (whose cocoon supply came almost entirely from the delta), 10 per cent from other delta filature centers, 11 per cent from Szechuan filatures, 15 per cent from Shantung filatures, 9 per cent from Hupeh-Hunan filatures, and 25 per cent from domestic reeling, primarily in the delta.[34] Cheap transportation made it possible for Shanghai to add to its monopoly of local silk marketing for export the silk of all the other leading areas except for Kwangtung itself.

Other Trade Goods

Shanghai was fortunate in that as China's monopolies of the tea and silk trade disappeared by about the turn of the century, the Yangtze continued to concentrate there for export a large proportion of the goods which now became the staples in China's more diversified foreign trade (table I). These goods: vegetable oils, hides, skins and bristles, eggs, and fibers, were staple products of the Yangtze basin, and their marketing in Shanghai was as logical as that of tea and silk. In this new trade, Hankow was the principal inland collection and distribution center, but as with tea, its direct exports overseas remained slight, and actually decreased after 1880 when steam navigation on the Yangtze had become firmly established.[35] Hankow sent the bulk of goods destined for export to Shanghai for transshipment.

Hankow's water connections enabled it to draw these goods not only from Szechuan, Hupeh, and Hunan along the Yangtze itself but also from Shensi, Honan, Kweichow, and Kwangsi via Yangtze tributaries. Szechuan led all the other provinces in the production of wood oil (t'ung oil), wax and tallow, and bristles, and was a leading producer of hides and skins, fibers, and other vegetable oils. Production of vegetable oils, raw cotton and other fibers, and eggs was also important in the lower Yangtze basin in Anhwei, Chekiang, and Kiangsu. While their production was less localized than was the case with tea and silk, and also because of this scattering, Shanghai had easier, cheaper, and quicker transport connections than any other leading port with these or other producing areas. The Yangtze also enabled Shanghai to exchange its foreign imports (and after 1920 increasingly its own industrial production) for export goods over a wider market and with greater ease and cheapness than rival commercial centers.

The disruptions of the Taiping Rebellion and attendant local uprisings (1850–1864) were heavy in the Yangtze delta, and the largest military campaigns were fought there. Shanghai itself acted as an invaluable base for the efforts of the Ch'ing government to suppress the rebellion, since with the support of foreign troops and volunteers, the city was able to hold out against a rebel tide which engulfed every other delta city of importance. It was from Shanghai that the famous "Ever Victorious Army" (composed of both Chinese and foreigners led by the American Frederick Ward and, after his death from wounds, by the British Major Charles ["Chinese"] Gordon) conducted its decisive campaigns on behalf of the Ch'ing government against the Taipings and retook all the delta cities before the eventual recapture of Nanking in 1864. Shallow-draft boats carrying both bombardment guns and troops and using the pattern of delta waterways leading from Shanghai gave this army a crucial advantage of mobility against the numerically greatly superior Taiping forces.

Shanghai's land and speculative boom and the defense of its boundaries during this period are briefly discussed above in Chapters One and Two, but two other results of the rebellion were of greater significance: the establishment of the Imperial Maritime Customs, with the commercial advantage which this gave to Shanghai (see below, Chapter Eight); and the damage to the tea and silk industries (which were concentrated in the delta and its immediate environs) together with the blocking of the normal trade routes, which was followed after 1862 by new opportunities for the expansion of a more diversified trade. Shanghai suffered substantially from the losses inflicted on its trade in these two key commodities. But the pliability of the Ch'ing government, in recognition of the fact that foreign military assistance from Shanghai was instrumental if not decisive in the suppression of this mass rebellion, played its part in the granting of free navigational rights on the Yangtze, more from apprehension than from gratitude. The foreigners, undismayed by the illogicality of their position from a diplomatic point of view (British naval and land forces were attacking Taku and Peking at the same time that British forces were fighting against the Taipings in the delta area), were encouraged by their military successes to press their demands for wider commercial opportunity. The rebellion revealed Shanghai's vulnerability as long as its trade was so heavily dependent on the two local or semi-local staples of tea and silk, and at the same time re-emphasized possibilities for a broader and larger trade in the Yangtze valley as a whole. Though the trade in tea and silk recovered rapidly after the fighting (see table I), stopped the marked growth in Shanghai's total trade was due predominantly to the opening of the Yangtze, and it was this new commercial sphere with its new commodities which after 1880 increasingly supported the city.

Shanghai's commanding position for marketing is revealed in the fact that between 1860 and 1930 it accounted for an average of 68 per cent by value of the total re-exports of goods from Chinese ports to Chinese ports. For the period 1925–1935, goods re-exported from Shanghai to Chinese markets went (according to percentages of the total value of such exports) to Kiangsu and other provinces as shown in the accompanying table.[36]

Kiangsu	18	Szechuan	8
Chekiang	17	Honan	6
Anhwei	16	Fukien	3
Hupeh	11	Shantung	2
Hunan	9	Other	1
Kiangsi	9	TOTAL	100

In a largely pre-industrial economy still characterized for the most part by local rather than regional or national markets, these figures show a truly remarkable areal extent over which Shanghai was able to market (and to purchase) its goods, and the degree to which Shanghai served as the dominant place of exchange for China as a whole. They suggest a close relationship between the size and areal distribution of the market and the waterways and sea routes which focus on the city.

Political and military events in 1926, and later during 1937 and after, re-emphasized the importance to Shanghai of this water network for the supply of its trade and industrial goods and for the distribution of its exports. Civil war was widespread in the middle and lower Yangtze basin during the latter half of 1926 as part of the campaign of the Kuomintang against the local and northern warlords. Commandeering of boats, including native craft and 13 out of the 31 Yangtze steamers of the China Merchants Steam Navigation Company by December 1926, led to the suspension of nearly all river sailings between Shanghai and Hankow by Chinese vessels before the end of the year. British and Japanese shipping firms continued to operate, but under difficulties, and they could not handle more than a small fraction of the normal volume of trade on the river. As a result, sales of piece textile goods in Shanghai had fallen by January 1927, to one quarter of their August levels. The kerosene trade out of the city was badly hit, and large stocks accumulated in warehouses. Imports of Chinese tobacco leaf to Shanghai virtually ceased by January, and forced the closure of several of the large cigarette factories. Egg imports to the city in January were less than 30 per cent of normal. By the end of 1927, with order restored in the Yangtze basin and navigation no longer interfered with, Shanghai's trade with its hinterland returned to normal levels. Both railway lines serving the city remained in regular operation for all but a few days during this period.[37]

In November 1937, in order to hamper Japanese naval movements on the Yangtze, the Chinese Government placed booms across the river at Kiangyin and Chinkiang, and fighting in the delta area and upstream from Nanking further disrupted traffic. The value of Shanghai's foreign trade fell by 76 per cent between July (hostilities began at Shanghai on August 13, 1937) and December 1937, as much because of the interruptions in transport as because of the local fighting, which ended at Shanghai itself in October. During the same period, the total value of the foreign trade of China as a whole decreased by only 2 per cent. Shanghai's relative decline continued through 1938, with a 49 per cent decrease in imports and a 63 per cent decrease in exports over the 1937 figures, while for the same period the total foreign trade of China increased by 8 per cent.[38] With its water connections disrupted, Shanghai could no longer compete commercially with rival centers, which despite the progress of hostilities over nearly the whole of east China by the end of 1938 increased the total of their trade at the expense of Shanghai.

But the disruptions of war should not obscure the fact that the Yangtze basin is the economic heart of China, nor that its river system will continue to be a basic element in China's transport pattern. The city at the mouth of the river will remain a metropolis under whatever conditions the future or the Communist Government of China may impose.

EIGHT

The Trade of the Port

Statistics make dull reading, but they may often tell an important and otherwise untold story, or illumine facts or ideas already grasped but imperfectly understood. With this latter end in view, graphs 4–8 and tables I–IV combine a great many statistics which would make dull reading indeed but which in this form may be less unpleasant and more expressive. In any case they are essential to an understanding of the history and nature of Shanghai's trade, and as charts they do a more effective job than they could as figures in the text, which they would very nearly bury, but which would mean little without them. The graphs and tables are the body of this chapter, and the text serves merely as the narrator of the events and patterns which they portray.

Foreign Trade Since 1850 [1]

The primacy of Shanghai in both the foreign and domestic trade of China was well established by at least 1865, and table III shows that this primacy was never thereafter seriously threatened before the Japanese attack on China in 1937. Shanghai's share of China's overseas commerce consistently totaled about one half from the opening of the Yangtze to foreign trade until the outbreak of full-scale hostilities with Japan. "The heart of foreign trade is Shanghai, and the other ports mere blood vessels." [2]

The export of tea and silk and the import of opium and cotton textiles dominate the greater half of the period since 1850 in Shanghai's, as in China's foreign trade. Despite Shanghai's key location for the trade in both tea and silk, however, the city's overseas imports exceeded its overseas exports in value in every year save two from 1864 (when the complete records of the Maritime Customs begin) to 1936. Until 1925, the excess averaged about 10 per cent annually, but between 1926 and 1936, when the growth of manufacturing in Shanghai required increased imports of expensive machinery and raw materials, the annual excess averaged about 15 per cent. This is characteristic of the trade of a transshipment point, which has an advantage in the distribution of imports (especially if they require repacking as well as reloading onto a different carrier) not equaled in the handling of exports, which can

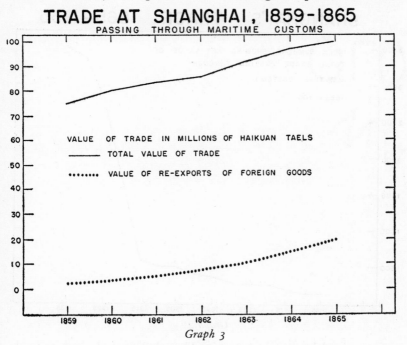

Graph 3

often move out in small lots directly from each production area to other regional or foreign markets as finished goods.

The most notable feature of the eighty years between 1850 and 1930 as shown in table I is of course the decline in the export of tea and silk from their commanding positions before 1890 to relatively minor importance after 1900.* While ample reasons can

* In 1868, the United Kingdom, consistently China's best tea customer, took 97 per cent of its tea from China, in 1888 40 per cent, in 1898 20 per cent, and by 1902 only 3 per cent.

be found for China's loss of her one-time monopoly of the trade in these two goods,[3] it needs to be emphasized that nearly all such monopolies of essentially agricultural or handicraft production are eventually broken. The cases of rubber, coffee, and sugar are examples of this rule which are familiar to all students of economic history. China held her monopolies of tea and silk probably longer than any other such monopolies have ever lasted. The monopolies

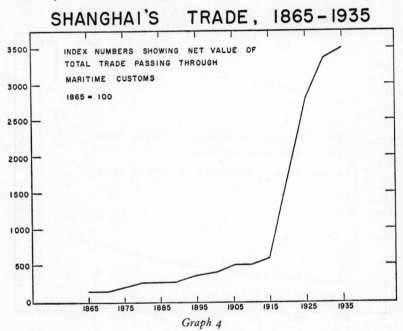

SHANGHAI'S TRADE, 1865-1935

INDEX NUMBERS SHOWING NET VALUE OF TOTAL TRADE PASSING THROUGH MARITIME CUSTOMS

1865 = 100

Graph 4

were retained long enough to give Shanghai an early start toward trade leadership in China by virtue of the city's favorable location for the tea and silk trade, and by the time that India, Ceylon, Java, and Japan among them had acquired the command of the world market for tea and silk (by about 1900), Shanghai's primacy was secure enough for the city to profit to the full from its equally favorable location for the newly diversified foreign trade of China.

The primary purpose of Robert Fortune's later visits to China in 1848 and 1853–56 (see above, Chapter Four) was the collection, on

TABLE I

Exports From Shanghai Through Maritime Customs to Foreign Ports

(Decenially, 1850–1930, by approximate percentages of
the total value of such trade in each year indicated.)

	1850	1860	1870	1880	1890	1900	1910	1920	1930
Raw silk	52	66	62	38	34	30	26	20	14
Tea	46	28	32	48	30	16	10	4	4
Miscellaneous	2	6	6	—	—	—	—	—	—
Miscellaneous raw materials	—	—	—	10	14	20	16	18	10
Vegetable oils	—	—	—	—	6	10	12	16	18
Miscellaneous manufactures	—	—	—	4	4	8	8	14	16
Textiles	—	—	—	—	—	—	4	8	16
Hides, skins, and bristles	—	—	—	—	8	10	10	12	14
Eggs and egg products	—	—	—	—	—	—	6	8	8
Raw cotton	—	—	—	—	4	6	8	—	—
TOTALS	100	100	100	100	100	100	100	100	100

SOURCES: Figures for 1850 and 1860 are estimates, based on Lanning (1923), p. 401, and Bannister (1932), p. 126. (Trade in 1850 did not of course move through Maritime Customs — see Chapter 8.) Data for 1870–1930 compiled from China: Maritime Customs, *Annual Reports and Returns of Trade.*

TABLE II

Imports Into Shanghai Through Maritime Customs From Foreign Ports

(Decenially, 1850–1930, by approximate percentages of
the total value of such trade in each year indicated.)

	1850	1860	1870	1880	1890	1900	1910	1920	1930
Opium	54	48	34	34	22	12	12	—	—
Cotton textiles	34	44	50	42	44	50	32	36	8
Miscellaneous	6	4	10	12	16	12	16	6	10
Cotton yarn	6	4	6	—	—	—	—	—	—
Coal	—	—	—	6	4	4	4	4	4
Metals and minerals	—	—	—	6	6	6	6	10	20
Machinery	—	—	—	—	—	6	8	16	28
Petroleum products	—	—	—	—	4	6	6	8	6
Raw cotton	—	—	—	—	—	—	4	8	14
Lumber	—	—	—	—	4	4	4	—	—
Tobacco	—	—	—	—	—	—	4	4	4
Sugar	—	—	—	—	—	—	4	4	—
Wheat (and flour)	—	—	—	—	—	—	—	4	6
TOTALS	100	100	100	100	100	100	100	100	100

Sources: Figures for 1850 and 1860 are estimates, based on Lanning (1923), p. 400, and Bannister (1932), p. 120. (Trade in 1850 did not of course move through Maritime Customs — see Chapter 8.) Data for 1870–1930 compiled from China: Maritime Customs, *Annual Reports and Returns of Trade*.

TABLE III

Foreign and Domestic* Trade of Leading Chinese Ports, 1870–1920

(Gross values of trade, in millions of hai-kuan taels, landed at or shipped from the leading treaty-ports in China in each year listed.)

	1870		1880		1890	
	Foreign	Domestic	Foreign	Domestic	Foreign	Domestic
Shanghai	90	96	88	112	101	136
Canton	28	24	30	26	28	24
Hankow	18	16	21	25	14	42
Tientsin	15	9	16	14	18	25

	1900		1910		1920	
	Foreign	Domestic	Foreign	Domestic	Foreign	Domestic
Shanghai	160	181	316	382	504	532
Canton	34	26	47	38	59	46
Hankow	15	52	13	58	13	73
Tientsin	32	38	64	68	108	117
Tsingtao	5	4	15	9	14	12

SOURCES: Figures compiled from China: Maritime Customs, *Annual Reports and Returns of Trade*.

* i.e., the domestic trade which was recorded by the Maritime Customs, only a part of the total volume of domestic trade at each port, or of China as a whole.

TABLE IV

Foreign and Domestic* Trade of Leading Chinese Ports, 1925–1935

(Average percentages of foreign and domestic trade by value passing through leading Chinese ports (exclusive of Manchuria) over the period 1925–1935).

Port	Foreign	Domestic
Shanghai	55	38
Tientsin	11	8
Canton	6	4
Hankow	4	6
Tsingtao	4	2

SOURCES: Recorded by the Maritime Customs. Data from Jones, 1940, pp. 58–9.

* i.e., the domestic trade which was recorded by the Maritime Customs, only a part of the total volume of domestic trade at each port, or of China as a whole.

behalf of the British East India Company, of information concern-
ing tea cultivation in China, and the procurement of cuttings of tea
plants. Fortune was able to transport tea cuttings from China to
London by growing them in tubs on shipboard en route, and
cuttings were subsequently sent from London to India.[4] From
India, tea cultivation spread to Ceylon, and by the end of the nine-

EXPORTS OF LOCAL ORIGIN

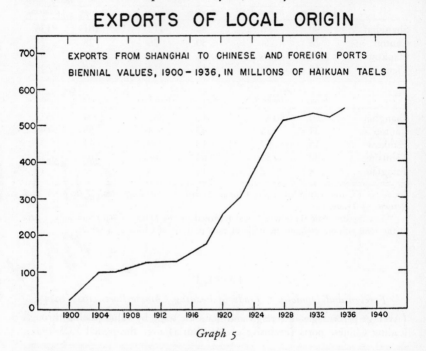

EXPORTS FROM SHANGHAI TO CHINESE AND FOREIGN PORTS
BIENNIAL VALUES, 1900 – 1936, IN MILLIONS OF HAIKUAN TAELS

Graph 5

teenth century Java and Japan (plus the Japanese colony of
Formosa) had joined India and Ceylon ahead of China in total
exports of tea.*[5] It should however be pointed out that the total
gross exports of both tea and silk from China, and from Shanghai,
continued to increase in volume by weight (although not by value,
due to overseas competition), from 1865 to 1929, with the exception

* Curiously enough, the Indian tea of commerce was ultimately derived from shrubs
found growing wild in Assam rather than from the plants introduced from China by
Fortune, a fact which helps to account for the difference between Indian and
Chinese teas. (See the account in Sir J. T. Pratt, *China and Britain* (c.1944), pp. 36–37.)

of three scattered years in which either the tea or silk crop failed.[6] The merchants in foreign trade at Shanghai deplored the success at their expense of tea cultivation in India, Ceylon, Japan, Java and Formosa, and of silk production in Japan. But they were nevertheless able to maintain the volume of tea and silk exports from Shanghai until 1930 at the same time that they were adding to the list of exports a variety of new goods which in the aggregate after 1890 were increasingly more important than tea and silk combined (table I).

Among the new exports were two new virtual monopolies: pig bristles and wood oil (t'ung oil), both produced predominantly in Szechuan and both marketed predominantly through Shanghai.*[7] But together with the increasing commercial exploitation of the entire Yangtze basin after 1860, in which wood oil and bristles played a prominent part, the end of the century also saw the rising importance of manufacturing in Shanghai. Agricultural and animal products (or raw materials in general) remained the majority of Shanghai's exports through 1930, but their prominence continued to decrease after 1890 as textiles and other manufactured goods increased in importance. Raw cotton disappeared from the list of major exports after 1910 as it was increasingly in demand in Shanghai textile mills, and exports of miscellaneous manufactures finally exceeded exports of miscellaneous raw materials in 1930 (table I).

Table II showing imports demonstrates that the relative decline in opium was not due to the prohibition of its import as much as to the spread of opium cultivation in China and the ease with which Szechuan opium could compete in Shanghai with foreign opium (see above, Chapter Seven). The table shows that by 1890 opium accounted for only 22 per cent of Shanghai's imports by value (as against an estimated 54 per cent in 1850), but the import of opium was not legally abolished until 1917 (an international convention in 1911 increased the duty on opium imports and fixed

---

* China's trade in pig bristles has recently been severely cut into by the use of nylon bristles, and the trade in wood oil has also been badly damaged by the increase in domestic production in the United States (China's chief market for wood oil) during and since the war, and by the use of substitutes and synthetics.

1917 as the last year in which opium could legally be imported). By 1910, opium and cotton textiles combined totaled only 44 per cent of Shanghai's imports, as against 88 per cent in 1850, and a variety of goods was coming in to feed not only the increasingly commercialized and Westernized market of the Yangtze basin for which Shanghai served as the transshipment point, but also Shanghai's growing industry.

In the trade of 1910 as shown in table II, imports of cotton textiles suffered their first notable relative decline, and imports of raw cotton appeared for the first time as a major item, destined for Shanghai's developing textile industry, for which domestic supplies of raw cotton were still inadequate. The disappearance of cotton yarn imports after 1880 indicates the disastrous effects of foreign textile goods imports on the traditional handicraft textile industry. By 1930, the two largest import categories were machinery, and metals and minerals, followed by raw cotton, with cotton textiles reduced to only 8 per cent. Shanghai manufacturing had become the most important determinant of the city's imports.

An even clearer picture of the growth of manufacturing in Shanghai is given by graphs 4 and 5. The first shows dramatically the coincidence between the boom in Shanghai manufacturing attendant on the removal of overseas competition during the first world war (and continued through the 1920's), and the meteoric increase in the trade of the port as a whole from 1915 to 1930. The second shows an equal correlation between the growth of manufacturing in Shanghai and the quintupling of the value of exports of local origin between 1914 and 1932.

Between 1860 and 1930, in sum, Shanghai, as the primary focus, first of the commercialization of the Chinese economy, and later of its industrialization, changed in its import trade from a position primarily as distributor of foreign consumption goods to its tributary area of the Yangtze basin to one primarily as consumer and distributor of foreign capital goods and industrial raw materials, while in its export trade it changed from the market for overseas shipments of the "noble articles" of tea and silk to the market for overseas shipments of the more mundane products of the Yangtze basin as a whole and of the goods produced by the city's own industry.

Shanghai as a Transshipment Point

The figures of the Maritime Customs are one of the few oases in the statistical desert of the Chinese economy.* The Chinese city at Shanghai was held by rebel forces during 1853 and 1854, and in the impotence of the Ch'ing customs officials, customs dues were collected on behalf of the Ch'ing government by the British and American consuls from their own nationals. Out of this temporary expedient grew the Imperial Maritime Customs (after 1911 called the Chinese Maritime Customs), an organ of the Chinese government headed by a British Inspector-General and staffed by both Chinese and foreigners.[8]

The advantages of this development for the foreign firms at Shanghai were great. Difficulties, and financial losses, inevitably involved in dealing with the native (original Chinese) customs had been frequent sources of complaint, despite the improvement over conditions in Canton (see above, Chapter Five). Like most official institutions in the declining years of Ch'ing, the customs was not only riddled with corruption, but thoroughly inefficient, and in any case neither capable nor disposed to expedite the foreign trade of the port, which was so largely in foreign hands and for foreign profit. The Taiping Rebellion provided the occasion for the removal of this obstacle, and the delay, red tape, squeeze, and cumbersomeness of the old system were replaced by a new body, which though hybrid was geared to the needs and techniques of the European trader. The change also redounded to the benefit not only of the Chinese in Shanghai, who increasingly shared in creating and profiting from the commercial expansion of the city which the new customs service facilitated, but to the whole of the Chinese economy where the stimulus of Shanghai was more and more being felt. The Maritime Customs represented a major step toward the creation of conditions under which Western-type

* The "Annual Reports and Returns of Trade," published every year from 1864 to 1941 for each of the treaty ports, itemize the imports and exports of each port and give figures for original exports, re-exports, coasting trade, and the origin and destination of imports and exports at each port. The Reports also give considerable information on trade and industrial developments in each province and treaty-port area, including the sources of the major trade goods of each port.

commercial growth, Shanghai in the van, could prosper with accelerating vigor.*

By 1864, offices of the new customs service had been established in all of the treaty ports, and its records of treaty-port trade are complete from that year. Maritime Customs figures for each treaty port, however, cover only the imports and exports to and from foreign countries, and the domestic coasting and river trade carried in foreign-built or foreign-type bottoms, whether Chinese- or foreign-owned (i.e., excluding junks, sampans, and rafts, but including lorchas, small sailing boats with a foreign-type hull and Chinese-type superstructure and sails). The trade carried in junks, sampans, and rafts, and the domestic overland trade, was the responsibility of the so-called "Native Customs," the original Chinese customs, which by the Boxer Protocol of 1901 was put under the control of the Maritime Customs at and within 15 miles of each treaty port. The figures of the Maritime Customs may be assumed reasonably accurate and complete for the categories which they cover, aside from smuggling, but the figures of the Native Customs are neither accurate nor complete. This is due in part to the inadequate numbers and inefficiency of the staff, and in part to the difficulty of regulating or measuring a trade brought into the port by a multitude of large and small water craft or by coolie and cart transport as well as by rail and truck.[†]

Perhaps a majority of the trade between Shanghai and the rest of China which was carried by coolies and carts, or by sampans, rafts, and junks by sea or by the variety of inland waterways leading from the city, was not recorded. Customs officials and other observers have estimated that as much as a quarter of the total domestic trade of Shanghai was not recorded.[9] Maritime and Native Customs figures for Shanghai also omit trade passing through the port on "trans-

---

* The steady revenue derived from Maritime Customs became a most important financial support of the Ch'ing government, in time its leading source of revenue, and thus made it dependent on the continuance of trade. Customs revenues were also used repeatedly as security for foreign loans and indemnities, symbols of the commercial and political processes at work. Thus was imperial China confounded by the merchants of the West.

† Complete statistical records of the Native Customs are unfortunately not available in this country.

shipment passes" to or from other Chinese ports, even though goods traveling on such passes may be stored, repacked, and reloaded at Shanghai. For all of these reasons, it must be assumed that the trade between Shanghai and the rest of China was considerably greater than recorded, and that the city's role as a transshipment point was thus more important than the combined customs figures would indicate.

With this major limitation, the customs figures nevertheless show that nearly half of the trade of Shanghai was transit trade. Graph 8 shows that re-exports (by value) to Chinese and foreign ports between 1885 and 1935 were consistently more than half of the total value of Chinese and foreign imports combined, and until after 1915 were greater in value than foreign imports alone. Until after 1920, the value of re-exports was more than half of the value of the gross trade, less exports of local origin. The break which comes between 1915 and 1925 is a reflection of the growth of manufacturing in Shanghai, which took increasing proportions of the city's foreign and Chinese imports and produced a sharp rise particularly in the value of exports of local origin, as well as in the value of all other trade categories except re-exports.

Graph 7 gives a similar picture of the city's trade, in terms of volume by weight. Discrepancies with graph 8 are due primarily to the greater weight per unit of value of imported industrial raw materials consumed in the city than of the imported finished goods subsequently re-exported. Nevertheless, re-exports in 1910 totaled about one half of combined Chinese and foreign imports by weight, and it was not until 1920 that manufacturing in the city claimed a majority of all imports by weight. In that year also, original exports equalled re-exports of Chinese goods and exceeded re-exports of foreign goods by weight. Slightly larger proportions by weight of Chinese than of foreign goods were re-exported in all of the three years represented in graph 7, indicating their greater weight per unit of value (predominantly food and unfinished goods) than foreign imports (predominantly finished goods). According to the Customs figures, Chinese imports into Shanghai in 1920 and in 1930 were, in rough order of value: coal, raw cotton, foodstuffs, raw silk, tobacco, tea, vegetable oils, hides, skins, and bristles, vegetable fibers other than cotton, and wool.

Graph 6 gives further details on what Shanghai did with its imports from the rest of China, and where it sent the growing volume of original exports produced by manufacturing after 1900. Through the entire period 1870–1930 as shown on the graph, Shanghai re-exported a total of well over half of the value of its imports of Chinese goods, and until after 1920 the proportion averaged about 90 per cent. (The value of foreign imports during most of this period is given in graph 8.) In every year shown on the graph, re-exports abroad were considerably greater by value than re-exports to the rest of China, a reflection of Shanghai's function in collecting from the Chinese hinterland and exporting to industrial economies overseas the assortment of raw materials shown in table I. However, Shanghai's original exports went about half and half to Chinese and foreign ports until 1910, and after 1920 went predominantly to the former, an indication of Shanghai industry's dependence on the domestic market. The sharp rise in Chinese imports and the fall in total re-exports between 1920 and 1930 indicate the increased proportion of the city's imports which were absorbed by manufacturing.

In 1893, the Commissioner of Customs at Shanghai described the trade of Shanghai as follows: "Excepting the small amount used locally, the bulk of the produce which comes here from Chinese ports or from foreign countries goes away again in some channel — the ocean, the river or the creeks — in a vessel which may be a large steamer or may be a little more than a sampan." [10] While the proportion of re-exports increasingly declined as manufacturing developed in Shanghai after 1895, the city's function as a transshipment point continued to depend in large degree on its water transport connections as they are described in the Commissioner's statement.* It is in measuring this domestic trade that accurate figures are unfortunately lacking, since so much of it was carried in

* At the risk of stating the obvious, it should be pointed out that this function of Shanghai as a break-in-bulk (or transshipment) point was an important factor in the rise of manufacturing in the city. This is of course an illustration of Cooley's classic theory (C. H. Cooley, "The Theory of Transportation," Publications of the American Economic Association, IX: 1–148 [1894]).

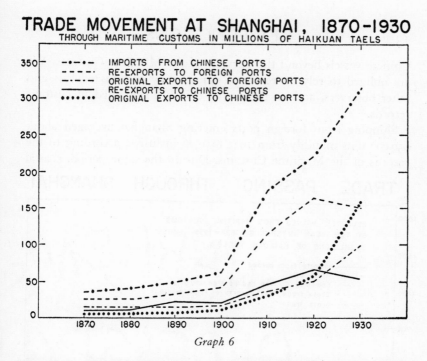

TRADE MOVEMENT AT SHANGHAI, 1870-1930
THROUGH MARITIME CUSTOMS IN MILLIONS OF HAIKUAN TAELS

-·-·- IMPORTS FROM CHINESE PORTS
---- RE-EXPORTS TO FOREIGN PORTS
-·-·- ORIGINAL EXPORTS TO FOREIGN PORTS
──── RE-EXPORTS TO CHINESE PORTS
••••• ORIGINAL EXPORTS TO CHINESE PORTS

Graph 6

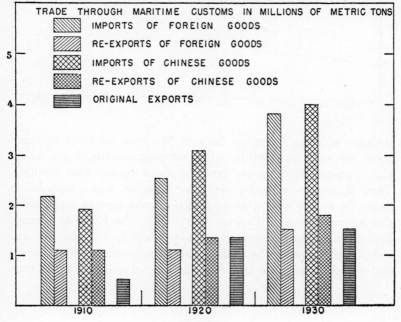

TRADE MOVEMENT AT SHANGHAI 1910-1930

TRADE THROUGH MARITIME CUSTOMS IN MILLIONS OF METRIC TONS

IMPORTS OF FOREIGN GOODS
RE-EXPORTS OF FOREIGN GOODS
IMPORTS OF CHINESE GOODS
RE-EXPORTS OF CHINESE GOODS
ORIGINAL EXPORTS

Graph 7

Chinese vessels beyond the purview of the Maritime Customs. We are obliged to rely on reasoned estimates by customs officials and other observers, and on the partial evidence contained in customs records.

Shipping from foreign ports entering Shanghai averaged about 650,000 tons monthly from 1933 to 1936 inclusive, according to the records of the Maritime Customs. During the same period, coastal

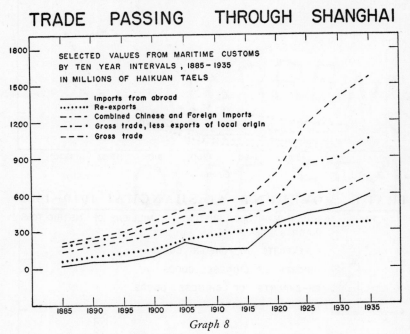

TRADE PASSING THROUGH SHANGHAI

SELECTED VALUES FROM MARITIME CUSTOMS
BY TEN YEAR INTERVALS, 1885-1935
IN MILLIONS OF HAIKUAN TAELS

——————— Imports from abroad
·········· Re-exports
— — — Combined Chinese and Foreign Imports
—·—·— Gross trade, less exports of local origin
— —— Gross trade

Graph 8

shipping entering Shanghai through Maritime Customs averaged about 640,000 tons monthly, while shipping entering from inland (i.e., Yangtze River) ports averaged about 250,000 tons monthly. These figures are exclusive of Native Customs, which recorded at Shanghai during 1930 a total of 54,410 junks entered and cleared (no tonnage given).[11] Combining the Maritime Customs tonnage figures, and adding a conservative 20 per cent for the recorded and unrecorded shipments by junk and sampan, gives a total for coastal and inland shipping (640,000 tons plus 250,000 tons plus 20 per cent, or 1,068,000 net tons monthly) 40 per cent greater in volume than shipping from foreign ports (650,000 net tons monthly). Among the domestic imports, food and industrial raw materials for the city, and among the exports, products of Shanghai manufacturing (or original exports) probably accounted (as we have seen in the above analysis of graphs 6, 7, and 8) for 50 to 60 per cent of these shipments to and from Chinese ports, but the remainder, or 40 to 50 per cent, was transit trade.*

Other published estimates corroborate the estimates of the relative importance of Shanghai's transit trade given above. The *Journal of The British Chamber of Commerce* at Shanghai in its issue for February 1920 estimates that about 65 per cent of the shipping of all types entering and clearing Shanghai was destined to or from coastal or Yangtze River ports, and only 35 per cent was engaged in overseas trade. Bowman estimates that about 50 per cent of Shanghai's imports of foreign goods were re-exported to ports on the Yangtze — 20 per cent to ports below Hankow, 15 per cent to Hankow itself, and 15 per cent to ports above Hankow.† In the cotton trade, Fong Hsien-ting estimates that between 1920 and 1930 Shanghai accounted for an average of 80 per cent of China's total exports of cotton piece goods, although less than 60 per cent of this 80 per cent was produced in Shanghai.[12]

Finally, published citations of the records of the Native Customs at Shanghai add a not inconsiderable figure to the total values of domestic trade as shown in graphs 6 and 8. The Native Customs in 1928 recorded total imports from Chinese ports to Shanghai to the value of approximately 65,000,000 Hai-kuan taels, and total exports from Shanghai to Chinese ports to the value of approximately 46,000,000 Hai-kuan taels, or a grand total of 110,000,000.[13] In 1930, this grand total had risen to over 114,000,000 Hai-kuan

---

* During the same period (1931–1936 inclusive), the railway line to Nanking carried into and out of Shanghai a monthly average of about 80,000 total tons of freight, and the line to Hangchow a monthly average of about 40,000 tons, according to Ministry of Communications, 1931–1936. These two figures combined are less than 12 per cent of the total domestic waterborne trade as estimated in the preceding paragraph (1,068,000 net tons).

† Bowman's estimates take into consideration the unrecorded trade carried in junks and sampans. Of the major Yangtze ports, only Chinkiang, Nanking, and Wuhu have direct rail connections with Shanghai.

taels.[14] Remembering that these records are far from complete and that the actual domestic trade carried in junks and sampans was probably at least 40 per cent larger, we must assume that the domestic trade of Shanghai was in fact between 20 and 30 per cent greater than it is shown in graphs 6 and 8. The proportion of transit trade was correspondingly greater.

As the first and the predominant focus of the opening of traditional China to Western commercial exploitation, Shanghai became, by virtue of its location and especially of its water connections, the great transshipment point for the trade of China which Western enterprise stimulated and directed into wider regional and international channels. Even after the growth of manufacturing in the city, at least half of Shanghai's commerce was transit trade. Trade repeated and transmitted the pattern of ideas, for Shanghai was the center and dispersing point of modern China's revolution.

NINE

How the City is Fed

■

Agriculture and Transport in the Delta

The portion of the Yangtze delta which we have called the fertile triangle (Chapter Four) stands out in dramatic relief as one of the richest agricultural areas in China. Maps 7, 10, and 11 show its place in the pattern of agricultural occupance and rice production. Shanghai lies at the apex of this largest area of high-fertility soil in China with adequate rainfall, and indeed so large a city could have developed nowhere else before the industrial revolution. With railway development still in its infancy in China, Shanghai has been able to maintain itself as a city of nearly four millions because it is located in what is in effect a huge truck garden.

The soil of the delta is of course alluvium, and its correspondingly high fertility is implemented by its fortunate median position between the semi-arid north and the humid south. Between Hangchow on the south and the Huai River on the north, average annual rainfall decreases from 58 inches to 34 inches. South of the line of the Huai River, leaching has removed much of the original lime content of the soils, but the prevailing gentle quality of the rains in the delta area and their relatively even distribution over the year * has prevented removal of all the lime. The line of the Huai roughly marks the division between the wheat-kaoliang-millet crop economy of the semi-arid north and the rice-tea-silk complex of the humid south, although the two major agricultural patterns overlap in the delta to some extent. Below Hangchow, rainfall increases sharply, and most of the soils of south China are thoroughly leached.

The fertile triangle thus avoids both the inadequate rainfall of

---

* Rainfall is concentrated from March through August, but no month has more than nine inches and no month less than two.

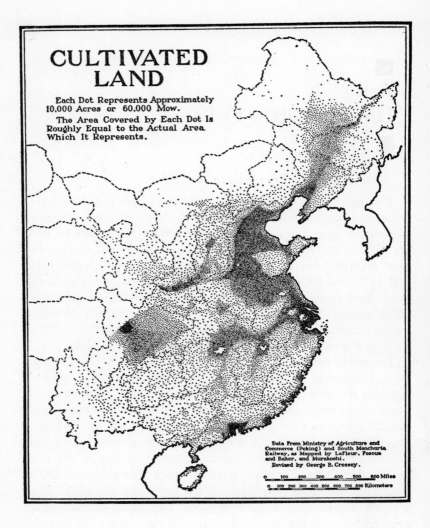

Map 10. *Distribution of Cultivated Land in China* (reproduced here by the courtesy of the McGraw-Hill Book Company, Inc., from G. B. Cressey, *China's Geographic Foundations* [1934]).

the areas immediately north and the leaching of the areas immediately south. It shares with most of south China however a soil which has a high clay content and is thus suitable for wet-rice cultivation in paddies. Of equal importance for the soil with the amount, distribution, and nature of the rainfall is the continual renewal of the alluvium by the Yangtze and its tributaries. While in the absence of frequent floods covering the whole of the area this renewal cannot keep pace with the soil exhaustion attendant on 2,000 years of farming, the material which the rivers bring down and deposit is a highly fertile mixture of well-varied origin containing in particular considerable calcium.[1]

Rainfall over the fertile triangle as a whole averages about 43 inches annually, and falls largely in gentle showers. The peak in late April, May, and June is especially favorable to agriculture, coming as it does during the planting season for most crops in this area and continuing through the first important weeks of early growth. These are the so-called plum rains (pai-yü), accompanying weak cyclonic storms whose effect is somewhat lessened by the counter influence of the monsoon wind system of east Asia. The growing season is long, averaging 287 days at Shanghai between killing frosts, 291 at Nanking, and 307 at Hangchow.

Relief forms almost no obstacle to cultivation. For the triangle as a whole, about 80 per cent of the total land area is cultivated (eliminating the area covered by lakes), the highest figure for an area of comparable size in China, according to J. L. Buck's figures.* The

* J. L. Buck, *Land Utilization in China* (1937). This is a highly statistical study, whose limitations are obvious in dealing with a largely illiterate peasant society where accurate or complete statistical information is unobtainable. Buck's figures have often been used too literally, but since they are virtually the only ones available on a national basis they may be used to advantage if it is realized that despite their detail they are no more than approximations, arrived at by Western methods whose applicability to the traditional Chinese society is questionable. Their safest use is as estimates of orders of magnitude. Subsequent citations here from Buck's work should be read with these considerations in mind.

Buck's figures have the advantage of considerable regional detail. Since the discussion of food production and marketing here is largely limited to the fertile triangle, Buck's statistics are more readily usable than others gathered or presented on a provincial basis. However, reference should be made to some of these more general studies by Chinese, of agriculture and of rice production, which bear on the problems treated here, and which I have used in a general way in addition extensive system of lakes articulated with Tai Lake is by no means lost to agriculture, since most of these bodies of water are shallow enough to permit widespread aquiculture of water chestnuts and lotus (whose roots form an important part of the local diet), as well as supporting a considerable fishing industry on both an exploitative and a farming basis.[2]

Cultivation within the triangle is at least as intensive as in any other part of the world. The growing season allows only one crop of rice, but winter crops of wheat and rape seed harvested in May occupy the rice fields after they are drained following the rice harvest in September-October. Cotton is planted in dry fields at the same time as rice in early May. Broad beans are usually inter-cultivated with the cotton. West and northwest from Soochow as far as the northern tip of Tai Lake as much as 20 per cent of the cultivated area is devoted to mulberry, but even here rice is dominant, and over the triangle as a whole occupies about 75 per cent of the total crop acreage. Vegetables are grown in small plots by nearly every farmer, and within a day's boat travel of Shanghai (approxi-mately 30 miles) they rank third (after rice and cotton) in total acreage.[3]

Intensive cultivation is decreed by the dense population character-istically associated with deltas in east Asia (the fertile triangle is one of the primary density areas of China), and made possible by the natural fertility of the soil and the ready availability of water. Common usage in the area of the triangle calls for the bodily exchange of soil once in every three years between rice paddies and

to depending on them at the specific points for which they are cited below. They would include C. C. Chang, Agricultural Statistics (1930), and *China's Food Problem* (1931), Chiang I-shih, Production of Various Cereals (1947), Chao Lien-fang, The Problem of Rice Production (1947) — including estimates from the early 1930's of the amount of cultivated land in rice, by provinces — Chiang Hsüeh-chai, A New Estimate of the Supply and Demand (1936), Feng Hu-fa, Source Materials (1935), Kuo Ming-hsüeh, Chinese Agricultural Resources (1948), Shen Tsung-han, Chinese Food Problems (1947), and *The Agricultural Resources of China* (1951), and T'ang Chi-yu, *An Economic Study of Chinese Agriculture* (1924) — including figures as of 1920 for rice production and cultivated land in the seven leading rice provinces. Wang P'ei-hsün, The Volume of China's Food Imports and Exports (1947), is a brief general discussion of China's foreign trade in food commodities as an introduction to selected statistics from individual ports.

fields growing other crops (primarily cotton), since this entails a thorough turning over of the soil which crop rotation alone would not accomplish. When the exchange is completed, the new surfaces are then overlaid with an average per acre of 70 tons of mud dug from the canals. Maintenance of navigability in the canals is a communal responsibility, and farmers are recompensed for their dredging labor by using the highly fertile calcareous mud (which as a rule has supported a heavy growth of water weeds as well as ultimately receiving considerable farm and village waste), also by making use of the canals to market their production and receive goods from outside.[4]

The farms are small, 93 per cent of them under 50 *mow* and 25 per cent under 5 *mow*, with an average size of 34 *mow*, according to a Chinese statistical study [5] (one *mow* equals approximately one sixth of an acre). Their cultivation is better described as gardening than as farming. Tools in general use are limited to the *t'u t'ou* (earth head) — a large-bladed hoe — and smaller metal-headed rakes, hoes, and mattocks, all designed for painstaking hand labor. Water is transferred from the canals to fields for irrigation by means of endless chains of small buckets mounted on inclined frames and driven by foot treadles.[6] The average number of total animal units per farm is lower in this area, according to Buck, than anywhere else in China.[7] This is due to the small size of the farms, and to the abundance of human labor, which cannot afford to allocate feed for animals in return for the labor, meat, and manure which they produce. Manual gardening gives a greater return than animal husbandry or farming with draft animals from this fertile and repeatedly refertilized soil in proportion to the food it consumes, and permits a population of 40 million people in the fertile triangle.

With such intensive cultivation, crop yields in the fertile triangle are among the highest in China. Buck's samplings show both rice and wheat yields in this area consistently among the upper five per cent of rice and wheat yields for the 161 localities in China covered by his study.[8] Within a thirty-mile radius of Shanghai, where the city's night soil is cheaper and more readily available than in outlying districts (see below, pp. 162–64), yields of all crops are exceeded by only two counties in China (both near Canton) reported by Buck. According to his figures, the grain production (or equivalent) per male adult of the population (or equivalent) within this thirty-mile radius averages 2594 kilograms, as compared with an all-China average of 1400 kilograms.[9]

The problem of how Shanghai is fed is, however, not answered merely by the facts of fertile soil, intensive cultivation, and high crop yields in its immediate hinterland. While the delta is clearly productive, it is equally clearly densely populated, and it is likely that a larger proportion of the total population of the fertile triangle lives in cities than is the case in any other area of comparable size in China (map 5).

Buck estimates that the consumption of food energy on farms in this area is 3486 calories per adult-male unit per day, a high figure for a so-called subsistence agricultural economy, and exceeded in Buck's figures for China only by the rice-tea area immediately to the south.[10] Far from being a subsistence economy, the triangle supports a relatively commercialized agriculture. Buck estimates for example, that the farmers of this area sell 61 per cent of their farm products immediately after harvest, and that 60 per cent of farm products are sold (i.e., first sale) as far away as the nearest market town, as distinct from the local village. Both of these figures are exceeded only by those from the double-cropping rice area of Kwangtung.[11]

Assuming that the favorable natural environment and the intensive farming methods result in a total food production great enough to allow a surplus for feeding the delta's cities, how is it marketed in this pre-industrial economy? Cities of the magnitude of Shanghai have hitherto never developed except where mechanization and technological improvement in agriculture have been accompanied by the growth of railways, and later, highways.* Shanghai, competing for the food surplus of the delta with Hangchow, Nanking, Soochow, and other large delta cities, added well over three millions to its population between 1843 and 1936, while agricultural practices in the delta remained in general just as they

---

* Ancient Rome and Peking, both cities of approximately one million long before the industrial revolution, might constitute exceptions. Both owed their size primarily to their administrative functions, and both depended heavily on water transport.

have been during the last 1,000 years. Improvements in transport facilities during the same period were slight. As stated above in Chapter Seven, the only railway lines serving Shanghai during the twentieth century were those to Nanking and Hangchow (opened in 1908 and 1909 respectively). They have never become large volume carriers on a Western scale. Highway development contributed even less to the total transport resources of the area. For a densely populated, highly productive area which also contains several large cities dependent in varying degrees on industry, this transport network is minimal.

The Shanghai Rice Market

Rice is the basic food commodity for Shanghai. A sampling survey of workers' families in Shanghai by the Bureau of Social Affairs during 1929 and 1930 * [12] showed the average worker's diet (by percentages of total money spent on food) to be 53 per cent cereals (of which rice was 90 per cent, wheat 5 per cent, and other cereals 5 per cent), 18 per cent vegetables and beans, 16 per cent meat, fish, and eggs, 8 per cent condiments, 3 per cent fruit, and 2 per cent miscellaneous. Since cereals may be presumed cheaper by weight than the other items in the list (as well as having a higher caloric value by weight unit), the importance of rice in the diet by weight (which is the leading consideration for transport problems) is thus greater than these figures indicate. Fortunately, statistics are more readily available for rice than for any of the other food items.

While no complete figures exist to show the rice supply pattern, trading in rice on the Shanghai market was recorded in considerable detail during most of the 1920's and 1930's, and an analysis of the published market reports provides a relatively clear quantitative picture of the main outlines of the city's food supply. The monthly reports issued by the General Chamber of Commerce of Greater Shanghai list supplies of rice entering the city according to source. [13]

* Chiang I-shih, Production, discusses regional differences in the consumption of cereals as between south China, the Yangtze region, and north China, and includes a table showing these differences for the major cereals, as of 1936. For the Yangtze region as a whole he estimates that rice formed 40 per cent of the cereal diet, wheat 20 per cent, minor cereals 14 per cent, and other food crops 26 per cent.

Most of the places so mentioned recur every month except during the rice planting season from early May to early June, and nearly all of them cluster within a relatively small area in the immediate neighborhood of Shanghai (map 5). In about half the cases they are *hsien* towns (county seats), which presumably draw on most of their respective *hsien* (counties), and in the other cases simply towns or villages which serve as collecting places for the rice-producing areas immediately around them. For the most part, they are located with indifference to existing road and railway networks. Most of the exceptions are large towns through which the road and/or railway are obliged to run in any case. The majority of the places however are located on main waterways, and in every case there is a direct water connection with Shanghai.

When the rice supply pattern for Shanghai as shown in these reports is compared with total figures for rice production in Kiangsu province by *hsien*,[14] it is seen that for the most part only the heavy rice-producing *hsien* which lie within about 75 miles of Shanghai send amounts to the city significant enough to be recorded consistently in the market reports. If a surplus exists in the other heavy rice-producing *hsien* * then either transport costs to Shanghai are too high for this rice to compete with areas nearer the city and it therefore moves to other consuming centers, or Shanghai can draw sufficient amounts from the nearer areas at a reasonable price to fill the majority of its rice needs.

For example, Kashing, an important rice marketing center on the railway 60 miles southwest of Shanghai sends little of its rice to Shanghai, although it does send large amounts of locally produced ginger. The comparatively high unit-value by weight of ginger can bear transportation costs which make shipment of rice uneconomic by either rail or water in this case. Another rice center, however, 19 miles farther south on the railway, sends large amounts of local rice to Hangchow 39 miles away. It is near enough apparently to be included in Hangchow's tributary rice area.[15]

Although water transport, especially in this delta area, is relatively easy and cheap, it is also relatively slow, and it is reasonable to find

---

* Kiangsu government figures indicate that this is the case — *Kiang-su sheng-chien*, cited above.

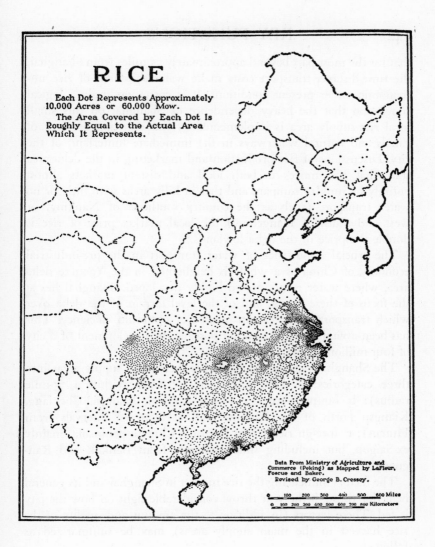

RICE

Each Dot Represents Approximately
10,000 Acres or 60,000 Mow.

The Area Covered by Each Dot Is
Roughly Equal to the Actual Area
Which It Represents.

Data From Ministry of Agriculture and
Commerce (Peking) as Mapped by LaFleur,
Fescue and Baker.

Revised by George B. Cressey.

May 11. Distribution of Rice Production in China (reproduced here by the courtesy of the McGraw-Hill Book Company, Inc., from G. B. Cressey, *China's Geographic Foundations* [1934]).

that for the most part beyond approximately 75 miles from Shanghai, the time-distance-transport costs make water shipment of rice uneconomic under present conditions. It is correspondingly a logical conclusion that the heavy dependence of Shanghai on this small local rice-supply area is implemented by the Venetian network of canals and natural waterways in the immediate hinterland of the city. Discussions of rice production and marketing in the delta area state that rice moves to both local and distant markets almost entirely by junk or sampan, and that in hilly areas with little or no water transport (such as the country southeast of Nanking, or west and south of Hangchow) the local market price of rice is double the price in the delta lowlands.[16]

The crucial importance of water transport in the pre-industrial economy of China as a whole is heightened in the Yangtze delta area, where water routes are so highly developed. Shanghai lies at the focus of these routes, and of the level terrain of the delta over which transport by water can operate at optimum efficiency. This has been a vital factor in making possible the development of a city of four million people.

The Shanghai rice merchants divide their main supply areas into three categories: a. local rice (roughly from within a 75-mile radius); b. out-province rice (from Anhwei, Kiangsi, Chekiang, Kiangsu north of the Yangtze, and at scattered intervals from Hunan); c. foreign rice (from the Indo-Chinese peninsula, mainly ex-Saigon, but including small amounts from Bankok and Rangoon).*

The factors influencing the rice market in Shanghai and its general behavior through the year throw considerable light on how the city is fed. These factors (in addition to the amount and quality of the rice harvest in the main supply areas) may be summarized as follows:

1. The price of foreign and out-province rice. Average monthly prices for the three area categories of rice for the period 1920–1936 were approximately as follows: a. (local rice), CNC$12.00 † per

---

* The export trade in rice from Indo-China, and to a lesser degree from Siam and Burma, is in the hands of overseas Chinese.

† Chinese National Currency — the Chinese dollar.

picul (the Shanghai rice picul during this period equalled 172 pounds); b. (out-province rice) CNC$12.40 per picul; c. (foreign rice) CNC$12.30 per picul.[17] At these levels the composition of the rice supply tended to remain stable, with local rice accounting for over 80 per cent of the total. Shanghai in general prefers to eat local rice even when its price rises slightly above that of foreign rice, as usually happens during the local planting season and at certain other times (see below). Foreign rice is a different type from the local product and there is prejudice in Shanghai against its taste and cooking properties. Any great change in these relative prices, however, upsets the balance. When foreign rice is relatively cheap, its Shanghai sales are large, but as fresh supplies continue to be ordered by the merchant groups, the Saigon price rises and the normal price and supply situation is restored.

2. The planting season for rice in the delta area, which lasts from early May to early June. During this period, movements of rice to Shanghai from the delta virtually cease, and the city draws on rice it holds in storage, plus foreign imports. The fact that the planting season usually coincides with the wet period of the plum rains means that the Shanghai price of rice rises sharply from late May to mid-June. New supplies of local rice come into the Shanghai market in early July (i.e., from the previous year's crop, which has been stored in the local collecting centers but which is not moved to Shanghai during the planting season, the greatest peak labor period of the agricultural year). The Shanghai price regains its normal level as a rule before the end of the month.

3. The weather. Hot and/or humid weather tends to rot stored rice, and thus depresses the price by forcing sales, or stimulates it by jeopardizing what is stored. Drought seldom affects harvests seriously in the delta with its network of canals to supply irrigation water. The greatest effect of rain is on the day-to-day movement of rice from local production areas to the Shanghai market. The delta waterways are easily flooded over their banks by rain and wind, and by both in combination with the tide in the stretches which receive tidal inflow from the Yangtze or the Whangpoo.*

* This might be deduced from the discussion of the delta above in Chapter Three, and it is referred to specifically in the two journals cited for this account of the rice

The boatmen on these waterways usually refuse to load or unload rice when it is raining (whether out of regard for their own safety or for that of their cargo is not clear), and the flow of rice to Shanghai stops almost entirely whenever it rains. The Shanghai rice market, including foreign and out-province rice, reacts with great sensitivity to the rain situation in the city, price changes for rice from all sources often following changes in the weather as closely as an hour.* The role of the weather in the Shanghai rice market as a whole underscores the fact that local sources of rice hold the commanding position, and that the rice moves to the city largely by boat. The monthly reports on the rice market refer repeatedly to water transport connecting Shanghai with the rice-producing areas of south central Kiangsu, but very little mention is made of railway transport of rice during the entire period 1920–1936. Highway transport of rice is not mentioned at all. The dominance of water is so marked that these monthly reports lay great stress on the weather, and conclude in one case that "Rain and wind make a great difference to the rice merchant's heart." [18]

4. Traditional festivals, especially the Chinese New Year (a lunar festival occurring as a rule in early February). Their effects may be summarized as follows: a. since the New Year is the time for settling of accounts as well as for feasting, the farmers need cash and sell their rice; the price falls as a result at the beginning of the festival period; b. however, the holiday on the farms decreases the amount of rice collected and transported to inland centers as the festival continues, thus counterbalancing the earlier selling; c. banditry resulting from inability to pay debts slows or stops move-

---

market on an average of ten or twelve times a year, principally from March through July.

* According to records kept by the Public Works Department of the International Settlement at Shanghai (printed each year in the Annual Reports of the Municipal Council from 1920 to 1939), rainy days occurred in the city from 1920 to 1939 on an average as follows:

	Jan.	Feb.	Mar.	Apr.	May	June	July	Aug.	Sept.	Oct.	Nov.	Dec.
Number of days on which some rain fell	3	4	6	6	8	14	7	5	5	4	4	1
Number of days with rain continuously 6 A.M.-6 P.M.	1	2	4	4	5	8	4	3	3	2	1	1

ment of rice by water to Shanghai. This last has the greatest effect on the rice market. In general, the Shanghai price of rice tends to rise at New Year about 5 per cent and at other festival times a little less. The above effects of festival periods also demonstrate the leading position of local rice supplies, since the entire Shanghai rice market (including the price of foreign rice imports) reacts at these times to purely local festival activities. Local rice being in short supply, foreign rice is at a premium.

5. Civil disturbances. Movement of local rice to Shanghai is notably interfered with during periods of local unrest, especially when troop movements occur. The boatmen fear commandeering of their boats and expropriation of the cargoes. This was a frequent occurrence during the unsettled political period of the late 1920's, and later during the Japanese attacks on Shanghai in 1932 and 1937, as well presumably as the wartime period and the large-scale civil war which shortly followed it. Civil order has unfortunately not been the rule in this area during the past thirty years. In October 1926, despite an excellent harvest just gathered, large amounts of rice already in storage in Shanghai and the accumulated demand in the city after the mid-autumn festival, a local uprising in Chekiang and troop movements connected with it in Kiangsu brought water transport to a complete halt in the delta south and west of Soochow. As a result, the Shanghai price of rice nearly doubled instead of falling as it otherwise would have done. The railways to Hangchow and Nanking were kept open during the entire period. In this case the rice supply situation was eased by shipments on special order from Tsingpu, Sungchiang, and other nearby areas removed from the trouble.*

* Rice was stored both in Shanghai and in the collection centers in the local producing areas. However, the Shanghai rice market was very sensitive to day-to-day changes in the supply arriving from the local areas. This suggests that relatively small amounts of rice were stored in Shanghai, and that the market depended on regular shipments. When these were interfered with, it was not possible for the Shanghai rice merchants to keep the Shanghai price from rising, since orders for foreign rice could not normally be delivered in less than two weeks. The hiatus in local supplies during the planting season was of course anticipated by the Shanghai merchants in the form of advance orders for foreign rice which were delivered during May and June, but even so the price of rice rose during this period, as indicated above, further evidence that the market was dominated by local supplies moving regularly to the city during most of the year.

The general impression from the foregoing summary of factors, and from the market reports themselves, is twofold: firstly, that there is an ample margin of rice supply for Shanghai, from various sources, at all times at least until 1936; and secondly, that by far the largest part of that supply comes from within a radius of approximately 75 miles and moves to the city largely by water transport. There is some statistical evidence which bears on the problem, and the following figures compiled from the records of the Maritime Customs provide as close a check as can be obtained at present.

Local, Out-Province, and Foreign Rice

The Food Commission of the Bureau of Social Affairs of the City Government (Chinese) of Greater Shanghai published in 1931 a statistical study of the sources of Shanghai's food supply, using figures taken from the records of the Maritime and Native Customs.[19] The study shows a yearly average during the period 1925–1930 of 780,000,000 pounds of rice brought into the city from all sources. This is stated as a rough estimate because there are no means of recording all of the small shipments arriving from the delta by junk and sampan via the many small creeks and canals which converge on Shanghai.

The total figure is broken down in the table below, according to means of entry into the city.

from inland areas via the Whangpoo, Yangtze, or Soochow Creek:	560,000,000 pounds
from the sea via the Yangtze:	160,000,000 pounds
domestic origin 30,000,000	
foreign origin 130,000,000	
via overland routes (means of transport not specified)	60,000,000 pounds
TOTAL	780,000,000 pounds

Railway haulage figures [20] indicate that nearly all of the 60,000,000 pounds arriving by overland routes came in by rail from cities and towns along the Yangtze toward Nanking, Tanyang, and Changchow in particular. Although these places are on or near the Yangtze, they are farther from Shanghai than its main rice supply areas so that rail transport to Shanghai can compete with water transport. Given the lines, one might assume that they would carry the most important product of the delta. The surprising fact is that they carry such insignificant amounts. Total figures given by the railway for rice haulage leave little or no margin for highway transport of rice, and we may assume that it is negligible.

The relatively small figure of 30,000,000 pounds given for arrivals by sea from domestic sources is probably accounted for by small-lot junk cargoes from the northern and southern shores of Hangchow Bay, and from the seaward-extending tip of Kiangsu just north of the Yangtze. South of Hangchow Bay all of the coastal areas import rice to balance their local rice deficits, and north China has no rice surplus for export.

Most of the foreign rice imports to Shanghai, according to the market reports referred to above, are ordered by rice brokers from Nanking, Tientsin, Hankow, and Ningpo operating at Shanghai as China's leading rice market, and this rice is then shipped from Shanghai to their respective cities. At certain periods when the Ningpo rice brokers ordered directly from Ningpo for Saigon rice, Shanghai's stores of foreign rice became superabundant and its price fell sharply, even producing a fall in the price of local rice during the planting season, as in May 1929. All of these cities are relatively more dependent on foreign rice imports than is Shanghai. The focusing of delta waterways on Shanghai, and the relatively less easy transport in the hilly or semi-arid hinterlands of the other cities mentioned, are certainly as important as the concentration of rice production in the delta in accounting for this difference.

The greatest period of foreign rice invasion on the Shanghai market for consumption in the city coincides roughly with the planting season, showing a natural lag of about one month during which Shanghai stores of local rice are drawn on. As soon as new supplies of local rice enter the Shanghai market in July, the situation returns to normal and prices are stabilized. Foreign rice is also ordered by Shanghai merchants when other natural or threatened hiatuses occur in the local supply due to weather, civil unrest, short supply in storage, or price stoppages. As a rule, these breaks in the local supply are short-lived or do not materialize.

With the exception of the planting season, the general price and supply situation is dominated by local rice.

Although considerable amounts (unfortunately there is no record of their size) of both domestic and foreign rice entering Shanghai are resold to or originally ordered by other cities, relatively more of the foreign imports fall into this category. The table on page 146 above should therefore be interpreted in the light of the ultimate destination of the several categories of rice shipments arriving in the city. Total sales of rice in Shanghai, for which relatively more accurate figures are kept, provide a different indication of the city's rice consumption. Sales are estimated by the Food Commission's study as averaging annually 860,000,000 pounds during the period 1925–1930.* Their report assumes that the difference of nearly 100,000,000 pounds between this figure and the total recorded entries of 780,000,000 pounds is accounted for by unrecorded shipments arriving by creek and canal from nearby sources. Shipment of much or most of the foreign rice from Shanghai to other cities would leave an even greater gap between the two figures as measures of Shanghai's consumption, and it is logical to assume that this also is filled from local sources.

The figure for total sales, however, may not be an accurate indication of total consumption if we attempt to estimate the average annual rice consumption of a Chinese adult and multiply it by the population of Shanghai in 1930. A Chinese economist [21] suggests four piculs per year (532 pounds), which, using 3,250,000 as Shanghai's 1930 population (graph I) gives a total city consumption of 1,730,000,000 pounds. Or if we use a lower estimate of 400 pounds,[22] which agrees more closely with the writer's experience, and scale down this figure to 380 to allow for children, for other cereals and foods in the Shanghai diet (see above, p. 139), and for the non-rice-eating foreign population of the city (38,000 in 1930), we still arrive at a figure of 1,235,000 pounds. This is equivalent to about 1,750 calories per day per capita from rice alone, certainly a minimum diet for a Chinese.

* This figure presumably includes spot sales of foreign rice by Shanghai brokers to dealers in other cities, but probably does not include foreign rice delivered in Shanghai on order from other cities.

We can be sure that the figures for foreign imports recorded by the Maritime Customs are reasonably complete and accurate, since smuggling of rice imports is hardly a profitable venture. If a discrepancy exists (and it is not considered that the calculations of the preceding paragraph do more than suggest the possibility of a discrepancy), it must therefore be attributed to unrecorded entries of rice by water transport from the delta area.

The Customs figures show great yearly fluctuations in the import of foreign rice to Shanghai, with a low in 1924 of 200,000 pounds and a high in 1926 of 300,000,000 pounds. 1926 was marked by prolonged and widespread civil war in the delta, culminating in the capture of Shanghai by the northern expeditionary forces of the Kuomintang in January 1927. The market reports referred to above mention interruptions in water transport to Shanghai from the local rice-producing areas more frequently in that year than in any other. They also describe it as an unusually rainy year, with floods over large areas of the delta during the spring and autumn. The reports make it clear that the rice crop in Shanghai's local supply area was not drastically affected by these conditions and totaled approximately 80 per cent of normal. The interruptions in water transport, however, caused by civil disturbances and weather, made it difficult to get the crop to market in Shanghai. They increased the price of what did come in so markedly that foreign rice was imported in unusually large amounts.

Foreign rice imports returned in 1928 to a more nearly normal level. Subsequently they rose and fell almost as radically in certain other years to give an average for the period 1920–1936 of 70,000,000 pounds yearly (as compared with the 1925–1930 yearly average of 130,000,000 pounds cited above from the Food Commission's Report). The following table lists annually foreign rice imports to Shanghai and notes after years of unusually large imports any exceptional conditions mentioned for those years by the market reports.[23]

Year	Foreign Rice Imports (lbs.)	Market Report Comments
1920	2,000,000	
1921	15,000,000	
1922	40,000,000	
1923	3,000,000	
1924	200,000	
1925	210,000,000	civil war in the delta
1926	300,000,000	civil war and floods in the delta
1927	120,000,000	civil war and floods in the delta
1928	80,000,000	
1929	40,000,000	
1930	40,000,000	
1931	200,000,000	floods in the lower Yangtze basin
1932	120,000,000	Japanese attack on Shanghai
1933	2,000,000	
1934	600,000	
1935	600,000	
1936	300,000	

The market reports imply (without giving any figures) that the drop in rice imports after 1932 was related to the fact that Ningpo, Tientsin, Hankow, and Nanking rice brokers decided in these years to order foreign rice directly for delivery to their respective cities without transshipment via Shanghai. But whatever the reason for the fluctuations in rice imports shown in the above table, it is clear that under normal conditions Shanghai could not and did not depend on foreign rice to any important extent. Given free movement of water transport in the delta, it was able to support itself almost entirely on what it drew from its local supply areas. Shanghai's population doubled between 1920 and 1936, yet imports of foreign rice to the city all but disappeared in one third of the years listed in the above table.

There is some evidence that even during the early years of modern Shanghai, before it reached a population of half a million, the city relied primarily on local sources of rice and depended on foreign imports only under unusual conditions. Trade reports of the British consul at Shanghai show large imports of rice in 1862, 1863, and 1864 while the city was for considerable periods besieged by rebel forces of the Taiping army. The consular reports specifically mention elsewhere that water transport in the delta to and from the city came to a standstill at frequent intervals during these years.[24] They also mention the Shanghai prejudice against eating foreign rice and state that it is consumed only when local supplies are unobtainable.[25] The Taiping Rebellion was suppressed and Nanking recaptured by the Ch'ing forces in June 1864. By 1865 the Shanghai consular report shows the virtual disappearance of foreign rice imports.[26] Apparently Shanghai was not at that period acting as an entrepôt for rice imports to other cities.

It has been a widespread opinion in China and outside it that the large cities of east Asia, including Shanghai, have depended for their growth on the import by sea of foreign rice from the surplus rice areas of Indo-China, Burma, and Siam. Various students of the problem have gone far enough to examine the rice import figures recorded by the Maritime Customs and to compare them with population growth, finding that in the case of at least the south China treaty ports overseas rice imports have increased faster than the population, and concluding that these cities would starve if overseas imports were cut off.[27] Aside from the fact that much of the foreign rice entering Shanghai is destined for other places, what statistics are available, when added to the evidence of the market reports, demonstrate that the part played by foreign rice is minor in the case of Shanghai.

If Shanghai is indeed an exception in this respect, an explanation may logically be found in the combination in its immediate hinterland of heavy rice production and highly developed water routes. There is no significant correlation between the size of the delta rice crop in different years and imports of foreign rice. The years of large import did however coincide with unusual conditions in the delta which affected primarily the movement of goods by water rather than the actual rice crop. Transportation rather than production would appear to be the key.

While the quantitative importance of foreign rice is minor within the general supply picture, it is certainly true that for recurrent short periods foreign rice has filled large gaps in the Shanghai market. Even in normal years, foreign rice came in during the local planting season, and in years marked by civil disorder or natural calamities in the delta it accounted for a quarter or a third of Shanghai's rice consumption of something like one billion pounds over the year as a whole. The supply situation was determined by price, and foreign rice was imported not necessarily because local rice was unobtainable but because its Shanghai price at certain periods rose considerably above the Shanghai price of foreign rice.

The price problem posed by the hiatus in local supply during the planting season might have been overcome without bringing in foreign rice, by carefully planned advance buying and by distributing price fluctuations for local rice more widely over the year as a whole. This solution was theoretically in the power of the Shanghai rice merchants, and it has since been applied at least to a degree by the Communist Government (see Chapter Eleven). But it is doubtful whether Shanghai could have existed without foreign rice imports during the periods of civil war and floods which disrupted its water connections with the producing areas. At such times, a high enough price in Shanghai could presumably have attracted to the city from the local areas adequate rice to feed its population despite the difficulties and dangers of water transport, but workers' families and other low-income groups, which constituted the great majority of the population, would have been priced out of the market.

The situation after 1936 was complicated by the Japanese invasion and conquest of the delta in 1937. Japanese military requisitions drained off increasing amounts of the delta's rice crop, and fighting over the area reduced total production and hampered the movement of rice to Shanghai. The city became increasingly dependent on foreign imports of rice, and by 1940 relied almost entirely on what it was able to import from Saigon. The unsettled political situation, in which the foreign settlements remained until Pearl Harbor in theory outside Japanese control but increasingly subject to Japanese influence and threatened with total absorption, encouraged hoarding and speculation. Curtailment of local supplies created an actual shortage, and these factors together resulted in a tripling of the Shanghai price of rice between 1936 and 1941.

Rice riots in the city became frequent, and Shanghai's normal dependence on its local rice supply areas was increasingly borne in upon all of the city's population. A leading commercial journal in the city remarked in 1940 that "Shanghai is an island cut off from the normal sources of supply of its staple food," and went on to point out that rice selling at that time in Wusih for CNC$15 per picul of 172 pounds sold for CNC$90 per picul in Shanghai, a price difference which certainly reflects transport difficulties as well as the abnormal situation in Shanghai. The Shanghai price of imported rice quite naturally rose to meet this level.[28] At scattered intervals during this period from 1937 to the end of 1941 when conditions permitted relatively safe water shipment to Shanghai from the delta, local rice appeared on the Shanghai market in large quantities and the price of rice from all sources dropped to nearly its pre-war levels.[29]

The part played by out-province rice is difficult to evaluate. The market reports already referred to indicate that except during the planting season out-province rice is unimportant on the Shanghai market, and at all periods under normal conditions is less important than foreign imports.[30] However, complete figures for out-province shipments of rice to Shanghai do not exist, doubtless due, at least in part, to the fact that much of it moves to the city in small boats, a flow difficult to measure. The market reports give the impression that most of Shanghai's out-province supply comes (in order of importance) from Wuhu (the chief rice center of Anhwei), the lowland areas of Kiangsi connected by lakes and rivers with the Yangtze, the lowland areas of northeastern Chekiang, and the western and southern shores of Tung Ting Lake in Hunan. All of these sources have direct water connections with Shanghai.

If the earlier opinion that Shanghai, among the other treaty ports, depended for its growth on overseas imports of rice is no longer tenable, it is perhaps reasonable to question whether at least Canton may not have profited from its similar location. The Hsi delta is the closest parallel in China to the Yangtze delta, although on a smaller scale. Like the Yangtze delta, it is a heavy rice-producing area which also contains a highly developed network of natural and artificial waterways. Kwangtung as a whole is a rice-deficiency area, and foreign imports of rice to Canton may not be destined entirely for consumption in the city. As in the case of Shanghai, Canton may act as an entrepôt for rice imports to other cities.

This may suggest that China as a whole produces enough to feed itself, even by traditional farming methods, if only the food could be transported cheaply enough. As it is, foreign rice moves only to the large coastal cities, because transport costs once it leaves the sea prevent further penetration. The rice comes in because at certain periods it is cheap, and it is cheap relative to Chinese rice primarily because of the difference in transport costs between sea and land. It may be found when full facts are available that the flow of rice to large Chinese cities, which depends on price, is governed predominantly by transport costs, as it is in the case of Shanghai, and that where cheap transport is possible, local sources form the major part of the supply.

Other Food Commodities

The Yangtze delta, and more especially the fertile triangle, is a specialized agricultural area, more so than most agricultural regions of China because of its greater degree of commercialization. Its special crop is rice, with cotton, mulberry, and vegetables the only other significant items. Some wheat is grown, but it is of relatively minor importance in the fertile triangle and is raised mainly as a dry-field winter crop between rice plantings. Shanghai's dependence on local sources for rice is thus not matched by the rest of its food supply. The significance of the city's water connections with other agricultural regions is apparent in the fact that in a largely pre-railroad and pre-commercial economy, Shanghai is able to depend on distant sources for many food items in a way, if not to a degree, which is in certain respects comparable to the food supply pattern developed for large cities in the United States and Western Europe.

Shanghai has its own truck- and market-garden area, much as large Western cities have, with the difference that vegetables in particular have always been grown there and that environmental conditions in the fertile triangle are virtually ideal for market-garden-type production. Near most Western cities, soil, climate, and relief must often be fitted with difficulty into the needs of the city for fresh local food. Vegetable production in the fertile triangle for sale in Shanghai is not only convenient but environmentally advantageous.

How much of the city's supply of vegetables comes from its market-garden area (a day's water travel, or about a 30-mile radius from the city, an area where vegetables rival rice as the leading crop), and how much from greater distances is difficult to determine with any accuracy in the absence of published records. The principal vegetable market in Shanghai is along both banks of Soochow Creek near its mouth, which suggests that vegetables come into the city by water from its immediate environs. Merchants and vendors there, including many farmers who bring their vegetables into the city by sampan for daily or twice weekly markets, speak only of the near neighborhood of the city as the source of their wares. About 15 square miles within the Municipality of Greater Shanghai itself are occupied by vegetable crops,[31] which can take the fullest advantage both of convenience to the market and of favorable environment in this fertile flat delta land. Vegetables undoubtedly come into the city in large amounts from greater distances, although it is unlikely that bulk shipments of such perishable commodities would move beyond the delta. The railways do not carry them in any significant quantities.[32]

Although its place in the Shanghai diet is relatively minor (see above p. 139), wheat is a major food commodity for the city because of the prominent place of the flour milling industry there. While over two-thirds of the flour milled is exported, principally to north China ports, the wheat must first be brought to the city even though most of it is not eventually consumed there.

Shanghai drew its domestic wheat largely from Kiangsu. Only a minor crop within the fertile triangle, wheat is of much greater importance in the drier and colder areas of Kiangsu north of the Yangtze, and in the western parts of the delta. This production, plus the wheat raised almost entirely for sale as a dry-field winter crop within the fertile triangle, can be carried to Shanghai from nearly every producing area via the water network of the delta, including the Yangtze itself. While the delta area is by no means a leading wheat producer, it is wholly unique among wheat areas in China in its cheap and easy transport connections with a large urban market. The semi-arid north, where most of China's wheat is grown, has almost no water transportation. Water in the delta has made it possible for wheat production there to become highly commercialized as Shanghai developed into a huge industrial market which water routes made accessible in terms of transport costs for bulk shipments.* This helps to explain the anomaly of Shanghai (rather than Tientsin — a close second) as the largest wheat-milling center in China despite its great distance from China's major wheat-producing areas where other industrial centers, notably Tientsin, also mill flour.

Domestic sources of wheat, however, accounted for slightly less than half of the city's supply during most of the 1920's and 1930's. Although Kiangsu sources held the commanding position domestically, wheat also came to the city especially from the major wheat area of Shantung, by sea from Tsingtao, where it was collected largely by rail. Shanghai's connections by sea thus implemented its water connections in the delta in ensuring a steady flow of low-cost cereals. Dependence on overseas sources for more than half of its wheat was more workable economically for Shanghai, with its location and harbor facilities, than for any other China port. It was cheaper for Shanghai to bring in wheat from Canada, the United States, and Australia (the three major overseas sources in order of importance) than for Tientsin, without inland water transport, to bring in wheat from the producing areas of north China beyond its immediate Hopeh region of the north China plain.

These imports of wheat from overseas fluctuated considerably from year to year according to price conditions. As in the case of rice, wheat imports were unusually high in years of civil disorder and (or) rain and floods in the delta area, notably in 1926, and decreased markedly in intervening years of political and climatic stability.[33] Again the inference is that stoppages of water transport in the delta were the key factor. As an ocean port near major world shipping lanes, Shanghai could import at a practicable cost whatever goods normally obtained from the delta which temporary cir-

* Water as rainfall, or as irrigation, also keeps wheat yields higher in the delta than the north China average.

cumstances interfering with inland transport made inaccessible locally.[34]

Other food commodities have a relatively higher unit-value by weight, and are therefore able to move to the city over greater distances, in some cases independently of the water network. Fruit, largely citrus, comes in principally from Chekiang which is just south of the delta but in many areas cut off from water routes by high relief. For this comparatively long-distance overland shipping, the fruit is packed in pine boxes and wrapped in sacking as a protection against frost. In the rugged areas of Chekiang it is carried by porter, and is transferred to junk or sampan when it reaches the edge of the delta.[35] Other fruit sources for Shanghai are even more distant, but most of them can ship to the city over at least part of the route by sea. Grapes and melons come to Shanghai from Hopeh and Shansi, oranges and lichees from Kwangtung and Fukien, and apples from Liaoning (southern Manchuria).[36]

Fresh meat is sold in the city only in limited quantities and is supplied (except for the tiny foreign consumption before 1941, which drew on refrigerated shipping from New Zealand and Australia) almost entirely from the immediate market-garden area. Fish and eggs are far more important elements in the average Shanghai diet than fresh meat, but some cured or salted meat is available from greater distances. Shanghai's main supply of cured hams comes from Chekiang, via Hangchow, and from Kiangsu and Anhwei by Yangtze steamer. Substantial amounts also come from as far as Szechuan and Yünnan, where the making of famous high-quality hams has long been a specialty. The tremendous cost of transporting hams from Yünnan does not apparently make their price prohibitive, although it does limit the market for them.[37] High unit-value is of course the basic factor.

Eggs have become industrial raw materials, in addition to their part in the city's diet, with the development of freezing and drying plants to prepare eggs for export. Fresh eggs are also exported from Shanghai in cold storage to places as distant as the United Kingdom. The Shanghai supply for this varied market is drawn from surprising distances. Within Kiangsu, eggs come to the city from all but two of the *hsien*.[38] These two are in the northernmost part of the province where arid north China fairly begins, and where water transport facilities are limited. Eggs also come to Shanghai from places up the Yangtze valley as far as Hankow, transported in bamboo crates holding from 500 to 1000 eggs and carried entirely by water. 40 per cent breakage in transport is given as an average figure.[39] This apparently does not make the longer hauls uneconomic, and implies that cheap transportation is an important factor.

Fish, however, after cereals and vegetables, is the most important protein-supplier in the city's diet, and Shanghai handles one third of the fish and marine products marketed in China annually for which there are market records. Seasonal variations in the catch and lack of adequate cold storage facilities make for violent fluctuations in the price of sea fish, in the case of one common species from a yearly low of CNC$3 per *shih* (200 pounds) to a yearly high of CNC$50 per *shih*. A good catch is often disastrous to the fishermen because it depresses the Shanghai price below cost, since in the absence of cold storage the fish must be sold within a few days.[40]

Shanghai's fishing fleet in the 1930's was about two-thirds sailing junks and one-third steam trawlers, both of which packed their catch at sea in iced barrels. In summer, spring, and autumn the packing preserved the fish for only about two days in this climate, and a premium was put on quick marketing. The fishing boats were allowed only a limited amount of salt for preserving, in order to prevent smuggling abuses. The main fishing grounds off the coast of central China are approximately fifty miles to the seaward of the Chusan Islands, or about 140 miles from Shanghai, a good two days' run for the junks and not much less than that for the trawlers. The catches are of course not all made in one day, so that fish arriving in Shanghai might be as much as four or five days old and in a questionable state of preservation.[41] Small fast power boats from Shanghai met the fishing fleet at the fishing grounds when the catches were good and rushed the fish to market in the city, but this stratagem greatly increased the cost and did not remove the need for making an immediate sale.[42] Dried and salted fish comes to Shanghai mainly from small villages and islands along the coast of northern Kiangsu and southern Shantung, where it is preserved, packed in barrels, and shipped to Shanghai by junk, but this supply also is irregular and its price fluctuates widely.[43]

The supply and price of fresh-water fish are much steadier. The catch from the lakes, canals, and rivers of the delta comes in alive in specially constructed boats with built-in wells floored with grating through which the water can circulate freely. The fish are fed en route with powdered egg yolk, and the average journey from source to Shanghai is about three days, or approximately 100 miles. These boats are built for the Shanghai trade, since fish do not travel alive for such relatively long distances to any other market. The boats avoid the lower reaches of Soochow Creek in approaching the city because they fear that its polluted water will harm or kill the fish.[44] Several alternate routes are available. Fish are also transported alive to Shanghai in tanks from places along the Yangtze as far as Wuhu, Hukow, and Kiukiang, the water being changed several times a day en route.[45] Although no complete figures exist, it is estimated that the supply of fresh-water fish and its sale in Shanghai are much greater than of sea fish.[46] This fact is certainly related to the ease of live shipment by water, which maintains a steady supply at a relatively constant cost.

Of the higher unit-value food items discussed above, only fruit and cured hams travel long distances independently of waterways. The extension of the egg supply area to as far as Hankow would seem to be related to the water connections between it and Shanghai. In the case of fish, although Shanghai is an ocean port near the main fishing grounds of the central China coast and served by a large commercial fleet, the city's fish market is dominated by a supply whose freshness, cheapness, and abundance at all seasons is the direct result of inland water transport.

Local Rice Surpluses, and the Future

There remain two principal unsolved problems. The first is accounting for a rice surplus in the densely settled delta where so many large cities compete for the food produced on these tiny farms by traditional farming methods. Only indirect explanations can be suggested, but it should be remembered that the Yangtze delta is by no means unique in this respect. The three great rice-exporting areas of Asia are all deltas, and all are of the same order of population density as the Yangtze delta: the lower basins of the Mekong, Menam, and Irrawaddy Rivers. Each of these deltas also contains a primate city, and in addition produces most of the rice for the entire population of each country (Indo-China, Siam, and Burma respectively). Yet each of them has continued, under peace-time conditions, to produce large yearly surpluses of rice for export.

The Sui emperor Yang Ti (A.D. 605–618) first joined together existing natural and artificial waterways into a connected system running from Hangchow in the south to northern Kiangsu and thence westward across Honan to the Sui capital at Ch'angan (modern Sian). This system of waterways linking the rich rice areas of the delta with the military and political centers of the north included several branches, among them a route to the Peking area which was later incorporated in the Grand Canal of the Mongols.* The southern half of the present Grand Canal was completed from Hangchow to Kaifeng during the northern Sung dynasty (A.D. 960–1127), inter alia, to bring rice for the supply of the court and capital at Kaifeng. During the Yüan (Mongol) dynasty (1260–1368) the canal was extended from Kaifeng to Peking, the Yüan capital, and up to the time of the late Ch'ing dynasty (1644–1911), with its capital also at Peking, rice to feed successive imperial centers in arid north China flowed in great volume out of the productive Yangtze delta.

Apparently a local surplus existed throughout this period, but it was not allowed to accumulate locally as the basis for a new population growth in the delta. By a coincidence which may or may not be significant, the end of the imperial system (the revolutionary Kuomintang overthrew the Ch'ing Government in 1911, and established its capital in 1927 at Nanking) came at about the beginning of Shanghai's major population growth (graph 1). It is certainly possible that instead of going to Peking, the delta rice

---

* Chi Ch'ao-ting, *Key Economic Areas in Chinese History* (1936), pp. 114–115, in giving an account of this development and its later extensions, shows that canals between the Huai and the Huang were built at least as early as the fifth century B.C., and that a through water route between the Yangtze delta and western Honan apparently existed by the third century B.C.

surplus began at this period to move to Shanghai and has continued to do so.

Grain shipments on the Grand Canal from the delta to Peking had actually become insignificant after the Taiping Rebellion (1850–1864), and ceased entirely in 1901. Sea transport of rice was substituted until 1911, but it never brought from the delta to Peking more than a small fraction of what had previously moved by the Canal. During the nineteenth century, Kiangsu and Chekiang had yearly quotas of tribute rice shipments to Peking of over one million piculs each, totalling for both over 320 million pounds,[47] or about one-third of the annual rice consumption of Shanghai alone in the 1930's. However Morse suggests[48] that the rice actually collected (much of which never got to Peking) may often have been six times the official quotas.

The population of Peking did not decline after 1911, since the city remained the seat of a northern warlord regime and became China's largest rail junction, especially with the economic development of Manchuria. Its estimated population total in 1936 was 1,400,000, in all likelihood the highest figure it had ever reached, as compared with about 800,000 in 1900. But it was no longer the seat of a court, garrison troops, and an extensive bureaucracy, recruited from all over China including the rice-eating south, and with power to command shipments of tribute rice, which made up part of many official salaries. After Peking ceased to function as the imperial capital, its population subsisted primarily on the millet and wheat readily obtainable from north China, while the flow of rice from the Yangtze delta followed economic rather than imperial dictates.

It does however seem possible that rice surpluses in the delta available for urban consumption have been greater since the twentieth-century growth of Shanghai (and of its many urban rivals in the delta) than during the imperial period. The following paragraphs suggest one explanation of this. Another might be that local farmers had less incentive to produce rice when most or all of the surplus went to Peking as tribute, or was absorbed as "squeeze," than when they could sell it in a reasonably free market for consumption in Shanghai.

In the early years of the foreign settlements when foreigners were permitted into the hinterland for half a day's travel from the city (since they were originally not allowed to spend a night beyond the Settlements), they moved very largely by boat, and "they inevitably met on the way dung boats, dung tanks, dung buckets, and dung carriers wherever they went." [49] Until 1923 (the 1925 population of Shanghai was approximately 2,300,000, including 29,000 foreigners), there were virtually no flush toilets anywhere in the city and no central sewage system. The human wastes (or night soil) and the garbage of the city, in common with the usual practice in east Asia, were carefully saved and "sold" to contractors, who were paid a small fee for their services in removing the wastes and distributing them for sale to the farmers of the delta. Up to 1923, when a central sewage system was installed, these night soil contractors collected the wastes at most of the houses in Shanghai, including the foreign houses, and were under contract to the Shanghai Municipal Council for the removal of wastes collected by the Council from public buildings and a few private houses within the International Settlement. The Council realized an average annual revenue between 1910 and 1920 of US$50,000 from these transactions. [50]

The Council made its first contract with the night soil collectors in 1867 because it was alarmed by the health menace presented by the promiscuous dumping of wastes of all kinds in the creeks which flowed through the Settlement. Night soil contractors had been operating in the Settlement for several years before this date, but they had not removed all of the wastes, and the Council in its new contract provided for a complete disposal system. [51] By 1932, the Health Commissioner of the International Settlement was defending this system as essential not only to the health of the Settlement but to the productivity of the farms which supplied it with food. [52] As a means of disposing of the city's refuse it also had notable advantages of economy, if not of attractiveness to the foreign residents. The Council estimated in 1920 that the cost of collection and disposal of household wastes in Shanghai over the period 1908–1919 averaged about 1s 2d per ton, as against an estimated cost in London at the same period of 9s 1d per ton. [53]

In 1923 the Council built the first central sewage system, which by 1934 included four sewage-treatment plants and two incinerators for household refuse. During the same period cesspools were dug for most buildings in the Settlement beyond the limits of the central sewage system. The night soil contractors continued to remove wastes from buildings without cesspools, and, by agreement with the Council, to drain the cesspools at regular intervals. Most of the sewage treated by the new plants was sold to the night soil contractors as before, but now in a concentrated form which was also less dangerous to health when used as fertilizer. Non-organic wastes were dumped at sea by the Council, or were used for raising low-lying land. Household garbage continued to be collected by the night soil contractors as before.[54] These malodorous cargoes went out from Shanghai entirely in barges, many of which were open and which were (and still are) to be seen on all of the waterways running through the city. It was these which attracted the adverse comment to which the Municipal Health Commissioner replied in the statement referred to above.

The night soil produced by two, three, or four million people and distributed to farmers must have been a not inconsiderable factor in maintaining or enhancing soil fertility and in making possible unusually high yields within a thirty- or forty-mile radius of Shanghai.* Existing figures for crop yields are unfortunately calculated on the basis of *hsien*, and *hsien* boundaries do not even approximately coincide with the thirty- or forty-mile radius. The Municipality of Greater Shanghai itself occupies 320 square miles (of which 210 square miles is listed as farm land) within the area of night soil distribution from the city. The effect of this distribution therefore cannot be measured with any accuracy in terms of crop yields, although the figures do show about 10 per cent higher yields of all crops in the *hsien* which have some part of their area within a forty-mile radius of Shanghai than in the remaining *hsien* in the Kiangsu section of the delta south of the Yangtze and east of Tai Lake.[55] Soil and land forms are generally uniform over this area. It is a readily observable fact that fields are greener and crops heavier and further advanced within a day's foot or water travel

* See above, p. 137. Buck's figure was compiled from surveys in only one district (about one quarter of one *hsien*) within this area.

from large Chinese and Japanese cities than in the remainder of the rural districts, into which the green fades off beyond 30 or 40 miles. This is particularly true at Shanghai, and is most clearly seen from the air, but it also strikes the eye on the trip by train from Shanghai to Nanking, or in walking through the country.

Night soil distribution could have provided an automatic increase in crop yields in the immediate vicinity of Shanghai as the city's population grew. In a country where even near the large coastal cities and under a system of relatively commercialized agriculture, chemical fertilizers are beyond the means of the farmers, the heavy use of night soil in the neighborhoods of large cities where it can be purchased at a price even the poorest farmer can afford can be assumed an important factor for agriculture. In the case of Shanghai, it may help to explain the apparent local surplus of rice from the delta which goes to feed the city.

The second problem concerns the future. Shanghai up to 1936 had managed to feed itself largely from its local supply areas. During the disturbed war years, virtually unbroken from 1937 to 1949, it was for long periods forced to depend on imported rice, although the inference is still that under normal conditions the local supply areas remain adequate. But can the city continue to grow on this basis, or will the population not eventually outrun the food supply as it has done repeatedly in the past throughout China? Obviously this is a possibility. It would lead to greater dependence on rice imports, and greater use of railways and highways as these expand and become cheaper carriers, to bring rice and other food into the city from longer distances. In the absence of figures and information for the period since the war with Japan comparable even to the inadequate data for the pre-1937 period, we have no reliable basis for judging whether Shanghai has already entered a new phase in this vital aspect of its economic life. As we can measure it, this huge city is a world anomaly in the pattern and mechanics of its food supply, but as China is increasingly drawn into the world economic pattern, with Shanghai leading and accelerating the change as before, this anomaly, like most of its others, will disappear.

TEN

The Geography of Shanghai Manufacturing

Shanghai is not only the primary industrial center of China proper, but has a virtual monopoly of large-scale manufacturing enterprises in nearly every field. Two factors are principally responsible for this concentration. First, Shanghai and its trading area represent by far the largest market in China; and second, despite the local absence of most industrial raw materials, cheap transportation makes it possible for Shanghai industry to produce competitively.

Evaluation of Data

More statistical work has been done on Shanghai manufacturing than on almost any other economic problem in China. It is therefore perhaps a commentary on statistical work in China that what has been done on Shanghai falls so short of reliability as measured by any criteria. A further difficulty is that no large-scale work has been published on the problem since 1936; this limits the use of statistics here almost entirely to the pre-war period. The standard study of Liu Ta-chün (1936) draws on the findings of six different surveys made during the late 1920's and early 1930's by the municipal governments of both the foreign and Chinese settlements and by private groups. The combined data of these six surveys do not cover more than two-thirds of Shanghai manufacturing, by workers or by industries. Where two or more surveys cover the same material, their data are almost invariably contradictory. In most of the surveys, and in Liu's compilation, totals are wrongly added, figures misplaced, columns transposed, and statistical paradoxes abound.

These faults are apart from the inherent difficulties of the problem. Until 1945 no one municipal authority had jurisdiction over the entire city, and it was impossible for any one survey to collect complete data, especially on matters such as wages, costs, and capital investment. A much greater difficulty was presented by the fact that something like 80 per cent of the manufacturing establishments in Shanghai employed fewer than 30 workers (and were therefore not liable to regulation or inspection under the National Factory Act of 1929) and operated in private houses. What statistics are used here must be read with the foregoing in mind, realizing that they are in nearly all cases approximations of limited reliability.[1]

While perhaps four-fifths of the total number of "factories" in Shanghai employed fewer than 30 workers, probably about two-thirds of the total industrial workers in the city were employed in factories with a labor force of over 30, and perhaps three-quarters of the total industrial production, by value, of the entire city was accounted for by these larger factories.[2] Most of the figures which will be cited here are based on investigations of these larger factories, and while they are to that extent incomplete, they do at least deal with the most important segment of Shanghai manufacturing in terms of labor force and of value of production.

The Pattern of Manufacturing

Estimates of the degree to which China's industry was concentrated in Shanghai before 1937 differ, but it is clear that Shanghai accounted for about half of the country's large-scale Western-type industrial production. Liu's figures [3] show in 1932–33 136 modern cotton mills in China, of which 64 were in Shanghai, 60 modern tobacco factories, of which 46 were in Shanghai, 83 modern flour mills, of which 41 were in Shanghai, and 2435 modern factories of all kinds in China, of which 1200 were in Shanghai. He estimated that 43 per cent of China's industrial workers in modern manufacturing were employed in Shanghai, and that the city accounted for 51 per cent of the value of China's industrial production.*

* Liu does not define "modern." According to his analysis of "modern" factories elsewhere in his work, the term means factories employing 30 or more persons and using power-driven machinery. However, on this basis his figure of 2435 "modern" factories for the whole of China in 1932–33 would seem too low.

Textile manufacturing was by far the leading industry in Shanghai in the period 1920–36, and included the spinning, weaving, and dyeing of cotton, wool, jute, flax, hemp, and ramie, and the spinning and weaving of silk. The pattern of manufacturing was in most respects typical of the early stages of industrial development, with textiles far in the lead and light consumer goods in general predominant. Shanghai, however, as the primary focus of the Westernization process in China in which a pre-industrial economy was suddenly confronted with the impact of a highly developed industrial economy, was also engaged to some extent in the production of capital goods to supply its own consumers'-goods production and that of most of the rest of China.

For the city as a whole in 1932–33, Liu estimated [4] that the textile industry accounted for 50 to 60 per cent of Shanghai's industrial workers and 40 to 50 per cent of the value of industrial output. Cotton spinning led the textile industries, followed by silk reeling, cotton weaving, wool spinning, and wool weaving in that order. Food industries were second, with 10 to 15 per cent of the industrial workers and 30 to 35 per cent of the value of industrial output. Flour milling was first in this category, closely followed by tobacco (cigarette manufacturing). Most of the rice entering Shanghai was milled in the hinterland collection centers and all of the relatively few rice mills in the city employed fewer than 30 workers.

Clothing industries ranked third, with 3 to 5 per cent of the value of the industrial output, leather and rubber goods fourth, with 2 to 3 per cent, paper and printing fifth, chemical industries sixth (including matches, soap, cosmetics, drugs, and production of industrial chemicals), and manufacture of machinery seventh.*

The Shanghai Municipal Council in its Report for 1935 published figures showing the distribution of factories and workers within the various industries located in the International Settlement, based on surveys conducted in 1934 and corrected to November 1935. In

---

* These figures for 1932–33 are representative for the period 1920–1936 despite the world depression, which affected Shanghai manufacturing relatively little and whose effect in Shanghai was delayed until late 1933 in most industries, with the exception of silk reeling and weaving, which were heavily dependent on the American market. See Liu Ta-chün, *The Growth and Industrialization of Shanghai* (1936).

the latter year, the government of the Chinese Municipality of Greater Shanghai collected similar figures for industries located in the Chinese Municipality (i.e., exclusive of the two foreign settlements).[5] The two sets of figures provide the most reliable indication available of the pre-1937 industrial pattern in Shanghai.

For the International Settlement

Industry	Number of Factories	Number of Workers
textiles	567	75,242
food, drink, and tobacco	155	35,886
machinery	1108	19,051
paper and printing	663	17,730
clothing	226	13,765
chemical (including soap, drugs, matches, and industrial chems.)	191	4,225
metal working	167	2,602
woodworking	98	2,010
bricks, pottery, and glass	45	1,637
vehicles (including boats)	20	1,292
leather and rubber goods	36	1,039
furniture	23	912
scientific and musical instruments and jewellers	22	640
public utilities	5	362
others	95	4,311
Totals	3421	170,704

The discrepancies of this list with Liu's figures on page 167 will be noted, in particular the relatively high place which it gives to machinery. It is obvious from the totals that the figures are not limited to factories employing over 30 workers, but the Council's Report indicates that they do not cover all the industrial establishments in the Settlement and are in general limited to those using power-driven machinery. This would help to account for the relatively higher place of machinery manufacturing, since the figures show that the average number of workers per factory producing machinery recorded in this survey is only 17. The figures also indicate the relatively larger-scale production in the textile, food-drink-tobacco, clothing, bricks-pottery-glass, vehicles, furniture, and public utilities industries, and relatively smaller-scale production in the paper-printing, chemical, metal working, wood working, leather-rubber, and scientific-instruments-jewellers industries.

For the Chinese Municipality

Industry	Number of Factories	Number of Workers
textiles	690	73,448
vehicles (including boats)	46	50,472
food, drink, and tobacco	84	32,379
clothing	344	16,621
machinery	720	16,708
rubber and leather	78	11,845
chemical (including soap, matches and industrial chems.)	121	7,426
power generating	8	5,267
wood working	25	4,101
brick, tile, cement and glass	61	3,370
iron works	169	3,224
building materials	31	1,796
scientific apparatus and jewellery	72	1,779
furniture	46	(no figures)
others	181	17,023
Totals	2676	245,664

Machinery is high on this list also, but the figures show an average of only 23 workers per factory producing machinery. The relatively high place of vehicles and the apparently large scale of production in this industry are presumably accounted for by the two shipyards attached to the Kiangnan Arsenal and by the five foreign-owned shipyards on the right bank of the river.[6] Power generating is necessarily a large-scale industry, but it may be doubted whether six of the eight plants listed here are independent establishments rather than adjuncts, and particularly whether as many as 5,267 workers are employed directly in this industry or whether at least half of this figure represents auxiliary labor outside the plants themselves, such as linesmen, service men, etc.

The relative importance of the other industries listed here is about the same as listed for the Settlement, despite slight differences in the categories. This second list also clearly includes many factories employing less than 30 workers, but again does not include all of the industrial establishments in the Chinese Municipality. We may assume that it too is largely limited to factories using power-driven machinery, but not necessarily that it includes all of these. 169 seems a large number of iron works, especially since this means an average of only 19 workers per factory; when it is considered that the Kiangnan Arsenal is included in this survey and that it alone employed about 700 men in 1932,[7] one may question the accuracy of these figures, or at least the nature of most of the other 168 iron works.

On the basis of an independent survey which he made in 1934, Liu estimated [8] that the eleven leading industries of the city as a whole, according to estimated annual value of output, were as shown in the table below.

Industry	Estimated Annual Value of Output in CNC$
cotton spinning	5,500,000
flour milling and wheat products	4,400,000
cigarettes	1,300,000
matches	720,000
silk reeling and spinning in steam filatures	430,000
chemical (soap, industrial chemicals, cosmetics, drugs)	330,000
cotton weaving	240,000
rubber goods	230,000
silk weaving	130,000
knitted goods	110,000
machinery	70,000

This list of course uses a different method of evaluation, and discrepancies with Liu's earlier estimates of 1932–33 will also be noted (see above, p. 167), but it re-emphasizes the major outlines of the city's industrial pattern as revealed in the other two lists above, namely, the preponderant position of textiles and of light consumers' goods generally, and the inclusion of some capital goods production among the leading industries.

One of the notable features of Shanghai manufacturing is the prevalence of small-scale production in private houses, or in dwellings slightly altered to house machinery which is tended by the residents of the house, often members of one family. These small industries are engaged in a bewildering variety of production, and despite their universal under-capitalization, most of them use electrically-driven machinery. "Factories" of this kind produce, for instance, machine tools, cast iron, electric appliances, soap, acids, textile machinery, power presses, boilers, and telephone parts, as well as a long list of light consumer goods, such as flashlights, light bulbs, thermos flasks, clothing, lamps, electric fans, and food products.[9] Despite crowding and poor working conditions, the quality of production in these plants was apparently high. American orders for telephone parts were placed in Shanghai from 1932 to 1935 for export to South America, and the contracts went predominantly to these small household operators.[10] There was a very high rate of turnover among these "factories"; their small scale and small capitalization enabled them to react with great sensitivity to market changes and to crowd or evacuate lines of production alternately as profits varied.*

Market and Raw Materials

Market considerations are the leading factor in the concentration of manufacturing as a whole in Shanghai. As the primate commercial and industrial center of China, not only were capital, relatively trained industrial labor, and electric power available there more abundantly and in most cases more cheaply than anywhere else in China, but Shanghai includes in its trade hinterland half of the country. With the notable exception of the textile industries, most of the raw materials necessary to maintain Shanghai's manufacturing were not available locally in its immediate hinterland. It was the market which attracted and held most manufacturing.

We may logically begin with the exception, the textile industries. Shanghai is located near the center of China's chief cotton-producing

* The *Chinese Economic Bulletin*, published in Shanghai, records many of these changes. For example, there were 11 industrial establishments in Shanghai in November 1930, producing "gourmet powder" (made mainly from wheat flour), 9 in October 1931, and none in June 1932, according to the *Bulletin's* weekly industrial news columns.

area. Kiangsu alone produced before the war about 30 per cent of China's total annual cotton crop. Shanghai's textile mills at this period consumed an annual average of about 3,800,000 piculs of raw cotton (one picul equals 133 pounds), of which it is estimated that 2,000,000 came from Kiangsu, 500,000 from Hankow, 500,000 from Tientsin by sea, and 800,000 from foreign ports, principally from the United States.[11] The foreign cotton imports were predominantly of long-staple varieties for the weaving of finer-count cloth for which the native short-staple Chinese cotton was not suitable. During the 1930's considerable progress was made in growing long-staple cotton in China from American seeds, including that grown in the Kiangsu area, so that by 1936 foreign cotton imports to Shanghai were only half of what they had been in 1920.[12] The ground thus gained was largely lost during the war years, but reports from China since 1946 indicate that self-sufficiency in all types of cotton is now again within reach, with Kiangsu still the leading producer.[13]

The major silk-producing regions of China are also near at hand. The delta areas of Kiangsu and Chekiang accounted for about half of the total Chinese production of raw silk in the 1920's and 1930's, as they had during most of the nineteenth century, and Shanghai remained the primary silk market of China. When silk-reeling, spinning, and weaving in the delta area became largely concentrated in factories after about 1910, rather than being done as before on a domestic basis, it was logical that the industry should center in Shanghai, as well as in the nearby cities of Soochow, Wusih, and Hangchow.

The rest of the textile industry is less closely related to the sources of its raw materials. About three-quarters of the raw wool used in Shanghai factories before the war came from the grazing areas of northwest China via Tientsin, by sea and rail. Less than one-tenth came from Kiangsu, and it was mainly "dead" wool of poor quality shorn from dead sheep and goats. The remainder was supplied largely from central China, via Hankow, by Yangtze steamer.[14] Ramie and hemp for Shanghai manufacturing came primarily from Hankow, in the center of the chief producing areas for both crops. Most of the jute consumed in Shanghai was imported from India.

Among the food industries, Shanghai's flour mills, as we have seen above in Chapter Nine, depended more heavily on foreign wheat imports than on what they drew from China. The six plants in Shanghai in the 1930's producing dried, powdered, or frozen eggs were all foreign-owned and all large-scale, employing an average of about 350 workers per plant.[15] The area from which they drew their eggs has already been outlined in Chapter Nine. While local sources were important in this industry, they did not fill the entire demand, and it was necessary to bring eggs from as far as Hankow. Shantung was also a large egg-producing center, but the factory production of preserved eggs in Tsinan and Tsingtao combined was less than a third of Shanghai's.[16] It is reasonable to suppose that a measure of this difference was accounted for by the water transport network feeding Shanghai and the lack of it in Shantung.

Of all the food industries in Shanghai, tobacco manufacturing was most notably divorced from major sources of supply. The cigarette industry in China had been started on a large scale by the American Tobacco Company in the late 1890's (it merged with British interests in 1902 to form the British-American Tobacco Company, the largest producer of tobacco products in China). During the first decade of the twentieth century, its foreign tobacco experts surveyed soil and climatic conditions in China and fixed on three main areas where American tobacco seed would grow best so that its leaf could be blended with the native Chinese leaf (which was produced in small quantities in most parts of central and north China but with the best quality leaf coming from the three areas selected by the foreign experts) to produce an inexpensive but good quality smoke. The three areas were located in south central Shantung, northwestern Anhwei, and central Honan. Large Chinese cigarette producers entered the field after 1905, drawing on the increasing domestic production of foreign-type leaf and blending it with Chinese leaf.[17]

In spite of the presence of large industrial centers (by Chinese standards) in or near these main producing areas (Kaifeng and Hankow for Honan, Kiukiang, Wuhu, and Nanking for Anhwei, Tsingtao and Tsinan for Shantung), approximately 60 per cent of all the factory-made cigarettes in China were produced in Shanghai from 1925 to 1935.[18] The Shanghai cigarette factories drew about half of their tobacco from Shantung, 20 per cent from Anhwei, and 20 per cent from Honan.[19] The remaining 10 per cent was imported, mainly from the United States, but the amount imported continued to decline as domestic production of foreign-style leaf increased, and by 1935 it was about half what it had been in 1925, the overall average for the period 1925–1935 being 10 per cent. The magnetism of the Shanghai market gave it a commanding position in spite of its distance from the leaf-producing areas.

Shanghai industries using large amounts of metal, and the rubber goods industry, were the farthest removed from their sources of raw materials. Virtually all of the steel, ferro-alloys, and non-ferrous metals (with the exceptions of antimony and tungsten) were imported. Until the recent subsidized development program of the Communist Government, large-scale modern production had not been profitable in China proper for either iron or steel, with the exception of three plants which produced mainly from local scrap and which served a local market.[20] These three plants were in Shanghai, and were therefore by definition market-oriented. Two plants in Pootung were established in 1918. One produced steel from local scrap in two open-hearth furnaces of 30 and 70 tons capacity respectively, and the other probably produced no steel (since its "blast furnaces" were of only 12 and 33 tons capacity respectively), but poured iron castings.[21] Both plants worked only sporadically until 1934, when they were shut down. They were reopened by the Japanese in 1938, presumably on a military, and therefore a non-paying basis.[22] (Iron and steel were made for a few years during the war in Chungking, but on a small and uneconomic basis.)

The third plant was the steel-casting unit of the Kiangnan Arsenal, which operated two 15-ton electric furnaces to produce regular plate, high-speed, and armour steel for its shipyards and munitions works, using entirely local scrap. It was dismantled in 1932.[23] Other engineering and metal-working plants in Shanghai had small iron- and steel-casting furnaces of a few tons' capacity, but such small furnaces are necessary in any modern industrial complex for re-working scrap. They do not add to existing stocks.

The reason for the absence of a steel industry in China, or in Shanghai, was the inability of the industry to meet the price of foreign imports. China's total iron ore resources are not inconsiderable, but in the Yangtze basin, where most of the production attempts have been centered, the ore deposits are small and scattered so that their exploitation imposes high costs. Small deposits of coal are also found in scattered localities along the lower Yangtze, but the combined costs of mining and of transport to production centers were too high to permit economic iron or steel making.[24] In the case of Shanghai, not only did these factors operate despite its water connections with the ore and coal deposits along the Yangtze, but as a seaport it could not produce iron or steel from domestic or foreign ore at anything like the price of seaborne imports of foreign iron and steel. Fortunately its maritime connections enabled it to draw on foreign sources for iron and steel and to produce finished metal goods at a cost which still allowed them to compete in the China market with foreign imports of finished metal goods.

Among the large metal-using industries, the vehicle plants (aside from the shipyards of the Kiangnan Arsenal before 1932) imported almost all of their finished steel plates, wire, rods, tubing, and other semi-finished steel products, and most of their cast iron, directly, or indirectly as recastings from iron and steel scrap. The same was true of the plants producing machinery, with their large use of more highly-finished steel products and special steels.[25] The nine large-scale modern shipyards produced primarily river and small coastal craft, the largest ship built up to 1932 being of 11,000 net tons. The steel, production machinery, and most of the engines installed in these ships were imported, and yet it was still apparently possible for the yards to compete in the China market with European, Japanese, or American yards. In 1930 the nine yards turned out a total of 71 ships with a gross tonnage of 17,839, and an average tonnage of 240.[26] There were also about 30 smaller shipyards building Chinese-style wooden craft, from canal sampans to large coastal junks.[27]

Among the other metal-using industries, the food canning and can-producing plants in Shanghai imported all of their tin plate, primarily from the United States.[28] China has significant deposits of tin and produced in the 1930's between 3 and 4 per cent of the world's tin ore. It is mined in the southwest tableland of Yünnan and Kwangsi, and in the hills which form the divide between the Hsi and Hsiang River basins (in Kwangsi and Hunan), but no tin was smelted anywhere in China until 1932, when a small plant was established at the largest Chinese mine in Yünnan. The ore, and the small amount of smelted tin were almost entirely exported. China before 1937 was the leading world producer of both tungsten and antimony, and Shanghai was able to fill its own small needs for these alloys entirely from domestic sources. Both ores were mined predominantly in the basins of the Hsiang and Yüan Rivers in Hunan, and over 90 per cent of the total production of both ores was exported, nearly all of it through Shanghai.

Hides for the leather industry in Shanghai, and for export, came to the city, in order of importance, from Manchuria by sea, Tientsin (which acted as the main collecting center for hides from the grazing lands of northwest China) by sea, Shantung (Tsingtao and Tsinan) by both sea and rail, and from Hankow (collecting center for the hides of central China) and Szechuan via the Yangtze. Hides from Kiangsu and Chekiang were considered greatly inferior as well as being very limited in quantity in this animal-poor area of intensive hand agriculture, and accounted for less than 3 per cent of Shanghai's total supply.[29] Rubber was of course entirely imported.

Shanghai's wood-working, furniture, and paper industries were almost entirely dependent on imported wood from Canada, the United States, and Scandinavia. The delta area produces no wood at all, and the nearest commercially usable stands are in the hills along the Chientang River south and west of Hangchow, but they are small and of poor quality. About one-tenth of the quantity of foreign imports came in by junk from south China, particularly from Foochow, the lumber center of the China coast by virtue of the heavily wooded slopes of the Wu Yi and Ta Yü ranges, too steep for agriculture and not crossed by any important transport routes.[30]

The two leading chemical industries, soap and matches, provide in the sources of their raw materials an illustration of Shanghai's position as a manufacturing center in an otherwise pre-industrial economy. There were about fifty soap factories in Shanghai in the

1930's, or about half of the large-scale mechanized soap factories in China. They drew 90 per cent of their raw materials from domestic sources. Lye (potash) was obtainable from plants in Shanghai. Vegetable tallow and vegetable oils (most importantly, cotton, peanut, rape seed, sesamum seed, and castor) came to the city via the Yangtze system from the major producing areas of central China.[31] The fruit of the tallow tree is gathered in central China in October and the oil pressed out during the winter, but it is not marketed in Hankow and sent to Shanghai until the spring rise of the waterways leading to Hankow makes easy navigation possible. A dry spring makes the market soar in both Hankow and Shanghai.[32]

The average Shanghai price before the war was nevertheless substantially below that of foreign vegetable oil imports (despite the production of coconut oil in southeast Asia). Vegetable wax from central China also largely replaced foreign imports of paraffin wax after 1930, when the *likin* (internal customs tax) was abolished by the Kuomintang government. The cheapness of domestic tallow, oils, and wax in Shanghai relative to seaborne foreign imports was clearly related to the use of inland water transport in bringing these products to the city. The fact that 80 per cent of Shanghai's soap production in the early 1930's was marketed outside Kiangsu also suggests that the city's water connections with its hinterland were basic in locating the industry there. Only 10 per cent of the Shanghai soap industry's raw materials were imported, largely coconut and olive oils for making especially high-quality soap for the domestic market.[33]

By contrast, the Shanghai match industry was almost entirely dependent on overseas sources for its raw materials. It imported all of its sulphur (largely from Japan), all of its paper and cardboard (from Sweden), and all of its match-making machinery (from Japan). Most of its phosphorous was also imported, but some was produced locally from animal bones. Ample sulphuric acid was produced in Shanghai. For this product of such high unit-value by weight, raw materials to which so much value was added by manufacture could economically be imported, and the finished matches were marketed in every province of China.[34] Shanghai was nevertheless industrially out of gear with the rest of China to such an extent that the match industry imported even its paper and cardboard.*

Chinese sources could maintain Shanghai's soap manufacturing, using relatively bulky agricultural raw materials, but the match industry, dependent on relatively finished and specialized materials, was obliged to rely predominantly on overseas sources. The city's market was able to hold both of these greatly dissimilar enterprises, each typical of much of its manufacturing complex.

The jade-cutting industry may be cited as a final illustration of the market-oriented character of Shanghai manufacturing as a whole. While jade-cutting would presumably be less likely than diamond-cutting to gravitate to primate financial and banking centers, it is equally dependent on specially skilled labor, which is most often found in the largest cities, and on the commercial services and connections of a primate market. Most of the world's jade is mined in northern Burma, but Shanghai, rather than Rangoon or Calcutta, was the world's leading jade center for cutting, polishing, and marketing. It imported its rough jade from Burma by sea, paying a 50 per cent export duty *ad valorem*, and sold the finished product not only in China but all over the world. Japanese attempts at competition in this industry during the 1920's failed to dislodge Shanghai from its leading position.[35] An early start and accumulated skill have been more important in this industry than in almost any other, but it was the Shanghai market which attracted and continued to hold it.

The Cost of Raw Materials

It will be useful to estimate the percentage of total costs which is represented in different Shanghai industries by the cost of delivered raw materials in order to throw light on the competitive position of the city as a location for manufacturing. The published estimates of costs are contradictory, and the implication is that accurate information is not available, an understandable condition in view of the

---

* The relative importance in Shanghai manufacturing of the industries discussed above (pp. 171–178) is indicated by the tables above on pages 168, 169, and 170. Consumption figures are unfortunately not available.

complex industrial and administrative picture in Shanghai as outlined in the first section of this chapter. The following figures should
therefore be read as the roughest kind of approximations, and con-
clusions should be drawn from them only with great caution.

The table below, according to Liu's survey of 1934, gives estimates
of the percentage of total costs represented by delivered raw
materials in each of the eleven leading Shanghai industries (by
value of output).[36]

Industry	Raw Materials' Percentage of Total Costs
cotton spinning	65
flour milling	73
cigarettes	40
matches	68
silk filatures	72
chemical (including soap)	45
cotton weaving	74
rubber goods	48
silk weaving	63
knitted goods	65
machinery	72

These figures are incredibly high, especially for the textile industries, where not only are local supplies of raw materials readily
available by water transport, but where the amounts of power and
labor necessary are relatively great. The figures must reflect very
low proportionate costs for labor and for power. The figures for the
textile industries are hard to reconcile with that for cigarettes
(which is itself about what one would expect — 40 per cent), considering the much greater distances over which the leaf tobacco must
move to Shanghai, and the difference is not explained away by the
relatively larger amounts of labor necessary in the cigarette industry.
The figure for the chemical industries seems reasonable, including
the separate figure for matches, as well as that for rubber goods,
considering the large proportionate amounts of labor necessary. The
figure for flour milling, however, also seems high, despite the large
importance of foreign wheat imports. Presumably it also reflects low

proportionate costs of labor and power. The same comment applies to the high figure for machinery.

In a generally more careful work dealing only with the cotton industry, Fong Hsien-ting, as shown in the accompanying table, provides a different estimate of costs in the production of cotton yarn in Shanghai in 1930.[37]

Cost Item	Percentage of Total Costs
raw cotton	42
labor	30
power	8
overhead and interest	20
	100

These seem much more reasonable, and they are generally substantiated by the findings of Moser and of Pearse.[38] Liu's figures for cotton spinning are also suspect because in 1934 a larger proportion of the mills' supply was the cheaper domestic cotton (see above, p. 172). If we may accept these figures of Fong's as a closer approximation to the facts than Liu's, we have at least some idea of the proportionate cost of delivered raw materials in Shanghai's largest industry, cotton spinning, and we may justifiably assume that this cost was of approximately the same order of magnitude in the other cotton industries and in the silk industries, since Liu's figures show a maximum spread of only 10 per cent among the raw materials' cost in the textile industries which he covers, and since both cotton and silk supplies came very largely from the local delta area. We have unfortunately no check on Liu's estimates of raw materials' costs in other leading Shanghai industries. Since with the exception of flour milling and machinery, these other figures seem reasonable, we can only accept them with caution.

Even after this revision, however, the best estimate which can be made of the proportionate costs of raw materials in Shanghai manufacturing still shows these costs to be high by Western standards.* There are two major reasons for this: the relatively low cost of labor, and the relatively high cost of transport. The first

---

* The United States Census of Manufactures for 1939 gives value figures for manufacturing costs in major categories of manufacturing in the United States in

condition operates to approximately the same degree in all Chinese industrial centers.[39] The second operates for all Chinese industrial centers, but not to the same degree.

Only two important carriers are involved: railways and water-ways. Highway transport by truck remains negligible in China, relative to the scale necessary for the maintenance of modern manufacturing, and with the shortage of fuel, vehicles, and parts as well as of adequate roads it is an impractically expensive carrier. Non-mechanized overland carriers in general use in China (porters, wheel-barrows, pack animals, carts) are also notoriously expensive, and are inadequate to handle volume movements.* Representative rates for railway transport of bulk goods (exclusive of coal) in carload lots in China during the 1930's ranged from the equivalents of US$.02 to US$.07 per ton/mile.[40] This compares with an average ton/mile rate on United States railways during the same period of about US$.01.[41] Accurate or even representative rates for water transport in China are not available, but the average for unobstructed inland routes may be estimated at between US$.018 and US$.02 per ton/mile during this period. In any case, where adequate water transport is available in China, it is a cheaper carrier than railways under present conditions, and can handle bulk shipments.

As we have pointed out above in Chapter Seven Shanghai is not a major rail center, and the two railways which serve it are not

---

that year under five headings. Expressed in percentage terms, these costs are tabulated, for United States manufacturing as a whole, and for the textile industry in the United States:

	All Manufacturing(%)	Textile Manufacturing(%)
labor and salaries	53	57
materials and supplies	37	35
fuel	2	1
purchased electric power	1	4
other	7	3
	100	100

"Materials and supplies" is not defined. No figure is given for overhead and interest, so that all of these figures must be scaled down in order to make them comparable with the figures cited for Shanghai.

* Average ton/mile rates for truck transport in China range from the equivalents of US$.30 to US$.50. For porter and wheelbarrow they often reach US$1.00 per ton/mile.

large carriers. The city's water connections, however, are uniquely good. (They have been outlined in some detail in Chapters Four and Seven.) It may be assumed that the cost of most delivered raw materials in other Chinese industrial centers was a higher percentage of total costs of production than in Shanghai. This assumption is borne out in the case of Tientsin. Tientsin is not only an ocean port through its association with Taku, but it lies on the Grand Canal and is, after Peking, the second most important rail junction in China. It lies at the focus of an even more extensive lowland (the north China plain and the basin of the Yellow River) than does Shanghai. Tientsin's water connections over this lowland are slight compared with Shanghai's water connections over the Yangtze basin, but with the possible exception of Hankow, Tientsin nevertheless has the most favorable orientation to transport routes of any Chinese industrial center after Shanghai.

Fong Hsien-ting found, in comparing production costs in the spinning of cotton yarn (also Tientsin's largest industry by value of output) that the cost of delivered raw materials in this industry in Tientsin averaged about 70 per cent of the total cost of production, as against an average of 42 per cent for Shanghai (see above, p. 180). Yet Tientsin also lies near the center of one of China's leading cotton-producing areas, through which three railway lines run to the city. Fong's cost estimates for the Tientsin cotton yarn-spinning industry, by percentages of total costs, are shown in the accompanying table.[42]

Cost Item	Percentage of Total Costs
raw cotton	70
labor	15
power	7
overhead and interest	8
	100

It does not seem possible that the costs could be divided as Fong has estimated. The figure for raw cotton seems too high, and that for overhead and interest too low. Power is cheap in Tientsin, due largely to the proximity of the Kailan mines at Kaiping, 82 miles north by rail, China's largest producer of coal, and the chief source of Shanghai's coal supply as well. The figure for labor costs is of course depressed by the high figure for raw cotton. Nevertheless it seems clear that Tientsin, despite its rail and water connections and its location in a major cotton-producing area, paid a considerably higher price than Shanghai for delivered raw cotton. If this was true for raw cotton, we may assume that it was true for most of the other industrial raw materials consumed in Tientsin, with the obvious exceptions of coal and the wool, hides and skins of north China, and the possible exception of wheat.* If Tientsin could obtain the necessary raw materials in these latter cases more cheaply than Shanghai, this is further evidence of the paramountcy of the Shanghai market and of the market-oriented character of its manufacturing. If Tientsin paid a higher price than Shanghai for most delivered raw materials, we may assume that other Chinese industrial centers did so too.

Water transport has been a key factor in the development of manufacturing in Shanghai. The city's railway connections are inferior to Tientsin's, and yet its manufacturing apparently paid less for most of its raw materials, and in fact was a greater consumer than Tientsin manufacturing of the leading industrial raw materials of north China: coal, hides, and wheat, all of which can move to Shanghai by sea from north China ports. In turn, the primacy of the Shanghai market depends in large measure on the water transport network which includes half of China in the city's tributary area. The market is able to exercise its attractiveness for manufacturing of all kinds by its ability to draw to its generally resource-poor area by sea and river transport the industrial raw materials which it needs.

Coal and Electric Power

The single most important industrial raw material, coal, has been left for final consideration, since it plays a major role in nearly every industry, directly, or in the form of electric power.

---

* Shanghai nevertheless led Tientsin in the 1920's and 1930's in the consumption of coal and in the production of leather goods and flour, and in fact shipped nearly 10 per cent of its total flour production to Tientsin on an annual average. (For comparative figures on consumption of coal and production of leather goods and flour, see respectively Leonard Ting, "The Coal Industry in China" (1937), p. 217; Chinese Year Book (1936), p. 1153; Y. C. Chang, "Flour Milling in China" (1922), p. 219).

Consular and Customs reports from Shanghai during the early decades of the modern city show that it depended almost entirely on overseas imports of coal. There was a large movement in ballast from England to Shanghai from the opening of the port to foreign trade in 1843 through the period of the 1860's, when foreign merchants had difficulty finding a market for foreign goods in return for China's tea and silk.[43] It was consumed largely by the coastal, river, and ocean vessels fueling at Shanghai.[44] This relatively cheap ballast coal from England was however gradually replaced after 1870 by even cheaper coal from Nagasaki in Japan and from the large Chinese government-operated Keelung mines (subsequently taken over by the Japanese in their conquest of Formosa in 1895) at the northern tip of Formosa, opened in 1875. Both of these new sources were on tidewater and coal from both could move to Shanghai as part of the growing volume of east Asian maritime trade.

The first large-scale coal mine in China was opened at Kaiping, Hopeh, in 1878,* (map 9), and the first shipment from Kaiping to Shanghai arrived in 1881, but this coal was unable to compete with Japanese imports at Shanghai until after the turn of the century. By 1930, the Kaiping mine accounted for 23 per cent of China's annual coal production.[45] Kaiping was connected by rail to Tangku and Tientsin in 1888 (the first permanent railway in China), and to Shanhaikuan, via Chingwantao, in 1894. At Chingwantao, 79 miles by rail north of Kaiping, a seawall and wharves were built between 1899 and 1902 to permit shipment of Kaiping coal from this port, where there was no bar as at Tangku.[46]

This facilitation of transport, and the relatively short rail-haul from the mines to Chingwantao, were undoubtedly factors in the increased ability of Kaiping coal to compete in the Shanghai market after 1902. In the 1890's, with the assistance of French capital, another new supply of coal appeared on the east Asia market, from Indo-China. The mines, located on tidewater near Haiphong (map

---

* This was the Kaiping Mining Bureau, organized at the instigation of Li Hung-chang in 1878, and later (1912), after a period of British control (1901–1912), reorganized as the Kailan Mining Administration, a joint Sino-British undertaking and one of the pioneer modern industrial enterprises in China. For a valuable account of its development, see Ellsworth Carlson, *The Kailan Mines* (1949).

9), could compete in Shanghai with Japanese, Formosan, or north China coal.

The table below estimates the relative rank of major sources for Shanghai's coal in the 1930's, by percentages of total tonnage of coal delivered in Shanghai in each year from all the sources listed.[47]

Source	1931	1932	1933	1934	1935	1936	Average 1931–36
Kaiping (Hopeh)	37	46	37	36	37	36	37.5
Tzuchuan-Poshan (Shantung)	7	6	11	17	19	22	14.0
Japan (ex-Nagasaki)	18	16	15	8	5	3	10.8
Fushun (Manchuria)	19	13	13	6	3	1	9.5
Anhwei (mines on Yangtze)	—	—	9	10	14	23	9.2
Chunghsing (Shantung)	8	8	6	12	12	8	9.1
Haiphong (Indo-China)	4	6	6	5	5	5	5.3
Shansi (mine(s) unspecified)	7	5	3	6	5	2	4.6
	100	100	100	100	100	100	100.0

Mainland places mentioned in the foregoing table will be found in map 9. The Poshan and Tzuchuan mines were located in the major coal field of Shantung. Both mines began to produce coal on a large scale in the late 1920's, after they were connected by rail to Tsingtao, approximately 175 miles away. Tzuchuan and Poshan coal moved to Shanghai largely by rail to Tsingtao and thence by sea, although there was some rail shipment via Nanking and thence to Shanghai via the Yangtze. Fushun was linked by rail with the port of Yingkow (Newchwang), 120 miles to the south at the mouth of the Liao River, as well as by limited water transport on the river, and by rail with Dairen, Manchuria's leading port, 210 miles to the south. The mines in Anhwei were located along the Yangtze, but production was not begun on a large scale until after 1932. The Anhwei coal deposits are relatively small and their exploitation is more expensive than in the larger Chinese mines, such as at Kaiping. Only their location along the Yangtze made their exploitation profitable as a source for Shanghai's coal supply. Coal from Chunghsing in Shantung moved 120 miles by rail to Haichow, and thence to Shanghai by sea. Shansi coal entering Shanghai came principally from the mines at Tzu-chou, and moved to both Tientsin and Haichow by rail, whence it traveled to Shanghai by sea.

The figures for coal imports from Japan and Manchuria in 1931, 1932, and 1933 listed in the foregoing table owe their size primarily to Japanese dumping of coal on the Shanghai market in these years at a price which was often less than two-thirds of the domestic price of coal in Japan. The table shows that while this dumping did not greatly affect sales of Kaiping coal in Shanghai, it did cut into the Shanghai market for Shantung coal in particular (Tzuchuan, Poshan, and Chunghsing). This may suggest, in the absence of complete available price figures, that Kaiping coal was relatively cheap in Shanghai and that Shantung coal was relatively expensive. A reason for this difference may be found in the long rail-haul necessary for coal moving from Shantung mines to Shanghai (120 miles from Chunghsing and 175 miles from Tzuchuan-Poshan), compared with the shorter rail haul of 79 miles for Kaiping coal to Chingwantao.

Railway figures show that coal shipments arriving in Shanghai by rail in the years 1931, 1932, and 1933 averaged less than one-quarter of the railway coal shipments recorded for 1930, 1934, 1935, and 1936.[48] Apparently direct rail haulage of coal from Shantung (or from other sources) to Shanghai was not profitable in the face of Japanese dumping in Shanghai. Figures of the Maritime Customs for these years show no significant falling off in seaborne cargoes of coal arriving in Shanghai between 1931 and 1933, and in fact record a slightly higher average for these three years than for the years immediately preceding and following them, readily explainable in terms of larger imports of the unnaturally cheap Japanese coal for inland distribution as well as for consumption in Shanghai. In any case, Kaiping coal apparently had no difficulty in maintaining its position on the Shanghai market despite Japanese dumping.

Shanghai drew most of its coal from sources closely oriented to water transport. Coal deposits are widely distributed over large areas of north and central China. While Shanghai received its largest supply from Kaiping mines near the coast, and a relatively constant supply from the mines on tidewater at Haiphong, it drew inland coal only from Fushun (on a navigable tributary of the Liao, and normally the cheapest pit-head coal in East Asia due to easy extraction from huge open-pit mines), Anhwei (deposits along the Yangtze), Shansi (China's major coal reserve), and Shantung (the nearest large coal deposits to Shanghai). The Chinghsing mines in Hopeh could not depend for transport on their largely unnavigable river connections with Tientsin, 190 miles away by rail.

The accompanying table lists the average annual production (in millions of tons) of the major coal-producing provinces of China in the early 1930's.[49]

Province	Production
Hopeh	7.7
Shantung	3.5
Shansi	2.7
Honan	2.1
Szechuan	.9
Hunan	.6
Anhwei	.6

Hopeh, with its Kaiping mines 79 miles by rail from the port of Chingwantao, supplied the largest share of Shanghai's coal for the period 1931–1936 (37.6 per cent). Shantung, immediately north of Kiangsu and the nearest large coal producer to Shanghai, but with limited water transport, supplied an average of only 23.1 per cent of Shanghai's coal during the same period. Inland Honan, Szechuan, and Hunan do not figure as sources of Shanghai coal. Anhwei, also without a seacoast, but with mines along the Yangtze, accounted for 23 per cent of Shanghai's coal supply by 1936. Landlocked Shansi, China's third producer of coal accounted for less than five per cent of Shanghai's coal supply for the same period. Overseas coal imports (Japan, Manchuria, and Indo-China) accounted for 25.6 per cent of Shanghai's coal supply for the period 1931–1936, or more than any Chinese province except Hopeh (see table above on p. 185).

Ting estimates that for China as a whole in the period of the 1930's domestic coal was moved 70 per cent (by weight) by rail, and

30 per cent by water.[50] Shanghai was thus in a relatively favorable position in being able to draw its coal supplies so largely over water routes. For the period 1930 to 1936, the city imported an annual average of 3.9 million tons of coal from all sources combined.[51] Figures of the Maritime Customs at Shanghai for the same period show an annual average of 3.5 million tons of coal arriving in the city by sea and river [52] (so that railway haulage accounted for less than 10 per cent). Even so, the distances separating Shanghai from its sources of coal made domestic coal more expensive there than for instance in Tientsin, where the cost of Kaiping coal was about 10 per cent less than in Shanghai. Shansi coal, selling for CNC$5 per ton at the pit-head, sold after its long rail haul for CNC$10 at Taku and CNC$12 per ton at Shanghai.[53] (Note that the price doubled between the mines and Taku, but increased by only 20 per cent between Taku and Shanghai, more than twice as long a haul, but by sea rather than by rail.) Shanghai has the advantage of central location, and can draw with equal ease on domestic or overseas coal as prices vary.

Consumption of coal in the city, according to C. A. Bacon, was divided approximately as shown below.[54]

Users	Approx. Annual Consumption, in Tons	
Public Utilities	1,475,000	
electric power companies		1,300,000
gas works		100,000
waterworks		75,000
Other Industries	1,100,000	
Households	500,000	
Shipping	400,000	
Railways	350,000	
Miscellaneous	50,000	
TOTAL	3,875,000	

According to these figures, 37 per cent of Shanghai's coal consumption was accounted for by the electric power companies. There were four of these companies in the 1930's, of which the Shanghai Power Company (sold by the Shanghai Municipal Council to an American company in 1929, and in 1949–50 taken over by the Communist government) was by far the largest. An official of the company estimated that it was responsible for an average of 83 per cent of the total sales of electric power in Shanghai for the period 1925–1934, and that 78 per cent of its sales during this period were to industrial users, distributed as shown in the accompanying table.[55]

Industry	Percentage of Total Industrial Power Sales
cotton mills	78
flour mills	7
rubber goods factories	2
miscellaneous textiles	2
other industries (less than 1 per cent each)	11
	100

The city's dominant industry, cotton textiles, was thus apparently heavily dependent on rented electric power. All of the five power plants in Shanghai were entirely carbo-electric. The Shanghai Power Company operated two plants, one at the northeastern tip of Yangtzepoo (the "Riverside" plant), and the other near the mouth of Hongkew Creek (map 3). Of the other three plants, one was owned by the French Municipality and was located on Siccawei Creek at the southern edge of the French Settlement, and two were Chinese-owned, located respectively in Nantao and Chapei. The silk-reeling industry does not appear in the above table because it used primarily steam power (and steam heat), which was produced on the factory premises from coal. Approximately 80 per cent of the industrially-used electric power was purchased from the power companies, and only about 20 per cent was generated by the industrial consumers themselves. Fully half of this 20 per cent was accounted for by the generators of the Kiangnan Arsenal.[56]

Shanghai produced in 1936 58 per cent of the electric power generated in China, and the "Riverside" plant of the Shanghai Power Company had a larger output in 1930 (450 million kilowatt-hours) than any single station in England.[57] The combined output of all four power companies in 1930 was greater than in any English city except London.[58] This power was sold at very low rates, special rate arrangements being made for large industrial users.

Rates during the period 1926–30 averaged for all users the equivalent of US$.008 (.025 taels) per kilowatt-hour, which the president
of the Shanghai Power Company claimed made his product the
world's cheapest power.[59] These rates were made possible, in spite
of the higher price of domestic coal in Shanghai than in Tientsin,
by the very high and constant annual 24-hour load factor, which
averaged nearly 70 per cent during the period 1930 to 1936, as compared with 42, 26, and 40 per cent respectively for Manchester,
Birmingham, and Liverpool during the same period.[60]

The load factor reflects a high intensity of industrial operation,
and a heavy dependence of Shanghai manufacturing on electric
power purchased from the power companies. It also reflects the
long working hours of nearly all manufacturing establishments in
Shanghai, which averaged between 11 and 12 hours a day six days
a week,[61] and the widespread Sunday and night-time operation
among nearly all of the household and smaller-scale manufacturing
establishments using electric power. The low power rates encouraged the spread of small-scale mechanized manufacturing in
private houses, and more important, made Shanghai an attractive
location for almost every form of manufacturing.

The case of electric power demonstrates again the role of the
Shanghai market in locating industry there. While coal was relatively easily and cheaply obtainable in Shanghai, it was even
cheaper in Tientsin, yet rates for electric power produced from coal
in Shanghai were among the lowest in the world. The availability
of cheap power must be counted one of the outstanding advantages
of Shanghai for manufacturing. Power was cheap because water
transport made a flexible and reasonably priced coal supply possible
at all times short of war in the Pacific, and because the volume of
industry already attracted to the Shanghai market by its transport
connections, and dependent on rented electric power, made for a
load factor which kept power rates exceedingly low.

Factory Location

As if to demonstrate a basic reason for its presence there, manufacturing within Shanghai is closely oriented to waterways, as
map 3 will illustrate. Manufacturing came relatively late in the

development of modern Shanghai, and has always been subordinate to the city's trading function. It has tended to occupy the urban margins and has not notably displaced older land-use patterns in the city. In a Western city this might give manufacturing an advantage of easy railway connections. Shanghai has at least part of a belt line, connecting the Hangchow, Nanking, and Woosung tracks, in addition to conveniently placed yards, but the railway lines touch important manufacturing areas only along Soochow Creek (the riverside industrial developments at Nantao and Woosung are relatively minor and are in both cases more closely related to the Whangpoo and its tributary creeks than to the railway). It is a surprising fact (by Western standards) that while manufacturing has spread toward the Yangtze along the left bank of the Whangpoo for about half the distance between Soochow Creek and Woosung, there is no manufacturing along the railway to Woosung from the station in Chapei (which is itself flanked on two sides by a residential area) to Woosung Creek. The greater part of this spur line passes through purely agricultural country.

The Yangtzepoo manufacturing area, the largest in the city and on the left bank of the Whangpoo, is nowhere nearer to the railway than one mile, and most of it is between two and three miles away. The manufacturing zone along Soochow Creek is mainly on the opposite bank from the railway and does not follow it when the lines leave the creek. The residential district of the French Settlement is also flanked on the south side by an industrial sector, articulated with Siccawei Creek and divorced from the railway. Manufacturing is absent from the left bank of the Whangpoo only along the well-guarded frontage of the Bund (see above, Chapter Three) and immediately downstream where wharves and docks have primary claim. Even Pootung, devoid of railway connections, but jutting into the Whangpoo in peninsular form, is an industrial area.

Power plants in any city must be located on or near large supplies of fresh water in order to cool their condensers. But of the five power plants in Shanghai, none has a direct rail connection, and all but two are considerable distances from the railway. The gas works, not heavily dependent on water for cooling purposes, but, like the power plants, a large consumer of coal, is on Soochow Creek, on the opposite bank from the railway.

Cotton textiles and flour, Shanghai's two leading industries by value of output, illustrate in the location of their manufacturing plants what is surely a unique economic phenomenon among modern industrial metropolises. Virtually all the city's cotton and flour mills are located on or near the navigable creeks by which they receive their supplies of raw cotton or wheat and send out their finished goods. The great majority of these mills had no other transport facilities, not being connected with either roads or railways.[62] Shanghai, for all its superficially Western appearance, is economically a blend in which Venetian characteristics are as discernible as British or American to the enquiring eye.

Changes in Industrial Location

Any city and any industrial center, once it reaches metropolitan size, tends to develop a seemingly automatic power of attraction for economic enterprises of all kinds. In particular once it has become a primate city, it seems to grow in snowball fashion and to corner for itself continually the lion's share of any new economic activity of the political or economic unit as a whole. This primacy in the case of Shanghai was undoubtedly in large part responsible for the continuing concentration there of trade, manufacturing, and finance. The more economic activity the city supported, in variety and volume, the more advantageous it became for new economic activity of any kind to center there.

By 1936, there were, however, signs that some new manufacturing was locating elsewhere more than in Shanghai, and even that certain industries were moving from Shanghai to other industrial centers. The cotton textile industries of China were increasingly dependent on domestic cotton through the early 1930's (see above, p. 172). This removed some of the double advantage of Shanghai's location in the major domestic cotton producing area, and near the main shipping lanes, where it could easily import long-staple foreign cotton. The growing of long-staple cotton in China from American seeds was first begun on a large scale in Shensi in the early 1930's, but it was still cheaper for Shanghai to buy its long-staple supplies from overseas. Tientsin, Hankow, and to a lesser extent Tsingtao, could, however, use this improved Shensi cotton, and by the early 1930's, although the production of long-staple cotton had spread into all the cotton-growing provinces, more of it was grown in Hopeh and Shantung than in Kiangsu.[63]

A further factor was China's recovery of tariff autonomy in 1929. Up to that time, the tariff on most imported and exported goods was fixed by successive treaties between China and the major Western powers (beginning with the supplement to the Treaty of Nanking in 1843) at 5 per cent *ad valorem*. In practice the rates had varied between 3 and 10 per cent, but the average between 1843 and 1929 had been close to 5 per cent.[64] The new tariff of 1929 promulgated by the Nationalist Government in that year and revised in 1931, 1934, and 1935 imposed duties on the import of raw cotton and cotton yarn which varied considerably but which averaged about 17 per cent *ad valorem* between 1929 and 1935.[65] While Shanghai normally drew about 20 per cent of its raw cotton from abroad, Tsingtao, Tientsin, and Hankow respectively drew 93, 95, and 98 per cent of their raw cotton supply from domestic sources by 1930.[66] The average price of raw cotton in Shanghai by 1935 was about 10 per cent higher than in these three other centers, and nearly 90 per cent of the new building in the cotton textile industry in that year was elsewhere than Shanghai, although Shanghai still contained 51 per cent of the cotton spindles in China in 1936, and although total production costs for cotton spinning were still about 10 per cent lower in Shanghai than in any other Chinese city.[67]

This may prove to have been only a temporary disadvantage, since in the face of higher duties on imported raw cotton after 1929, and currently of China's desperate attempts to become independent of foreign imports, steps have been taken to increase the production of long-staple cotton, especially in Kiangsu where Shanghai manufacturing is so heavily dependent on it. The work of the Cotton Industry Commission of the National Resources Commission during the 1930's indicates that the goal of complete self-sufficiency in all types of cotton was realizable within five or ten years, under an effective administration.[68] Recent reports from China suggest that domestic cotton production, while still inadequate to supply Shanghai's textile factories, is now again approaching a self-sufficient level.[69]

Until 1927, the silk-reeling industry had been larger, by value of output, in Hangchow and in Wusih (where it was more closely oriented to the major silk-producing areas) than in Shanghai. With the stimulus of civil war in the delta in 1926, many of these mills moved to Shanghai, where they could get cheaper coal and electric power, abundant capital, and the general commercial advantages of a large market, as well as being able to draw their raw silk from the producing areas by water transport at nearly the same cost as in Hangchow or Wusih. By 1936, however, Wusih again led Shanghai in silk-reeling, due apparently to lower labor costs in Wusih, local skill, newer and hence more efficient plants, and the drop in the Wusih price of coal brought from Shanghai by barge trains pulled by steam tugs.[70]

A major and continuing development of the 1930's was the large Japanese investment in Manchurian heavy industry, notably in the Mukden area. Following the Japanese conquest of north China in 1937–38, this development was extended to include the Peking-Tientsin area, although on a much smaller scale. While these were primarily strategic or military rather than economic investments, they laid the foundation for a new heavy manufacturing center, closely oriented to its sources of bulk raw materials, and confined to the north. In addition to the logical association with coal and iron deposits, this project was geographically an obvious one for Japan to undertake from her original Korean and Manchurian base, and it did not include Shanghai, especially after the widening of the war from 1941 on made seaborne imports of raw materials into Shanghai increasingly difficult.

Japanese war-dictated industrial investments have now however become a legacy of great value for China, and heavy manufacturing is still virtually restricted to the north. In time, a second manufacturing center of this type may develop at Shanghai, dependent on cheap transportation for the assembling of bulk raw materials and shipping of finished products, cheap electric power, skilled labor, and continued market attractions. But in the current acute capital shortage in China, which is unlikely to be alleviated soon, such a development cannot be considered imminent.

Industrially Shanghai has been an anomaly, by Western standards, since it has reached its dominant position in China in the local absence of most of the essential materials of manufacturing. This is especially striking in the case of coal, the single most important industrial material. The city's development has nevertheless proceeded rapidly once industrialization began in China (Shanghai's population doubled between 1920 and 1936) because it remained the cheapest point of assembly within China proper for the resources on which Chinese industrial structure rested. Manufactured goods which the city produced could also be marketed more cheaply than from any other location. Assembly costs and distribution costs are after all the ultimate locational considerations, and the actual presence of raw materials is important only in those terms. But Shanghai's position is a reflection of the level of the Chinese economy as a whole. As China moves from a pre-industrial economy to an industrial economy, with the accompanying expansion in transportation facilities, Shanghai may lose some of its particular advantage. By 1936 and up to the present, such a development has by no means occurred, but there are signs that it may have begun.

ELEVEN
Shanghai Today and Tomorrow

Shanghai, with the rest of China, has lived in a state of nearly unbroken war since 1937. "Normal conditions" has been almost a meaningless phrase since the first Japanese attack on the city in 1932. As of late 1952, the Nationalist blockade and accompanying United Nations embargo continue to reduce Shanghai to a virtual state of siege. For a city whose economy depended closely on free access by sea to a variety of raw materials, producer and consumers' goods, and markets, this situation cannot help but have affected its economic life in fundamental fashion. Shanghai's industrial production and commercial facilities are of the greatest importance to the Communist regime, whose success depends on its ability to raise China's living standards through increased production and easier exchange. As the greatest single producer and exchanger, Shanghai provides tools, machines, and markets for agriculture, transportation equipment, and capital and consumers' goods for the support of a huge economy where such things are otherwise notably lacking.

Since Shanghai's productivity is so vital to the new government, it is understandable that accurate information on the state of the city's economy is difficult to obtain, or difficult to deduce from the mass of propaganda-style news releases on the city in current Chinese periodicals and official statements.[1] The Communist armies occupied on May 27, 1949, a city which had suffered almost no physical destruction, either as a result of the Japanese war or during the civil war and the "battle" for Shanghai (which was in effect fought north of the Yangtze), but whose industrial plant had barely begun to recover its pre-war production levels. In particular, the flow of goods and raw materials into the city by sea was still far below minimum needs, as it had been since at least 1939, due to shipping shortages and to delayed recovery of many of the areas from which the city drew its supplies, especially in north China, where civil war had quickly succeeded international war.

The pinch which these conditions imposed on the Shanghai economy was nowhere more apparent or more important than in the case of coal. Coal normally came to the city primarily from north China (Kaiping, Fushun, Shansi, and Shantung), and the acute shortage of this essential and universal raw material slowed Shanghai's industrial recovery to a walk during the four years of Nationalist control from 1945 to 1949.* Other essential supplies were also curtailed, especially industrial machinery, liquid fuels, rubber, chemicals, semi-finished metal goods, and prime movers, all of which normally came to Shanghai for the most part from overseas and had been largely cut off during the Japanese occupation after 1941 as well. Runaway inflation, bred in part of current and forseen shortages, had a disastrous effect on the entire urban economy.

Shanghai's skilled industrial labor force, which before the war had constituted at least half of the China pool, had been dissipated through eight long war years during which many workers migrated to Free China (and to Japan and Manchuria), and technical and managerial personnel were similarly decimated. Inland routes supplying the city were choked off periodically as the civil war progressed. A major part of Communist military strategy was the destruction of railways over which the Nationalist armies could move their originally greatly superior military equipment, and the lines feeding Shanghai were repeatedly cut, both between the city and Nanking, and north of the Yangtze where the interruptions were only slightly less awkward for Shanghai. More importantly, civil unrest and actual fighting in the delta and along the Yangtze recurrently brought water transport there to a halt.

The inland routes the Communists could reopen, and this was

* The textile industry enjoyed a brief recovery in mid-1948 (after electric power production had been momentarily restored nearly to its pre-war level), based on the removal of Japanese competition, especially in the southeast Asia market (see Université Aurore, "L'état présent de l'industrie à Shanghai" [1949]. But unlike the earlier boom during and after the first world war, this was extremely short-lived, as the Communist armies closed in on the city in the months before May 1949, and increasingly stifled its vital economic relations with China as a whole.

done with dispatch soon after Shanghai had been taken. By the end of 1949, railways destroyed in the delta area during the civil war had been restored to operation, and by the end of 1950, most of the lines in China as of 1936 had been rebuilt, plus considerable new mileage. Great stress has also been put on maintaining a high level of commodity flow by water transport from the Yangtze and the delta to Shanghai. Numerous hydraulic improvements were undertaken in 1949, 1950, and 1951, including the widening, deepening, and regulating of existing waterways, the building of additional carriers of all types,* and in November 1950 the commencement of a very large five-year project for the regulation of the Huai River, designed primarily to prevent its disastrous floods, but also to facilitate navigation.[2]

But the sea routes, equally vital to the city's economic life, remain largely closed. Political capital has been made of this unfortunate situation, since it has in effect called the Communists' bluff in their repeated assertions that Shanghai was a foreign sore on the Chinese body politic and should be integrated with China rather than with its kindred economies overseas.

The new Shanghai . . . is closely linked by commerce and the interflow of goods with the rest of the country. Facing inland instead of across the sea, it is integrated politically, economically, and culturally with the nation whose needs it serves. From being a source of infection in China's economic life, Shanghai has today become a source of strength to the new China.[3]

This is cold comfort. Shanghai can be a source of strength to China only if it produces, and it cannot reach more than a part of its industrial potential while the sea routes which feed it are closed. The shortage of coal in the city remains, if one may read between the lines of official statements and news releases. Electric power is rationed; new users are discouraged, and one gathers that current users are unable to get enough to increase their production. Remembering the crucial importance of cheap and abundant electric power for all of the city's industry, as we have discussed it above

* 192 inland water craft were built in Shanghai alone in 1950, totalling 28,000 tons displacement, according to Ching-Chi Chou-Pao for January 4, 1951, p. 9.

in Chapter Ten (it constituted probably Shanghai's outstanding advantage for manufacturing), the present situation is discouraging. We may assume that the newly rebuilt railways are now carrying much larger amounts of coal from north China to Shanghai than they did before the war, but this greatly increases its price as against sea shipment, and is unlikely to have the necessary capacity. Industrial machinery, liquid fuels, rubber, chemicals, and the other goods which were imported from overseas and which are vital to Shanghai's industrial recovery are also short under the combined Nationalist blockade and United Nations embargo.

Ocean shipping using the port virtually disappeared during 1949 and most of 1950. Toward the end of 1950 it reappeared on a very small scale, and now averages perhaps two or three ships a month, all in the coasting trade. The entrances to the Yangtze have been mined by the Nationalists, and the main ship channel in the estuary has not been dredged since 1937. Sunken ships, to which floating mines still occasionally add, further block the river. Until early 1951 there was a small trade with Hong Kong, but this has now nearly disappeared with the adoption of the United Nations embargo in December 1950, and the few ships which call at Shanghai are restricted almost entirely to the trade with Tientsin, Tsingtao, and Dairen. Rates are prohibitively high, and all imports and exports through the port of Shanghai are rigidly controlled by the government. Luxury goods and most consumers' goods are excluded from the list of admissable imports. The city's busses and most of its other gasoline vehicles have been converted to run on charcoal gas. Export and import licenses can be obtained only where it is considered in the national interest, but buyers to whom exports might be sent are in many cases unreachable, as witness the consistent import surplus for Shanghai itself of 100 to 120 per cent over exports during 1951.* [4] Such conditions are crippling for a city which

---

* The Soviet bloc however seems now to be filling the gap in China's foreign trade left by the shrinking of commercial relations with the West, judging from current reports. (See Ch'en Han-seng, "The Future of China's Foreign Trade" (1952), *New China News Agency Bulletin*, September 29, 1951, *Hsin-Hua Yüeh-Pao*, October 1951, *Ching-Chi Chou-Pao*, September 27, 1951 and April 24, 1952, *Peoples' China*, August 1, 1952.) But for trade with the Soviet bloc, though it is still a new development whose permanent outlines are uncertain, Shanghai is in a relatively

not only depended heavily on seaborne supplies, but which had a large and important transit trade.

As if in a commentary on the nature of the city's food supply, food, in particular rice, has remained cheap and plentiful throughout the period of Communist control. Order was quickly restored in the delta in 1949, and the flow of low-cost food to the city was maintained despite a nearly universal food shortage or famine in the rest of China during the winter of 1949–50, and despite the Nationalist blockade, which prevented any substantial amounts of food from arriving in the city by sea. The Communist Government has apparently been able to solve, at least to a degree, the problem of local rice supply during the planting season and at festival periods, by controlling prices and arranging for large government purchases which are released on the market at stable prices whenever the situation requires. There is no suggestion that local food supplies are not entirely adequate to meet the city's demands under such a system of management. While no official figures have been released, it is unlikely that Shanghai's population is substantially less than the four millions it had reached in 1936; it may have risen closer to the five million mark, since the great influx of people after the Japanese war has not apparently been balanced by the still limited exodus.*

Nationalist bombings during the winter of 1949–50 did only minor industrial damage, and came to an end by late 1950 with the arrival of jet defense planes from the Soviet Union and the Nationalist loss of the Chusan Islands, which had been the major base for the bombings of the city. A continuing deterrent to industrial recovery however has been the still inadequate domestic production of raw cotton. Several cotton textile factories in the city were obliged to shut down entirely during 1949 and 1950 for lack of raw cotton, and while all or most of these have subsequently reopened, not enough cotton is coming in to maintain peak production.†

---

poor position, and its economy has in the past been closely geared with that of the West.

* See above, p. 21. Foreign and Chinese press reports still consistently refer to Shanghai as the fourth largest city in the world, with a population given variously as 5 or 6 million.

† *Hsin-Hua Yüeh-Pao* for November 1951, 130–131, reports that while production

Cotton production is gradually increasing, and the expectation is that within the next two or three years enough will be available domestically (mainly in the delta area) to occupy Shanghai's full textile potential, which is still the largest of any city in the country.

Much shuffling around of the industrial pattern has resulted from government regulations on the types of manufacturing which may be licensed and may obtain the necessary power and supplies. During 1950 nearly 500 "factories" closed down, through financial failure and through inability to obtain licenses because they were considered non-essential under the new regulations. Most of the casualties were presumably small-scale manufacturers operating in private houses, who were before the war engaged in a great variety of production, mostly of consumers' goods. Many of these have since reopened, but in different production lines more in keeping with the government's new policy, and for which a market is available under the current austerity program. The government has for example refused reopening licenses to tobacco manufacturers, restaurants, hotels, and funeral establishments.[5]

The problem most frequently referred to in Chinese reports on economic Shanghai since 1949 is that of keeping pace with increased rural demand and rural purchasing power. This may be designed as an advertisement of the accomplishments of the land reform program in raising rural living standards, but it is repeatedly stated that industrial production in the city runs behind the demand in the country. Industries in the city showing the greatest profits during this period have been those producing light consumers' goods for which there is a ready local market. Dyeing leads the list, since the delta peasants are now sufficiently well off, if one may take the published reports at face value, to buy colored and printed clothing made in Shanghai. Western-type medical supplies are also listed, which would indicate a revolution indeed in the *mores* and income of the Chinese peasant. One report gives as an example of increased

---

of cotton textiles for China as a whole in 1950 and in the first six months of 1951 was between 20 and 30 per cent greater than the pre-1937 peak, domestic production of raw cotton is still inadequte to meet the demands of the textile industry. For an earlier post-war report, see Shen Wen-fu, The Increase in Cotton Production, (1948).

rural purchasing power the large domestic sale of Shanghai-made thermos bottles, and others cite the increasing domestic demand for flashlights, soap, and stationery made in the city.[6] Times have changed. Among the heavier industries, cement and machinery production in Shanghai also lag behind demand,[7] as might be expected in view of the general shortage of such production over China as a whole and of the ambitious industrialization program of the Communist Government. Apparently, if these reports can be accepted, Shanghai need not be concerned for domestic markets despite the closing of its normal sea routes.

Earlier Communist talk of moving industry out of Shanghai (see above, pp. 27–8) has tended to disappear. During 1949 and early 1950 some small cotton textile factories were moved to Tientsin and Hankow, and a few other small manufacturing plants to Tientsin and Tsingtao (including a bicycle works, a printing establishment, and a furniture plant). These were minor removals, and no plans were made to move any of the larger factories or the heavier industries. Occasionally during this period there were general remarks in official speeches and news reports encouraging commercial enterprises to go out into the countryside, and encouraging Shanghai workers to help with the industrial reconstruction program in Manchuria, but more recently the prevailing attitude has been one of pride in Shanghai and enthusiasm for its own program of recovery. Criticism was natural while the Communists were on the outside looking in, but now that the new regime is in full control, and has full responsibility, it is more clearly aware of Shanghai's vital importance, and more clearly aware as well that no other location in China offers equal advantages for the kind of manufacturing which has grown up in the city and which the government is now trying desperately to maintain.

In future, a measure of Shanghai's advantage may disappear as railways bind the Chinese economy more closely together and as light and heavy industrial production continues to grow in Manchuria and north China where raw materials are close at hand. The coal and iron reserves of Shansi may also in time support a major industrial development there, as part of a thoroughly commercialized economy based on a mature railway system. Hankow and the three

Wu-Han cities may grow into another important industrial center, combining transport advantages, nearness to agricultural raw materials, and location near the population center of the China market as its purchasing power gradually rises. In time the potential hydroelectric power of the west and southeast, in combination with local mineral resources and markets, may lead to large manufacturing developments in cities like Chungking, Changsha, Amoy, and Canton. Electric power in all of the cities mentioned, however, with the possible exception of Manchuria, is a problem whose solution is neither currently nor foreseeably within reach, and Shanghai remains virtually the only city in China proper where power facilities are adequate and power costs low enough for large industrial growth.

While the long-term changes in China's overall economy which would permit such developments would probably remove much or all of Shanghai's industrial primacy, they would help to increase the city's absolute production and commercial importance as they simultaneously reduced its relative rank. When we consider that in 1936 Shanghai accounted for about half of China's modern industrial production and half of its foreign trade, it is apparent that there is ample room within the Chinese economy as a whole for many new industrial and commercial centers to develop without reducing the actual part which Shanghai would play in a more completely industrialized China.

In the long run, however, Shanghai's economic growth will depend on a restoration of free access by sea to the whole of East Asia and to the rest of the world. Its trading and commercial functions have been even more important to its growth and prosperity than its industrial development, and those functions have depended not only on its location within China but on its geographic orientation to the entire world of commerce. Shanghai may never again serve, as it has in the past, as the funnel for the penetration of China by the West and as the major seed bed of economic change in China. As China is increasingly drawn into the world economic order by the changes now in progress there, other points of entry and other breeding grounds for modernization will become increasingly prominent until the economy as a whole is unified. But economic change of the order indicated in China cannot be accomplished without the catalytic action which an already established industrial and commercial center like Shanghai can provide. In the process of the change, Shanghai would be more likely to grow than to decline.

As a trade center, its advantages would remain even in a railroad-based economy.* Its physical location midway on the China coast and at the mouth of the Yangtze River would merely be implemented by a network of rails. For China as a whole, the change from waterways to railways as a major carrier is still far in the future, not only because a change of this kind and on this scale is necessarily slow, but because China has been endowed by nature with an enviable network of waterways. Unlike the United States, China's great rivers, preeminently the Yangtze, flow from west to east, draining commercially, with their tributaries, most of the country. Complementary to this inland system is the east coast, providing a north-south water highway which connects most of the large cities. Railways will supplant these two great trunk routes only slowly, if at all, and they are unlikely ever to reduce the absolute importance of water transport in China. China might be compared in this respect with maritime western Europe and the United Kingdom, where ice-free rivers drain most of the productive heart of the area and where the surrounding sea links all of its parts. Water transport there has increased in absolute volume since the beginning of the industrial revolution despite the building of a dense railway net, and has continued to play a vital role in Europe's economy. Shanghai might be taken as the Asian counterpart of Rotterdam, a city whose commercial and industrial position has certainly not declined during the last two hundred years and which rests now as it has always done on its location at the mouth of the Rhine midway along the coast of maritime Europe.

Industrially, Shanghai's advantages are also not likely to be removed. Cheap transportation, reflected in every aspect of its eco-

---

* Since at least 1950, Hong Kong has of course pre-empted Shanghai's functions as a trade center, transshipment port, and point of contact with the West for China as a whole. However long political conditions may continue this situation, it is nevertheless an artificial one, and is not considered in this general evaluation of Shanghai's economic potential within China and within a "normal" east Asian market. Indefinitely cut off from access to sea routes as it now is, Shanghai must obviously wither, in greater or lesser degree.

nomic life, has been and will continue to be its major attraction. Cheap transportation means low power costs, costs which would remain relatively low even after hydro-electric development in China has progressed. Cheap transportation offers a variety of advantages for every industry dependent on bulk raw materials or bulk shipments of finished goods, including iron and steel manufacture, which could certainly be carried on in Shanghai as the market for it increases, in successful competition with Manchuria, north China, Japan, or India. No other Chinese location can assemble the necessary raw materials and market the finished products as cheaply as Shanghai. As inexpensive transportation attracts industries dependent on it, other industries find it advantageous to be there as well, and the manifold economies and conveniences of location in the market take on a self-perpetuating power of attraction. This is reflected again in the high and constant load factor which continues to keep power costs low. Power costs do not end with the assembling of coal or the production of a few kilowatt hours.

Whatever new industrial areas may arise elsewhere, Shanghai is likely to remain near the center of the China market as a whole, to which the Yangtze River system will continue to give it low-cost and easy access. Capital will be relatively plentiful in Shanghai as long as the city maintains its trading, commercial, and financial importance, and these functions are unlikely to be usurped in the foreseeable future. Skilled labor and technical management tend to gravitate to such centers, and to be produced by a pre-existing industrial structure. Industrially and commercially, Shanghai has much to gain and little to lose in the gradual process by which the rest of China puts into practice the economic pattern which Shanghai was the first to create.

So long-term a view may not be in the minds of current government planners in China. Shanghai is still too new a possession, and too new a responsibility. But the geographic logic of the city's economic leadership is likely to prove more powerful and more convincing than any political argument. Great cities do not arise by accident, and they are not destroyed by whim. The geographic facts which have made Shanghai will prosper it in the future once peace has been restored in East Asia.

Bibliography

Notes

Index

Bibliography

Abend, Hallet, *Treaty Ports in China* (New York, 1944).

Abor, Raoul, "Le Port de Changhai," *Revue du Pacifique* 14: 7–29 (1935).

Ahlers, J. A., "Shanghai at the War's End," *Far Eastern Survey* (Nov. 25, 1945).

Arnold, Julean, *China: A Commercial and Industrial Handbook* (Washington, 1926).

—— *China: A Commercial Handbook*, 2 vols. (Washington, 1920).

Bacon, C. A., "The Coal Supply of Shanghai," *Chinese Economic Journal* 6: 195–218 (1930).

Bain, H. F., *Ores and Industry in the Far East* (New York, 1933).

Bank of China, Research Department, *The Position of China as a Producer of Raw Materials and a Consumer of Manufactured Products* (Shanghai, 1934).

Bannister, T. W., *A History of the External Trade of China, 1834–1931* (Shanghai: Maritime Customs, Decennial Reports for 1921–1931, 1932), pp. 1–193.

Barnett, R. W., *Economic Shanghai: Hostage to Politics* (New York, 1942).

Blakiston, T. W., *Five Months on the Yangtze* (London, 1862).

Blanchard, F. S., *The Textile Industries of China* (New York, 1944).

Boston First National Bank, *China's Tea Trade* (typed MS., 1919).

Bowman, C. H., *Shanghai: Its Port, Industries, and Trade* (Shanghai, 1928).

Brandl, L. T., "Improvements in the Yangtze River Delta," *Journal of the Association of Chinese and American Engineers* 16: 12–19 (1935).

Brunhes, J. A., "La France de Changhai," *Journal de la Marine marchande* 5: 1057–68 (1923).

—— "Le Port de Changhai," *Journal de la Marine marchande* 5: 1081–93. (1923).

Buchanan, R. E., *The Shanghai Silk Market* (New York, 1929).

Buck, J. L., *Land Utilization in China*, 3 vols. (Chicago, 1937).

Bureau of Public Roads, *The Soochow-Kashing-Hangchow-Shanghai Highway* (Nanking, 1933).

Carlson, Ellsworth, *The Kailan Mines, 1878–1912*, Papers on China, III, 24–77, Mimeographed (Committee on International and Regional Studies, Harvard University, 1949).

Chang, C. C., *China's Food Problem* (Shanghai, 1931).

—— "Ko hsien nung-yeh kai-k'uang ku-chi pao-kao" (Agricultural Statistics of *hsien* in Kiangsu Province), *T'ung-chi yüeh-pao* (Statistical Monthly) 2. 7: 31–52 (1930).

Chang, Y. C., "Flour Milling in China," C. F. Remer, *Readings in Economics for China* (Shanghai, 1922), pp. 217–223.

Chao Lien-fang, "Chung-kuo tao-mi sheng-ch'an wen-t'i" (The Problem of Rice Production in China), *Chung-nung yüeh-k'an* (Monthly Review of Chinese Agriculture) 8. 11: 4–12 (1947).

Chao, T. K., "Shanghai Today and Tomorrow," *Science and Technology in China* 1: 41–46 (1948).

Chen, C. H., and Sun, Y. S., "The Electric Power Industry in China" (MS.) (Nanking: National Resources Commission, 1947).

Ch'en Han-seng, "The Future of China's Foreign Trade," *China Monthly Review*, 15–19 (July 1952).

—— *Industrial Capital and Chinese Peasants* (New York, 1939).

Chen Kung-p'o, "Self Sufficiency in Food Supply," *Chinese Economic Journal* 17: 97–110 (1935).

Ch'en Wei-ch'i, "Hsin Chung-kuo ti fang-chih kung-yeh ho fa-chan chien-tu" (New China's Textile Industry and the Outlook for its Development), *Hsin-hua yüeh-pao* (New China Monthly), 130–131 (November 1951).

Chi Ch'ao-ting, *Key Economic Areas in Chinese History* (New York, 1936).

Chiang Hsüeh-chai, "Chung-kuo shih-liang kung-ch'iu chih hsin ku-chi" (A New Estimate of the Supply and Demand of Food in China), *Kuo-chi mao-i tao pao* (Foreign Trade Journal) 8. 6: 51–67 (1936).

Chiang I-shih, "Chung-kuo tsa-liang sheng-ch'an" (Production of Various Cereals in China), *Chung-nung yüeh-k'an* (Monthly Review of Chinese Agriculture) 8. 11: 21–31 (1947).

Chiang Kai-shek, *China's Destiny and Chinese Economic Theory*, with notes and commentary by Philip Jaffe (New York, 1947).

Chiang, P. N., *Sur les Concessions de Changhai* (Nancy, 1932).

China Journal 16.5 (1932), Special Number on Shanghai.

China: Maritime Customs, *Annual Reports and Returns of Trade*, annually (Shanghai, 1864–1948).

—— *Decennial Reports on the Trade and Development of Ports Open to Foreign Trade*, Statistical Series No. 6, 1872–1881 (Shanghai, 1882); 1882–1891 (1892); 1892–1901 (1902); 1902–1911 (1912); 1912–1921 (1922); 1922–1931 (1932).

—— *Opium in China*, Special Series No. 9 (Shanghai, 1884).

—— *Reports on Trade at the Ports in China Open to Foreign Trade, 1859–1870* (Shanghai, 1872).

—— *Silk*, Special Series No. 3 (Shanghai, 1881).

—— *Tea*, Special Series No. 11 (Shanghai, 1889).

—— *The Trade of Shanghai* 1878–1905 (Shanghai, 1906).

—— *Trade Statistics of the Treaty Ports, 1863–1872* (Shanghai, 1873).

China Press, Supplement, *Greater Shanghai* (October 10, 1948).

—— *Shanghai Today* (August 10, 1946).

China Weekly Review, Greater Shanghai Number (December 4, 1926).

The China Yearbook, ed. Woodhead, irregularly (Shanghai and Tientsin, 1912–1939).

Chinese Repository 18: 8–22 (1849) unsigned translation of the 1812 edition of *Chia-ching Shang-hai-hsien chih* (Official Gazeteer of Shanghai).

The Chinese Yearbook (Shanghai, 1936).

Chou Chih-hua, *Chung-kuo chung-yao shang-p'in* (Important Commercial Commodities of China) (Shanghai, 1931).

Ch'ou-pan i-wu shih-mo (Complete Account of Our Management of Barbarian Affairs), 80 *chüan* (volumes) covering the period 1836–1850 (reproduced and printed, Peking, 1930).

Chu Chi-hua, *China's Postal and Other Communications* (London, 1937).

Chu, T. H., *The Tea Trade of Central China* (Shanghai, 1936).

Chung Jui-chi, "The Cigarette Industry in China," *Chinese Economic Journal* 16: 629–39 (1935).

Chung-kuo ching-chi nien-chien (Chinese Economic Yearbook), 2 vols. (Shanghai, 1934).

Chung-kuo kung-yeh chien: Kiang-su (China Industrial Handbooks: Kiangsu) (Nanking, 1934).

Clark, Grover, *Economic Rivalries in China* (New Haven, 1932).

Collis, Maurice, *Foreign Mud* (New York, 1947).

Cooley, C. H., "The Theory of Transportation," *Publications of the American Economic Association* IX, 1–148 (1894).

Cordier, H. A., *Les Origines des Etablissements Français à Changhai* (Paris, 1896).

Cressey, G. B., *China's Geographic Foundations* (New York, 1934).

—— "The Fenghsien Landscape," *Geogr. Rev.* 26: 396–413 (1936).

—— "The Geology of Shanghai," *China Journal* 8: 334–45; 9: 89–98 (1928).

Crow, Carl, *Foreign Devils in the Flowery Kingdom* (New York, 1940).

—— *Four Hundred Million Customers* (New York, 1937).

Darwent, C. E., *Shanghai: A Handbook* (Shanghai, 1920).

Davis, S. G., *Hong Kong in its Geographic Setting* (London, 1949).

Dechevrens, M. F., "The Climate of Shanghai," *Journal of the North China Branch of the Royal Asiatic Society* 12: 231–46 (1881).

Descourtils, L., *La Concession Française de Changhai* (Paris, 1934).

Dyce, C. R., *The Model Settlement* (Shanghai, 1906).

Fairbank, J. K., "The Provisional System at Shanghai in 1853–54," *Chinese Social and Political Science Review* 18: 455–504 (1935); 19: 469–514 (1936); 20: 42–100 (1936).

Far Eastern Review 33.1 (January 1937), "The Future of Far Eastern Ports" (unsigned article).

—— 26.6 (1930), Greater Shanghai Number.

Fauvel, A. T., "Le Port de Changhai," *Bull. de la Soc. geogr. commerciale* 32: 569–93 (1910).

Feetham, R. C., *Report to the Shanghai Municipal Council*, 3 vols. (Shanghai, 1931).

Fei Hsiao-t'ung, *Peasant Life in China* (London, 1939).

Feng Hu-fa, *Chung-kuo nung-ts'un ching-chi tzu-liao* (Source Materials on China's Agricultural Economics) (Shanghai, 1935).

Fong Hsien-ting, *The Cotton Industry and Trade in China*, 2 vols. (Tientsin, 1932).

—— *Industrial Capital in China* (Tientsin, 1936).

—— *Industrial Organization in China* (Tientsin, 1937).

—— *Toward Economic Control in China* (Shanghai, 1936).

Fortune, Robert, *A Journey to the Tea Countries of China and India*, 2 vols. (London, 1852).

—— *Three Years' Wanderings in the Northern Provinces of China* (London, 1846).

—— "Travels in Kiangsu," *Chinese Repository* 16: 569–76 (1851).

Gamewell, M. N., *Shanghai, Gateway to China* (New York, 1916).

Gould, Randall, "Shanghai During the Takeover, 1949," *Annals of the American Academy of Political and Social Science* 277: 182–92 (1951).

Greenberg, Michael, *British Trade and the Opening of China, 1800–42* (Cambridge, 1951).

Gull, E. M., *British Economic Interests in the Far East* (London, 1943).

Hall, W. H., *The Nemesis in China* (London, 1848).

Hatch, Margaret, "The Port of Tientsin," *Geogr. Rev.* 25: 367–81 (1935).

Hauser, E. M., *Shanghai, City for Sale* (New York, 1940).

Haushofer, Karl, "Schanghai: die Wehrgeographische Problematik der Grosstadt im Kriegsgetriebe," *Zeitschrift für Geopolitik* 9: 250–64 (1932).

Havret, Henri, *L'ile de Tsong Ming* (Shanghai, 1901).

Heidenstam, A. V., "The Great Yangzte Bar," *Transactions of the American Society of Civil Engineers* 93: 102–126 (1929).

—— "The Growth of the Yangtze Delta," *Journal of the North China Branch of the Royal Asiatic Society* 53: 21–36 (1922).

Her Majesty's Foreign Office, *Commercial Reports from H. M. Consuls in China* (London, 1863, 1864, 1865, 1866, 1867, and 1870).

Herrmann, Albert, *Atlas of China* (London, 1935).

Hinder, E. M., *Life and Labour in Shanghai* (New York, 1944).

—— *Social and Industrial Problems of Shanghai* (New York, 1942).

Hinton, Harold, *The Grain Tribute System of China, 1845–1911: An Aspect of the Decline of the Ch'ing Dynasty* (PhD Thesis, Harvard University, 1950). A later and shorter version of this study appeared as "The Grain Tribute System of the Ch'ing Dynasty" in *Far Eastern Quarterly*, 339–354 (May 1952).

Hommel, R. P., *China at Work* (New York, 1937).

Hsia, C. L., *The Status of Shanghai* (Shanghai, 1929).

Hsieh, C. Y., *Iron Deposits of the Lower Yangtze* (Nanking: National Geologic Survey of China, Series A, No. 13, 1935).

Hsü Shih-yü, "Kiang-su sheng chih kung-lu yün-sung (Highway Transport in Kiangsu), *Kuo-min ching-chi chien-shih* (National Economic Reconstruction) 1: 77–89 (1936).

—— "Kiang-su sheng chih shui yün-sung" (Water Transport in Kiangsu), *Kuo-min ching-chi chien-shih* (National Economic Reconstruction) 2: 53–70 (1937).

—— "Kiang-su sheng chih t'ieh-lu yün-sung" (Railway Transport in Kiangsu), *Kuo-min ching-chi chien-shih* (National Economic Reconstruction) 1: 34–48 (1936).

Huang, K. C., "Factors Determining the Choice of a Site for the Port of Shanghai," *Proceedings of the Fourth Pacific Science Conference* (Java, 1929), vol. 2, pp. 351–62.

Huang Yuan-hu, "Agricultural Regions of Kiangsu," *Geogr. Rev.* 37: 609–17 (1947).

—— "Kiang-su sheng chih nung-ch'an ch'u-yü" (Agricultural Regions of Kiangsu), *Ti-li-hsüeh pao* (Journal of the Geographical Society of China) 1.1 (1934), no pagination.

Hubbard, G. E., *Eastern Industrialization and Its Effect on the West* (Oxford, 1935).

Hunter, W. C., *The Fan Kwae at Canton Before Treaty Days* (London, 1882).

Jefferson, Mark, "The Law of the Primate City," *Geogr. Rev.* 29: 226–32 (1939).

Johnstone, W. C., *The Shanghai Problem* (London, 1937).

Jones, F. C., *Shanghai and Tientsin* (New York, 1940).

Kann, Edmund, *Currency in China* (Shanghai, 1927).

Keeton, G. W., *The Development of Extraterritoriality in China*, 2 vols. (London, 1928).

Kiang-su sheng-chien (Kiangsu Provincial Handbook), Chao Ju-heng ed., 2 vols. (Shanghai, 1935).

King, F. H., *Farmers of Forty Centuries* (New York, 1928).

Ko Siang-fang, *L'organisation de la Production, Crédit, et Echange en Chine* (Lyons, 1929).

Kotenev, A. L., *Shanghai, Its Mixed Court and Council* (Shanghai, 1925).

—— *Shanghai, Its Municipality and the Chinese* (Shanghai, 1927).

Koung Hsien-ming, *Travailleurs Chinois* (Louvain, 1927).

Ku Ling, "New Shanghai," *People's China* 4: 21–23 (1951).

Kuo Ming-hsüeh, "Chung-kuo nung-yeh tzu-yüan" (Chinese Agricultural Resources), *Chung-nung yüeh-k'an* (Monthly Review of Chinese Agriculture) 9.2: 1–9 (1948).

Labonne, Roger, "Shanghai," *Revue de Paris*, 144–178 (March 1, 1936).

Lai Kwok-ko, *Etudes sur la Marche du Change de Changhai* (Lyons, 1935).

Lamson, H. D., *The American Community in Shanghai* (unpublished doctoral thesis, Harvard University, 1935).

Lang, A. G., *Shanghai Considered Socially* (Shanghai, 1875).

Lanning, George, and Couling, Samuel, *A History of Shanghai* (Shanghai, 1923).

Lee, B. Y., "Shanghai, World's Largest Jade Manufacturing Centre," *Chinese Economic Journal* 6: 677–84 (1930).

Li Ping-jui, *Modern Canton* (Shanghai, 1936).

Lillico, Stuart, "Food for Shanghai," *China Journal* 22: 328–33 (1935).

———— "Keeping Shanghai Warm," *China Journal* 23: 222–28 (1935).

Lin, K. C., "Shanghai's New Fish Market," *Chinese Economic Journal* 16: 599–615 (1934).

Lin Wei-ying, *China and Foreign Capital* (Chungking, 1945).

Lindsay, H. H., and Gützlaff, Karl, *Report of Proceedings on a Voyage to the Northern Ports of China, Extracted from Papers, Printed by order of the House of Commons* (London, 1834).

Little, Archibald, *Through the Yangtze Gorges* (London, 1888).

Liu Nan-ming, "L'importation du Riz en Chine," *Annales de Geographie* 16: 199–205 (1936).

Liu Ta-chün, *China's Cotton Industry* (Shanghai, 1928).

———— *China's Industry and Finance* (Peking, 1927).

———— *The Growth and Industrialization of Shanghai* (Shanghai, 1936) A Chinese version of this work was published at Changsha in 1940.

———— *The Silk Industry of China* (Shanghai, 1941).

———— *Shang-hai kung-yeh-hua yen-chiu* (Studies in Shanghai's Industrialization) (Shanghai, 1934).

Lo Chih-ju, *T'ung-chi-piao chung chih Shang-hai* (Shanghai Statistics) (Nanking, 1932).

Macfarlane, W. H., *Sketches in the Foreign Settlement and Native City of Shanghai* (Shanghai, 1881).

Macllelan, J. W., *The Story of Shanghai* (Shanghai, 1889).

Matheson, A. M., "The Geology of Shanghai," *Far Eastern Review* 29: 440–48 (1933).

Maybon, C. B., *Histoire de la Concession Française de Changhai* (Paris, 1929).

Medhurst, W. H., "A General Description of Shanghae and Environs, Extracted from Native Authors," *Chinese Miscellany* 4: 3–17 (1850).

———— *A Glance at the Interior of China Obtained During a Journey Through the Silk and Green Tea Districts Taken in 1845* (Shanghai, 1849).

———— "Reminiscences of Shanghae's Opening to Foreign Trade," *Chinese and Japanese Repository* 12: 14–23 (1864).

Miller, G. E., *Shanghai, the Paradise of Adventurers* (New York, 1937).

Ministry of Communications, *Statistics of the Chinese National Railways*, published annually (Nanking, 1917–1936).

Ministry of Industry, *Ch'üan-kuo shih-yeh tiao-ch'a pao-kao chih i: Kiang-su sheng* (National Industrial Investigation Reports: Kiangsu) (Nanking, 1933).

Montalto, J. C., *Historic Shanghai* (Shanghai, 1909).

Moser, C. K., *The Cotton Textile Industries of Far Eastern Countries* (Boston, 1932).

Morse, H. B., *The International Relations of the Chinese Empire*, 3 Vols. (New York, 1918).

—— *The Trade and Administration of China*, 3rd revised edition (London, 1921).

Oberhummer, Eugene, "Schanghai," *Mitteilungen der geographische Gesellschaft im Wien* 45: 5–27 (1932).

Orchard, J. E., "Shanghai," *Geogr. Rev.* 26: 1–31 (1936).

Otto, Friedrich, "Correlation of Harvests with Imports of Cereals Into China," *Chinese Economic Journal* 15: 388–99 (1934).

Owen, D. E., *British Opium Policy in China and India* (New Haven, 1934).

Parker, A. P., "A History of Old Shanghai Town," *Journal of the North China Branch of the Royal Asiatic Society* 47: 87–112 (1916).

Pearse, A. D., *The Cotton Industry of China and Japan* (Manchester, 1929).

Pelcovits, N. A., *Old China Hands and the Foreign Office* (New York, 1948).

Peng Hsin-wei, *Shanghai Money Market* (New York, 1946).

Playfair, G. M. H., "The Grain Transport System of China," *The China Review*, III. 6: 354–364 (May–June 1875).

Pott, F. L., *A Short History of Shanghai* (Shanghai, 1928).

Powell, J. B., *My Twenty-five Years in China* (New York, 1945).

Powell, S. J., *A Deep-water Harbour for Shanghai* (Shanghai, 1915).

Pratt, Sir J. T., *China and Britain* (London: Collins, c. 1944 [no date given]).

Ratepayers' Association, *Land Regulations of 1845, 1848, and 1854* (Shanghai, 1855).

Read, T. T., "China's Iron Industry," *Geogr. Rev.* 33: 42–55 (1943).

Remer, C. F., *Foreign Investments in China* (New York, 1933).

—— *The Foreign Trade of China* (Shanghai, 1926).

—— *Readings in Economics for China* (Shanghai, 1922).

—— *A Study of Chinese Boycotts* (Baltimore, 1934).

Richard, Louis, *A Comprehensive Geography of China* (Shanghai, 1908).

Richtofen, Baron von, *Letters to the Committee of the Shanghai Chamber of Commerce* (Shanghai: North China Herald Offices, 1871).

Robertson, D. B., "Cotton in China," *Journal of the North China Branch of the Royal Asiatic Society* 1: 302–308 (1859).

Sau Ug-yee, *Le Port de Changhai* (Toulouse, 1935).

Schmidt, C. E., "Extracts from the History of Shanghai," *Journal of the North China Branch of the Royal Asiatic Society* 16: 234–48 (1874).

The Shanghae Almanac for 1852 to 1857 (Shanghai: North China Herald Offices, 1858).

Shanghai British Chamber of Commerce, *Minutes* (Shanghai, 1861).

Shanghai Bureau of Social Affairs, *Shang-hai chih nung-yeh* (Agriculture in Shanghai) (Shanghai, 1933).

—— *Shang-hai kung-jen sheng-huo ch'eng-tu ti i-ko yen-chiu* (A Study of the Standard of Living of Shanghai Workers) (Shanghai, 1934).

—— *Shang-hai shih chi-chih kung-yeh* (Machine Industry of Shanghai) (Shanghai, 1933).

—— *Shang-hai shih-liang wen-t'i* (Food Problems in Shanghai) (Shanghai, 1931).

Shang-hai Chih-nan (Guide to Shanghai) (Shanghai, 1926).

Shanghai Civic Association, *Shanghai Statistics* (Chinese and English) (Nanking, 1934).

Shanghai General Chamber of Commerce, *Minutes* (Shanghai, 1865).

—— *Report of Delegates on the Trade of the Upper Yangtze* (Shanghai, 1869).

Shanghai International Testing House, *The Silk Industry of Central China* (Shanghai, 1925).

Shanghai Mercury, *Shanghai, the Model Settlement* (Shanghai, 1893).

Shanghai Municipal Council, *Annual Reports* (since 1880).

Shang-hai shang-wu kung-hui (Shanghai Chamber of Commerce), *Shang-hai chih yen-chiu tz-liao* (Shanghai Research Materials) (1936).

Shang-hai shih nien-chien (Shanghai Yearbook), 1 vol. (1935) and 2 vols. (1936), Shang-hai t'ung chih-kuan (Gazeteer Office of the City of Shanghai).

Shen Tsung-han (with Mei Chieh-fang), "Chung-kuo liang-shih wen-t'i yü mai-liang ch'an hsiao" (Chinese Food Problems and the Production and Marketing of Wheat), *Chung-nung yüeh-k'an* (Monthly Review of Chinese Agriculture) 8. 11: 13–20 (1947).

—— *The Agricultural Resources of China* (Cornell University Press, 1951).

Shen Wen-fu, "Ching-chi fu tiao-sheng chung chih yüan-mien tseng-ch'an" (The Increase in Cotton Production During Economic Maladjustments), *Chung-nung yüeh-k'an* (Monthly Review of Chinese Agriculture) 9. 3: 9–15 (1948).

Shih Kuo-heng, and Levy, Marion, *The Rise of the Modern Chinese Business Class* (New York, 1949).

Sketcherly, S. B., *The Future of the Port of Shanghai* (Shanghai, 1894).

Smith, H. C., "Shanghai and its Hinterland," *Journal of Geography* 38: 173–80 (1939).

Sowerby, A. C., "Houseboating in Kiangsu and Chekiang," *China Journal* 12: 196–201 (1930).

Spencer, J. E., "Junks of the Yangtze," *Asia* 28: 466–70 (1938).

—— "Trade and Transshipment in the Yangtze Valley," *Geogr. Rev.* 28: 112–23 (1938).

Sun, L. T., "Kiang-ning hsien chi ch'i fu-hsin t'u-jang chien-pao" (Soil survey of Kiangning hsien, Kiangsu), *Ti-li-hsüeh pao* (Journal of the Geographical Society of China) 3. 1 (1936), no pagination.

Tamagna, F. M., *Banking and Finance in China* (New York, 1942).

T'ang Chen-shu, "River Navigation," *National Reconstruction Journal* 3: 24–37 (1945).

T'ang Chi-yu, *An Economic Study of Chinese Agriculture* (PhD Thesis, Cornell University, 1924).

Tao, L. K., and Lin, S. H., *Industry and Labour in China* (Shanghai, 1931).

Thomas, J. A., *A Pioneer Tobacco Merchant in the Orient* (Durham, N. C., 1928).

Thorp, James, *The Geography of the Soils of China* (Peking, 1939).

Ting, Leonard, "The Coal Industry in China," *Nankai Social and Economic Quarterly* 10: 32–75, 193–277 (1937).

—— "Recent Developments in China's Cotton Industry," *Nankai Social and Economic Quarterly* 9: 398–445 (1936).

Ting Wen-chiang and Wong Wen-hao (eds.), *Chung-hua min-kuo hsin ti-t'u* (New Atlas of the Republic of China) (Shanghai, 1934).

Trewartha, Glen, "Ratio Maps of China's Farms and Crops," *Geogr. Rev.* 28: 102–112 (1938).

Ts'ai Ch'ien and Cheng Yu-k'uei, *Chung-kuo ko-t'ung-sheng k'ou-an tui ko-kuo chin-ch'u k'ou mao-i t'ung-chi, 1919, 1927–31* (Statistics of the Foreign Trade of Chinese Ports with various Foreign Countries, 1919, 1927–31) (Shanghai, 1936).

Tsai Kung-wei, "Shanghai's Foreign Trade," *Chinese Economic Journal*, 9: 963–81 (1931).

Tsao, E. A., "Chinese Rice Merchants in Indo-China," *Chinese Economic Journal*, 11: 450–63 (1932).

Tseng T'ung-ch'un, *Chung-kuo ssu-yeh* (The Chinese Silk Industry), (Shanghai, 1933).

Tsha, Y. T., "Wage Rates in Shanghai," *Nankai Social and Economic Quarterly* 8: 459–510 (1935).

U. S. Department of Agriculture, *The Foreign Wheat Trade of Shanghai* (Washington: Bureau of Agricultural Research, 1928).

Université Aurore, "L'état présent de l'industrie à Shanghai (début de 1949)," translation of a report published in *Kung-yeh wen-t'i ts'ung-k'an* (February 1949), printed in *Bulletin de l'université de l'Aurore*, 298–315 (April 1949).

Wade, F. W., *Boat and Gun* (Shanghai, 1886).

Wang Chung-chi, *Navigation du Yang Tseu* (Paris, 1932).

—— "Wu-hsi chih tou-shih ti-li" (Comprehensive Geography of Wusih), *Ti-li-hsüeh pao* (Journal of the Geographical Society of China) 2. 3 (1935), no pagination.

Wang Kung-p'ing, *Controlling Factors in the Future Development of the Chinese Coal Industry* (New York, 1947).

Wang P'ei-hsün, "Io-kuo liang-shih chin-ch'u-k'ou shu-liang yü ti-yü fen-pu" (The Volume of China's Food Imports and Exports and Their Regional

Distribution), *Chung-nung yüeh-k'an* (Monthly Review of Chinese Agriculture) 8. 11:73–102 (1947).

Ware, E. M., *Business and Politics in the Far East* (New Haven, 1932).

Wetmore, W. S., *Recollections of Life in the Far East* (London, 1887).

Whangpoo Conservancy Board, *The Port of Shanghai* (Shanghai: General Series No. 8, 1932).

Wong, J. G., "The Port of Tsingtao and Its Trade," *Far Eastern Review* 21: 734–38 (1925).

Worcester, C. R., *Junks and Sampans of the Yangtze* (Shanghai, 1947). Vol. II appeared in 1949.

Wright, S. F., *China's Struggle for Tariff Autonomy, 1843–1938* (Shanghai, 1938).

—— *Hart and the Chinese Customs* (Belfast, 1950).

—— *Timber Rafts on the Yangtze* (Shanghai, 1918).

Wu Yung-ming, "Kiang-su chih mi-ch'an" (Rice Production in Kiangsu), *Kuo-min ching-chi chien-shih* (National Economic Reconstruction) 2: 101–123 (1937).

Yang Chi-ch'eng, "Sung-chiang mi-shih tiao-ch'a" (The Rice Market at Sungchiang), *Shih-hui ching-chi yüeh-pao* (Social and Economic Monthly) 3: 21–37 (1936).

Yang Teh-hui, "Shang-hai chih ch'i-ch'uan yü-yeh" (Steamboat Fishing Industry of Shanghai), *Shang-yeh yüeh-pao* (National Journal of Commerce) 15: 43–57 (1935).

Yen Chung-p'ing, *Chung-kuo mien-yeh chih fa-chan* (The Development of China's Cotton Industry) (Chungking, 1943).

Yu Hsüeh-hsi, "Io-kuo yü ts'ao chih ti-li fen-pu" (Geographical Distribution of Tobacco Production in China), *Chung-nung yüeh-k'an* (Monthly Review of Chinese Agriculture) 9. 2: 20–23 (1948).

Yung, Bartlett, "The Water Supply of Greater Shanghai," *Journal of the Association of Chinese and American Engineers* 11: 31–37 (1930).

Notes

■

CHAPTER ONE. INTRODUCTORY

1. R. C. Feetham, *Report to the Shanghai Municipal Council* (1931), I, p. 306.
2. *Shanghai Mercury* (1893), p. 59.
3. *Ibid.*, p. 95.
4. *Ibid.*, p. 30.
5. *Ibid.*, p. 30.
6. *Shun Pao* (December 3, 1934).
7. F. L. Pott, *A Short History of Shanghai* (1928), p. 181.
8. E. M. Hauser, *Shanghai, City for Sale* (1940), p. 85.
9. J. W. Maclellan, *The Story of Shanghai* (1889), p. 56. J. C. Montalto, *Historic Shanghai* (1909), p. 166.
10. *Shanghai Mercury* (1893) p. 19.
11. *Ibid.*, p. 23.
12. *North China Herald* (August 12, 1937).
13. Robert Fortune, *Three Years' Wanderings in the Northern Provinces of China* (1846), p. 196.
14. Shanghai Municipal Council, Annual Report for 1939, p. 175.
15. Feetham, *Report*, II, 55.

CHAPTER TWO. POLITICS AND POPULATION

1. For a detailed account of this complex problem, see Hallet Abend, *Treaty Ports in China* (1944); P. N. Chiang, *Sur les Concessions de Changhai* (1932); Feetham, *Report*; E. M. Hinder, *Social and Industrial Problems of Shanghai* (1942); C. L. Hsia, *The Status of Shanghai* (1929); W. C. Johnstone, *The Shanghai Problem* (1937); and A. L. Kotenev, *Shanghai: Its Mixed Court and Council* (1925) and *Shanghai, Its Municipality and the Chinese* (1927).
2. *The Nation* (November 19, 1949).
3. Figures from Shanghai Municipal Council, Annual Report for 1936, p. 24.
4. For a discussion of this problem, see N. A. Pelcovits, *Old China Hands and the Foreign Office* (1948).
5. Chiang Kai-shek, *China's Destiny and Chinese Economic Theory* (1947), pp. 85–87.
6. *China Digest*, August 10, 1949, p. 10.
7. Statement cited in the *China Digest* for September 21, 1949, p. 9.

CHAPTER THREE. SITE

1. A. V. Heidenstam, "The Growth of the Yangtze Delta" (1922), p. 22.
2. *Ibid.*, pp. 22–26; G. B. Cressey, "The Geology of Shanghai" (1928), p. 341.
3. Henri Havret, *L'ile de Tsong Ming* (1901), *passim*.
4. Cressey, "The Geology of Shanghai," pp. 338, 340.
5. Maclellan, *The Story of Shanghai*, p. 46.

6. S. J. Powell, *A Deep-water Harbour for Shanghai* (1915), p. 23.

7. It is described in H. H. Lindsay, *Report of Proceedings* (1833), p. 74.

8. See A. G. Lang, *Shanghai Considered Socially* (1875), p. 23.

9. George Lanning, *A History of Shanghai* (1923), p. 134.

10. See discussion of this question in *Shanghai Mercury* (1893), p. 78.

11. See Pott, *A Short History, passim.*; C. E. Darwent, *Shanghai: A. Handbook* (1920), p. 64.

12. For factual reference on this discussion of Shanghai's water supply, see Darwent, *Shanghai*, pp. 64, 127, 181; Shanghai Civic Association (1934): *Shang-hai shih nien-chien* (1936); Bartlett Yung, "The Water Supply of Greater Shanghai" (1930).

13. Montalto, *Historic Shanghai*, prints on p. 21, an old Chinese map showing Shanghai and the two streams in about the sixth or seventh century A.D.

14. Montalto, p. 28; Lang, *Shanghai*, p. 18.

15. Whangpoo Conservancy Board (1932), pp. 113–114.

16. *Ibid.*, pp. 114, 119.

17. See statement by Robert Dollar in the *North China Daily News* for January 12, 1931.

18. See *China Press* (1948), pp. 23–29.

19. Figures from *China Press* (1948), p. 23.

20. See *Far Eastern Review* (1937), *passim*.

CHAPTER FOUR. LOCATION

1. Edward Gibbon, *The Decline and Fall of the Roman Empire* (London, 1783), chap. lxxi.

2. See Chi Ch'ao-ting, *Key Economic Areas in Chinese History* (1936).

3. Cressey, *China's Geographic Foundations* (1934), p. 85; Chu Chi-hua, *China's Postal and Other Communications* (1937), p. 128; Hsü Shih-yü, Water Transport in Kiangsu (1937), p. 55.

4. Fortune, *Three Years' Wanderings*, p. 57.

5. Yeh Chou, "Hsinkang — China's New Northern Port," *People's China*, pp. 26–28 (December 1, 1951).

6. Estimates, except for the Shanghai figure, are compiled from Cressey, *China's Geographic Foundations*; Julean Arnold, *China: A Commercial and Industrial Handbook*; China: Maritime Customs, Decennial Reports for 1922–1931. For a discussion of the "primate city," see Mark Jefferson, "The Law of the Primate City" (1939). According to his definition, Shanghai is a double primate city, since it is larger than the second and third cities combined.

CHAPTER FIVE. THE OPENING OF THE CITY

1. Quoted in T. W. Bannister, *A History of the External Trade of China, 1834–1931* (1932), p. 39.

2. For a contemporary account of the Cohong and the Canton system, see W. C. Hunter, *The Fan Kwae at Canton Before Treaty Days* (1882); for a highly readable (though historically unreliable) recent account, see Maurice Collis, *Foreign Mud* (1947).

3. Lindsay, *Report*.

4. A weekly average of 550 ships averaging 158 tons entered the port of London from 1840 to 1842. Figures for London quoted in J. E. Orchard, "Shanghai" (1936), p. 6, from Tables of the Revenue, Population, Commerce, etc., of the United Kingdom and its Dependencies (1840–1842).

5. Lindsay, p. 85.

6. See Bannister, *External Trade*, p. 3; Michael Greenberg, *British Trade and the Opening of China* (1951), p. 1.

7. Lindsay, p. 87.

8. Text of the treaty from H. B. Morse, *The International Relation of the Chinese Empire* (1918).

9. *Loc. cit.*

10. For factual reference on the origins and history of the foreign settlements, see Chiang, *Sur les Concessions*; Lanning, *History of Shanghai*; C. B. Maybon, *Histoire de la Concession Française de Changhai* (1929); Ratepayers' Association (1855).

11. Bannister, pp. 86–88.

12. Montalto, pp. 35–36.

13. Report of Mr. Robert Thom to Sir Henry Pottinger, dated 1845, cited in Lanning, p. 400.

14. Morse, *International Relations*, I, 357.

15. Bannister, pp. 74, 103.

16. *Shanghai Mercury* (1893), p. 21.

17. Figures compiled from China: Maritime Customs, Annual Reports and Returns of Trade.

18. Fortune, *A Journey to the Tea Countries of China* (1852), I, 97–98.

19. *Chinese Repository* (1849), *passim*.

20. See C. R. Dyce, *The Model Settlement* (1906), for one of many contemporary accounts of foreign Shanghai in the 1860's and 1870's.

21. Dyce, pp. 68–79.

22. *Ibid.*, p. 99.

23. *Ibid.*, p. 202.

24. For contemporary accounts of this life, see Dyce; F. W. Wade, *Boat and Gun* (1886); W. S. Wetmore, *Recollections of Life in the Far East* (1887).

25. W. H. Medhurst, *A Glance at the Interior of China* (1849), p. 24.

26. Quoted in Pott, p. 100.

27. S. B. Sketcherly, *The Future of the Port of Shanghai* (1894), pp. 47, 68.

28. Sau Ug-yee, *Le Port de Changhai* (1935), p. 84.

29. *Shanghai Mercury* (1893), p. 36.

30. *North China Herald* (April 24, 1875), pp. 388–389.

31. Dyce, p. 53; Sketcherly, *The Future of the Port*, pp. 46–49.

32. *Shanghai Mercury* (1893), p. 95.

CHAPTER SIX. THE POLITICAL FACTOR

1. Feetham, I, 5.

2. *Ibid.*, p. 261.

3. *Ibid.*, p. 279.

4. *Ibid.*, pp. 279–80.

5. Figures on the German trade at Shanghai from China: Maritime Customs, Annual Reports and Returns of Trade, 1913–1930.

6. Feetham, I, 312–315.
7. *Ibid.*, II, 140.
8. *China Weekly Review* (December 4, 1926), p. 15.

CHAPTER SEVEN. TRANSPORT ROUTES AND TRADE
IN THE HINTERLAND

1. Ministry of Communications (1930–1936); *Statistics of Railways in the United States,* published annually by the United States Government Printing Office, Washington.
2. Ministry of Communications (1936).
3. Bureau of Public Roads (1933), p. 14.
4. See Hsu Shih-yü, Highway Transport in Kiangsu (1936). No figures are available to show the volume of highway transport in this area.
5. Shanghai Municipal Council, Annual Report for 1920, p. 159.
6. Shanghai General Chamber of Commerce (1869), p. 34, quotes these figures, which agree in general with the writer's observations.
7. Shanghai General Chamber of Commerce (1869), pp. 38–39.
8. Consular Report of April 11, 1850, quoted in Shanghai General Chamber of Commerce (1869), p. 47.
9. H. M. Foreign Office, Commercial Report of the Consul at Shanghai (1864).
10. H. M. Foreign Office (1863, 1864, 1865, 1866, and 1867).
11. Shanghai General Chamber of Commerce (1869), *passim.*
12. China: Maritime Customs, Special Series #9 (1884), *passim.*
13. H. M. Foreign Office, Commercial Report of the Consul at Shanghai (1864).
14. China: Maritime Customs (1884).
15. Dyce, p. 56.
16. Baron von Richtofen, *Letters to the Committee of the Shanghai Chamber of Commerce* (1871).
17. Fortune, *A Journey to the Tea Countries,* I, p. 228.
18. Bannister, p. 94. For an account of the Chinese side of these events, see *Ch'ou-pan i-wu shih-mo* (1930), chüan LXVII, 40–45; LXVIII, 13–31.
19. Richtofen, *Letters to the Committee,* p. 12.
20. T. H. Chu, *The Tea Trade of Central China* (1936), p. 12.
21. For a detailed description of the leading tea areas of central China, see Chu, *The Tea Trade.*
22. T. H. Chu; H. M. Foreign Office, Commercial Reports of the Consul at Hankow (1863, 1864, 1865).
23. H. M. Foreign Office, Commercial Report of the Consul at Shanghai (1867).
24. Richtofen, p. 13.
25. Medhurst, *A Glance,* pp. 42, 176 ff.
26. Fortune, I, 223 ff. See also Richtofen, p. 8, on this point.
27. H. M. Foreign Office, Commercial Report of the Consul at Shanghai (1867).
28. Bannister, p. 27; H. M. Foreign Office, Commercial Report of the Consul at Shanghai (1864).
29. These figures are estimates only, compiled from China: Maritime Customs, Special Series #13 (1881), and Shanghai International Testing House (1925).
30. Liu Ta-chün, *The Silk Industry of China* (1941).
31. Morse, I, 358–59.

32. Bannister, p. 26.

33. H. M. Foreign Office, Commercial Report of the Consul at Shanghai (1864); China: Maritime Customs, Annual Reports and Returns of Trade (1930).

34. Shanghai International Testing House (1925), p. 36.

35. China: Maritime Customs, Annual Reports and Returns of Trade.

36. China: Maritime Customs, Annual Trade Reports (Shanghai, 1925–1935). The figures are not broken down further, and it is therefore not possible to distinguish between areas served by sea and by river transport.

37. *Finance and Commerce* (December 1926; January, September 1927).

38. *Finance and Commerce* (December 15, 1937; January 25, 1939).

CHAPTER EIGHT. THE TRADE OF THE PORT

1. For more detailed accounts of the history of Shanghai's foreign trade, see the Decennial Reports of the Maritime Customs (a valuable but so far little-used source); China: Maritime Customs (1906); C. H. Bowman, *Shanghai: Its Port, Industries, and Trade* (1928); Sau Ug-yee, *Changhai.*

2. *North China Herald* (June 2, 1869).

3. For a discussion of the causes of the relative decline on the world market of Chinese tea and silk, see China: Maritime Customs (1889); T. H. Chu; Liu Ta-chün, *The Silk Industry.*

4. See Fortune, II.

5. Bannister, pp. 140 ff.

6. *Ibid.*, pp. 22, 144.

7. China: Maritime Customs, Annual Reports and Returns of Trade; unsigned articles in the *Chinese Economic Journal* on "T'ung Oil and Its Trade Development in China," 19:109–23 (1936), and "The Szechuan Bristle Trade," 14: 381–90 (1934).

8. For an account of the origins of the Imperial Maritime Customs, see J. K. Fairbank, "The Provisional System at Shanghai in 1853–54" (1935, 1936); for its later development, see Morse, *The Trade and Administration of China* (1921), chap. xii.

9. China: Maritime Customs, Annual Reports and Returns of Trade; *Shanghai Mercury* (1893), pp. 71 ff. — a report on the trade of Shanghai by R. E. Bredon, at that time Commissioner of Customs at Shanghai; Morse, *Trade*, chaps. x and xii (Morse was for many years an official of the Maritime Customs at Shanghai); Bowman, *Shanghai*, pp. 114–15.

10. *Shanghai Mercury* (1893), p. 74.

11. Native Customs figures cited in Whangpoo Conservancy Board (1932), p. 67.

12. Fong Hsien-ting, *The Cotton Industry and Trade in China* (1932), I, 308.

13. Figures cited from the Native Customs in Feetham, I, p. 296.

14. Figure cited from the Native Customs in Whangpoo Conservancy Board (1932), p. 67; no import-export breakdown is given.

CHAPTER NINE. HOW THE CITY IS FED

1. On soils in this area, see L. T. Sun, "Soil survey of Kiangning" (1936); James Thorp, *The Geography of the Soils of China* (1939).

2. *Kiang-su sheng-chien* (1935); unsigned article, "The Fishing Industry of Kiangsu," *Chinese Economic Journal*, 3: 833–845 (1928).

3. For a detailed discussion of crops and land-use patterns in the delta, see Y. H. Huang, "Agricultural Regions of Kiangsu" (1947).

4. See Fei Hsiao-t'ung, *Peasant Life in China* (1939), for a sociological field study of the Tai Lake region in which is included a discussion of the role of the delta waterways in the communal life of the area.

5. C. C. Chang, Agricultural Statistics of *hsien* in Kiangsu Province (1930). These figures are for the fertile triangle.

6. See F. H. King, *Farmers of Forty Centuries* (1928), pp. 150–163, for a detailed account of farming methods in this area. R. P. Hommel, *China at Work* (1937), is a series of photographs and descriptions of traditional farming and craft tools in China.

7. J. L. Buck, *Land Utilization in China* (1937), I, 251.

8. *Ibid.*, III, *passim*.

9. *Ibid*, II, table 13.

10. *Ibid.*, I, 71.

11. *Ibid.*, I, 349.

12. Shanghai Bureau of Social Affairs (1934).

13. The reports were published in the *National Journal of Commerce* and in the *Journal of the General Chamber of Commerce of Shanghai*.

14. Figures given in *Kiang-su sheng-chien*.

15. Unsigned article, "Two Agricultural and Commercial Centres of Chekiang," *Chinese Economic Monthly*, 3. 8: 327 (1926).

16. Unsigned articles in the *Chinese Economic Monthly*, "Rice: Its Production, Consumption, and Marketing," 3:432–454 (1926); "Rice Markets of Chekiang," 3: 51–64 (1926); unsigned article, "The Cultivation and Marketing of Rice," *Chinese Economic Journal*, 9: 878–893 (1931); Yang Chi-ch'eng, The Rice Market at Sungchiang (1936); Wu Yung-ming, Rice Production in Kiangsu (1937).

17. Figures compiled from the two journals cited above on p. 139. For additional price data, see Feng Hu-fa, *Source Materials on China's Agricultural Economics* (1935), pp. 135 *et seq*.

18. *Journal of the General Chamber of Commerce of Shanghai*, report on the rice market for January 1926, VII, 126.

19. Shanghai Bureau of Social Affairs (1931). All rice figures are cited in the study in *shih*, a Chinese unit of weight. They will be cited here in pounds, taking the Shanghai rice *shih* of this period as equivalent to 200 pounds.

20. Ministry of Communications (1920–1936).

21. Chen Kung-p'o, "Self Sufficiency in Food Supply" (1935), p. 102.

22. Friedrich Otto, "Correlation of Harvest with Imports of Cereals into China" (1934), p. 393.

23. Figures compiled from China: Maritime Customs, Shanghai Annual Trade Reports, Statistical Series #6 (1920–1936), and from the Annual Reports and Returns of Trade. Piculs converted to pounds at 133 pounds to the picul.

24. H. M. Foreign Office (1863), p. 46; H. M. Foreign Office (1864), p. 67.

25. H. M. Foreign Office (1864), pp. 66 and 67.

26. H. M. Foreign Office (1865).

27. For example, Otto, "Correlation of Harvests"; *Bank of China Monthly Review*, V, 23–68 (1932), unsigned article entitled "Rice in China"; Chiang Hsüeh-chai, A New Estimate of the Supply and Demand of Food in China (1936).

28. *Finance and Commerce* (October 9, 1940).

29. For reference on this discussion, and for a more detailed treatment of the food problem in Shanghai between 1937 and 1942, see Hinder, *Life and Labour in Shanghai* (1944), pp. 93–102; R. W. Barnett, *Economic Shanghai: Hostage to Politics* (1942), p. 54.

30. This is corroborated by *Kiang-su sheng-chien*, pp. 44–53.

31. Shanghai Bureau of Social Affairs (1933), p. 74.

32. Ministry of Communications (1920–1936).

33. China: Maritime Customs, Annual Reports and Returns of Trade.

34. For reference on this discussion of wheat, see Shen Tsung-han, *Chinese Food Problems* (1947); United States Department of Agriculture (1928); an unsigned article entitled "Wheat and Flour in Shanghai," *Chinese Economic Bulletin*, 9: 81–84 (1926); an unsigned article entitled "Wheat and Flour Markets in Shanghai," *Chinese Economic Journal*, 1: 287–291 (1927); and *The China Handbook*.

35. Unsigned article, "Citrus Fruit in Chekiang," *Chinese Economic Journal*, 11: 389–397 (1932).

36. Unsigned article, "Fruit Production and Marketing in China," *Chinese Economic Journal*, 9: 1132–1145 (1931).

37. Unsigned article, "The Shanghai Ham Trade," *Chinese Economic Journal*, 19: 184–193 (1936).

38. *Kiang-su sheng-chien*.

39. Unsigned article, "Chinese Eggs and Egg Products," *Chinese Economic Journal*, 14: 157–168 (1934).

40. K. C. Lin, "Shanghai's New Fish Market" (1934), *passim*.

41. Yang Teh-hui, "Shang-hai chih ch'i-chu'an yü-yeh" (1935), *passim*; unsigned article, "The Fishing Industry of Kiangsu," *Chinese Economic Journal*, 3:833–845 (1928).

42. Yang Teh-hui, "Shang-hai."

43. Lin, "Shanghai's New Fish Market," p. 612.

44. C. R. Worcester, *Junks and Sampans of the Yangtze* (1947), pp. 237–241.

45. Lin, pp. 608–609.

46. *Ibid.*, p. 606.

47. On tribute rice shipments, see G. M. H. Playfair, "The Grain Transport System of China" (1875); Harold Hinton, *The Grain Tribute System of China* (1950).

48. Morse, *The Trade*, p. 96.

49. Montalto, p. 43.

50. J. B. Powell, *My Twenty-five Years in China* (1945), p. 27.

51. Shanghai Municipal Council, Annual Report for 1920, p. 126 ff.

52. His statement was printed in the *China Journal*, 16: 215 (1932).

53. Shanghai Municipal Council, Annual Report for 1920, p. 127.

54. Shanghai Municipal Council, Annual Report for 1940, p. 98 ff.

55. Chang, "Agricultural Statistics."

CHAPTER TEN. THE GEOGRAPHY OF SHANGHAI MANUFACTURING

1. For the standard study of Shanghai manufacturing see Liu Ta-chün, *The Growth and Industrialization of Shanghai* (1936), and his references to the surveys on which his work is based.

2. These figures are estimates, compiled from Liu Ta-chün, *Growth and Indus-*

trialization, and *Shang-hai ḳung-yeh-hua yen-chiu* (1934); Ministry of Industry (1933); Shanghai Bureau of Social Affairs, Machine Industry of Shanghai (1933); and corrected for contradictions among these studies and against the overall nature of the Shanghai economy.

3. Liu Ta-chün, *Growth and Industrialization*.

4. *Ibid.*

5. These latter figures are reported in the *Journal of the British Chamber of Commerce* at Shanghai for August 1935, pp. 165 ff.

6. Whangpoo Conservancy Board (1932), pp. 30–36.

7. Liu Ta-chün, *Growth and Industrialization*.

8. Liu Ta-chün, *Shang-hai*.

9. See Shanghai Municipal Council, Annual Reports for 1932, 1934, and 1935.

10. Shanghai Municipal Council, Annual Report for 1935, p. 88.

11. Unsigned article, "The Raw Cotton Trade of Shanghai," *Chinese Economic Journal*, 3: 681–92 (1928).

12. Leonard Ting, "Recent Developments in China's Cotton Industry" (1936), p. 421.

13. Shen Wen-fu, The Increase in Cotton Production During Economic Maladjustments (1948). See also "Current China," fortnightly column in *People's China*, published fortnightly at Peking since January 1, 1950; and *Hsin-hua Yüeh-pao* (New China Monthly), 130–131 (November 1951).

14. Unsigned articles, "China's Raw Wool Trade," and "Cotton and Woolen Weaving Mills in Shanghai," *Chinese Economic Journal*, 18: 863–77 (1936), and 4: 454–59 (1929), respectively.

15. Unsigned article, "Chinese Eggs and Egg Products," *Chinese Economic Journal*, 14: 157–68 (1934).

16. *Ibid.*, p. 159.

17. For factual reference on the foregoing paragraph, see J. A. Thomas, *A Pioneer Tobacco Merchant in the Orient* (1928); Chung Jui-chi, "The Cigarette Industry in China" (1935); Ch'en Han-seng, *Industrial Capital and Chinese Peasants* (1939); Yu Hsüeh-hsi, Geographical Distribution of Tobacco Production in China (1948).

18. Chung Jui-chi, "The Cigarette Industry," p. 630.

19. *Ibid.*, pp. 633–34.

20. Liu Ta-chüan, *Growth and Industrialization*; T. T. Read, "China's Iron Industry" (1943).

21. Read, "Iron Industry," p. 49.

22. *Far Eastern Review* for March 1940, p. 120.

23. Read, "Iron Industry," p. 40.

24. For a detailed discussion of this problem, see Liu Ta-chün, *China's Industry and Finance* (1927), pp. 56–128.

25. Unsigned article, "The Iron and Steel Industry in China," *Chinese Economic Journal*, 2: 1–16 (1928).

26. Whangpoo Conservancy Board (1932), pp. 50–51.

27. Ministry of Industry (1933), p. 28.

28. Unsigned article, "The Food Canning Industry of Shanghai," *Chinese Economic Bulletin*, 15: 934–41 (1934).

29. Unsigned article, "Hides and Skins on the Shanghai Market," *Chinese Economic Journal*, 3: 1048–58 (1928); 3: 846–54 (1928); and 9: 671–85 (1935).

30. China: Maritime Customs, Annual Reports and Returns of Trade.

31. *Ibid.*

32. See a series of articles on oil seeds on the Shanghai market, in the *Chinese Economic Journal*, 5: 864–71 (1929); 10: 314–22 (1932); 13: 515–19 (1933); and 19: 109–23 (1936).

33. Unsigned articles: "The Vegetable Tallow and Wax Trade in Shanghai," and "The Soap Industry in China," *Chinese Economic Journal*, 19: 42–50 (1936), and 10: 113–26 (1932), respectively.

34. Unsigned article, "Shanghai Match Factories," *Chinese Economic Journal*, 3: 864–69 (1928).

35. B. Y. Lee, "Shanghai, World's Largest Jade Manufacturing Centre" (1930).

36. Liu Ta-chün, *Shang-hai*, p. 118.

37. Fong, *The Cotton Industry*, I, 89.

38. C. K. Moser, *The Cotton Textile Industries of Far Eastern Countries* (1932), p. 74; A. D. Pearse, *The Cotton Industry of China and Japan* (1929), p. 128.

39. For comparative wage statistics, see Y. T. Tsha, "Wage Rates in Shanghai" (1935).

40. Ministry of Communications (1930).

41. *Statistics of Railways in the United States*, published annually by the United States Government Printing Office, Washington, D. C.

42. Fong, I, p. 103.

43. China: Maritime Customs, Reports on Trade at Ports in China Open to Foreign Trade (Shanghai, 1859–70).

44. *Loc. cit.*

45. Ellsworth Carlson, *The Kailan Mines, 1878–1912* (1949), pp. 37, 50; Ting, "The Coal Industry in China" (1937), pp. 32, 75.

46. Carlson, *The Kailan Mines*, p. 36.

47. Estimates compiled from C. A. Bacon, "The Coal Supply of Shanghai" (1930) and Carlson; China: Maritime Customs, Annual Reports and Returns of Trade; Ting, "The Coal Industry"; Wang Kung-ping, *Controlling Factors in the Future Development of the Chinese Coal Industry* (1947).

48. Ministry of Communications (1930–1936).

49. Figures from Ting, "Coal," p. 56.

50. Ting, "Coal," p. 224.

51. *Ibid.*, p. 217.

52. China: Maritime Customs, The Foreign Trade of China (1930–1936).

53. Ting, "Coal," p. 219.

54. Bacon, "The Coal Supply," p. 208.

55. Unpublished correspondence from an official of the Shanghai Power Company, cited in Orchard, "Shanghai," p. 26.

56. Unsigned article, "Shanghai Public Utilities," *Chinese Economic Journal*, 8: 381–94 (1931).

57. C. H. Chen and Y. S. Sun, "The Electric Power Industry in China" (1947), p. 7.

58. Unsigned article, "Public Utilities in Shanghai," cited above, p. 386.

59. Statement by P. S. Hopkins, president of the Shanghai Power Company, "World's Cheapest Power Supplied by Shanghai Power Company," *China Press*, August 29, 1931.

60. Figures cited in Barnett, *Economic Shanghai*, p. 82, from the Annual Reports of the Shanghai Power Company.

61. Liu Ta-chün, *Growth and Industrialization*.
62. See Y. C. Chang, "Flour Milling in China" (1922); Pearse, *The Cotton Industry*.
63. Fong, I, 231.
64. S. F. Wright, *China's Struggle for Tariff Autonomy* (1938), *passim*.
65. Chinese Year Book (1936), pp. 1260–1274.
66. Ting, "Recent Developments," p. 429.
67. *Ibid.*, pp. 426, 431.
68. See Fong, *Toward Economic Control in China* (1936), pp. 62–63.
69. See *Hsin-hua Yüeh-pao*, 130–131 (November 1951); "Current China," fortnightly column in *Peoples' China* (since 1950).
70. Liu Ta-chün, *The Silk Industry*, pp. 123, 212.

CHAPTER ELEVEN. SHANGHAI TODAY AND TOMORROW

1. Material for this chapter has been drawn from the files of *Ching-chi Chou-pao* (Economic Weekly), published at Shanghai since 1947; *Hsin-hua Yüeh-pao* (New China Monthly), published at Peking since November 1949; *China Digest*, published monthly at Hong Kong from 1944 to 1949, when it was superseded by *Peoples' China: Peoples' China*, published fortnightly at Peking since January 1, 1950; *Daily News Release*, published daily at Peking since July 1, 1949; and from the verbal accounts of friends returned from Shanghai to the United States during 1951 and 1952. Specific statements of recent or current fact for which no reference is given in a footnote are in most cases based on these verbal accounts.
2. See Yeh Tseng-ke, "The Huai River Battle," *Peoples' China*, 21–23 (Aug. 16, 1951).
3. Ku Ling, "New Shanghai," *Peoples' China*, 21–23 (Sept. 1, 1951).
4. *Ching-chi Chou-pao*, 183–87 (Sept. 6, 1951).
5. See *Ching-chi Chou-pao*, 7–8 (Jan. 4, 1951).
6. *Ching-chi Chou-pao* (March 22, 1951, Jan. 24, 1952); *Hsin-hua Yüeh-pao*, 1309–1311 (October 1951).
7. See *Ching-chi Chou-pao* (March 22, 1951).

INDEX

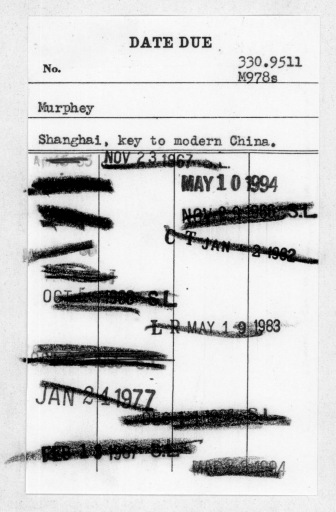